Birth
NEW

MAVEN PRESS

Copyright © Laura Elizabeth
First published in Australia in 2022
by Maven Press
Roleystone WA 6111

Cover Design by Kristy Jamieson

Edited by Tara Caetano

All rights reserved. No part of this book may be used or reproduced by any means, graphic, electronic, or mechanical, including photocopying, recording, taping or by any information storage retrieval system without the written permission of the copyright owner except in the case of brief quotations embodied in critical articles and reviews.

Because of the dynamic nature of the Internet, any web addresses or links contained in this book may have changed since publication and may no longer be vaild. The views expressed in this work are solely those of the author and do not necessarily reflect the views of the publisher and the publisher hereby disclaims any responsibility for them.

 A catalogue record for this work is available from the National Library of Australia

National Library of Australia Catalogue-in-Publication data:
Birth New/Laura Elizabeth

ISBN: 978-0-6453230-4-7
(Paperback)

ISBN: 978-0-6453230-5-4
(Ebook)

FOREWORD

We live in a time when menstrual shame and birth trauma are considered normal. Mothers are lied to, coerced and manipulated into making choices that don't serve their best interests. Fundamentally they are betrayed and babies are traumatised for life.

Let's hope we are at the end of this kind of this terrible disrespect and that it is heralding a new way, a time when we *Birth New* ways for us all to understand and respect birth, mothers and babies.

This time in our history will be known more for the brave voices of the women that stood up and spoke, than for the men who abused their power. This book is a collection of those voices, voices from women who trusted their intuition and their bodies and those who nourish and nurture other women to do that.

Women have known they are midwives and medicine women for longer than they haven't.

Our herstory tells us that the ways of this time now, known for its oppression of women and suppression of feminine knowledge, has not always been the way. So much has been taken away from us and for so long that we have forgotten it belongs to us.

There is much talk in our world about the rising of the divine feminine, of women joining together, of healing the wounded sisterhood, of reclaiming feminine wisdom, knowledge and power, and the brave voices that speak here, in this book, gathered together and helped by Laura Elizabeth ,represent this feminine force rising.

By telling our stories of courage, bravery, vulnerability, strength, cleverness, ruthlessness, strategy etc., we are telling ourselves back into our power. The lens through which we see the world as women in 2022, and how we see ourselves as women in the world, is a result of our enculturation, and that lens is basically created and reinforced at our rites of passage.

* At birth – however we are gestated, birthed and cared for as a newborn sets up our nervous system's patterned responses and our degree of resilience.

* At menarche (our first period) – whatever happens then teaches us how a woman is valued in our culture and therefore how we have to behave to be accepted as a woman. This experience creates the mindset, the imprint, the brainwashing that happens there and plays out for the rest of our lives until we realise we're doing it and want to do the healing to change it. And our menarche experience affects how we give birth. One rite of passage leads to the next.

* Every pregnancy, including pregnancy loss or abortion, results in a birth, whatever ends the pregnancy is a birth, and how the woman is treated during her pregnancy, birth and postnatal time, teaches her how her culture values mothers and therefore how she should behave.

As mentioned, a woman's experience of giving birth is impacted by her menarche and also by her experience of her menstrual cycle and how connected she was to her body's wisdom through her cycle, or not.

* And then this all either heals, explodes or implodes at menopause.

We must remember some basics – we live in a patriarchal culture which means that women and the feminine are oppressed, which means fundamentally we are not safe. We are animals, mammals – and mammals require safety to give birth.

Our experiences of our rites of passage create who we believe we are and how we behave. And, we can hack/change the culture with conscious rites of passage and healing from traumatic experiences.

Be inspired by this collection of stories to tell your own stories.

Let us tell ourselves back into our power as we awaken and shift the power balance so that women are respected at birth, are treated with kindness and all babies are treated with gentleness and care.

It's up to us.

Thank you, Laura Elizabeth, for bringing these brave women's voices together to share with us all.

Jane Hardwicke Collings
Women's Mysteries Teacher

ACKNOWLEDGEMENTS

In unity, we honour and pay our respects to the custodians of Whadjuk Noongar Boodjar country, the lands on which this book was first seeded.

We pay our respects to the Elders both past and present and to those emerging.

The stories within these pages may contain sensitive content and/or memories of loved ones who have passed on, which may activate a response within you.

Please read with awareness and care.

CONTENTS

Laura Elizabeth
THE VISION 1

Vicki Hobbs
GIVING BIRTH BACK TO WOMEN 7

Emma Woodham
SHEDDING THE SHAME 21

Jenna Richards
BEAUTIFUL BEGINNINGS – CONNECTIONS BETWEEN BIRTH AND BREASTFEEDING 32

Nicole Aly
HONOURING HER 44

Claire In't Veld
YOU AS THE MIRACLE OF BIRTH 55

Laura Van Der Meulen
BIRTHING WITH WISDOM AND POWER 67

Emily Schoeman
MY JOURNEY THROUGH MATRESCENCE 80

Ashley Rose
THE VILLAGE 91

Tara Caetano
MY BIRTH, MY BECOMING 102

Tania Henderson
JUST PERFECT 114

Hayley Leonard
CLAIMING YOUR POWER IN THE BIRTH SPACE 125

Melissa Arnott
MY FIRST BIRTH AND MY REBIRTH 138

Rachelli Yaafe
WE HAVE THE BIRTH WE NEED TO HAVE 151

Emma Snelgar
STORIES FROM THE SYSTEM 167

Bonnie Collins
CONNECTION 180

Sarah Elise
TRUST IN YOUR POWER, REMEMBER YOU'RE MAGIC 192

Cat Fancote
BIRTH HAS CHANGED ME 204

Shani-Faye Chambers
BIRTHING ON MY TERMS 217

Sarah Howard
BIRTH BROUGHT ME HOME TO ME 229

Sara Evans
UNRAVELLING THE MYSTERY 240

Kirtsen Lyle
A SACRED RITE OF PASSAGE 251

Brigitte Benary
RED NECTAR 263

Laura Elizabeth
THE VISION

We are the midwives.
The portals of exponential potential
Through all time and space.
The ushers of light at the end
Of the long and transformative tunnel.

We are the midwives.
We have no fear of pain.
We simply accept and surrender
To the expansion that follows faithfully
After each and every contraction.

We are the midwives, the witches, the seers.
We remain focused and unswayed.
We are the keepers of truths
Stored deeply within the folds
Of our collective womb.
Accessible each time we vibrate
In accordance with her frequency.

Laura Elizabeth

We are the midwives, the guides, the channels.
We are the vortices
Spreading hope in the darkness
For light currents to flow through.
Supporting her

Through the birthing and creation
Of an incredible new world.
We are the midwives.

– Laura Elizabeth

Sometimes I must remind myself that all experiences are necessary for personal growth. They become the road map, the string line, and the breadcrumbs in our navigation toolbox. They are the truth, vulnerability and warrior that exists within our very cells. The foundations of the wise woman, the medicine woman, the midwife inside us all.

I knew deep in my bones when the inspiration dropped in for *Birth New* that this book was truly something special.

I felt the current of its energy rippling through my body at light speed. I saw these stories awaken the midwives and medicine women within us all. Inspiring and offering guidance to those drawn to the mystery of conception, pregnancy, birth and beyond. A reference point for anyone fascinated by the birthing process and hungry to learn from those who have birthed before them, or the angels who serve us in the birthing world.

From a young age I was curious about the magic and miracles of birth. I always wanted to be a mother, and had a deep sense of trust and knowing that my body was capable of birthing with ease. I was made for birthing, and no-one could convince me otherwise. When I conceived my first child, I set my intention to birth my baby in water.

It was during this pregnancy that I received my first insight into the lack of education, fear and trauma surrounding birth. My colleagues at the time ridiculed me for entertaining the idea of a waterbirth.

"Haha! Yeah, good luck with that, love! As soon as labour starts you'll be begging for that epidural."

I found it genuinely puzzling that everyone felt the need to give me unsolicited advice, particularly if the choices I was making were different to the ones they had made for their own pregnancies and births. It was like there was some kind of score keeping to see *who had done it better* rather than cheering each other on.

As intended, I birthed my son in water, and 17 months later my daughter was born in the gentle waters of the same birth pool (albeit in about half the length of time).

By the time it came to baby number 3, the call to birth at home was an overwhelming yes. I knew he was my last baby, and I longed for that homebirth experience. Four years had passed since my first pregnancy. I was surrounded now by a strong tribe of mama friends. Some of which had experienced homebirth for themselves and were so much more supportive.

I booked an appointment with my GP to request a homebirth referral. I felt disappointed and angry when she advised that she 'couldn't fathom anyone risking a homebirth without any obstetric care'. I was told that I was irresponsible and she was reluctant to sign my referral paperwork.

I remember feeling extremely letdown by the guilt trip and lack of support. I somehow found courage to maintain my voice and let her know that after 2 previous low-risk births, with midwifery-led care, I felt confident that my body knew how to birth at home. She signed the documents and I never went back there.

In absolute trust and surrender, my 3rd beautiful baby was born at home.

My children, without a doubt, have been the catalyst to finding my voice. I've learned to trust my body and my intuitive intelligence for myself and for them. Even now, as my eldest prepares to start high school,

Laura Elizabeth

I am constantly gifted opportunities to find my fearless voice and set an example for these 3 incredible humans I have birthed into this world.

Please know that I do understand that there are most definitely times when birth doesn't always go to plan, and challenges can be thrown at us. It's important for us to have a platform and safe space to share all sides of birth in order to obtain an objective view. It's true that birthing people and/or babies do sometimes need a little help to reach earthside, and times when things do reach crisis point. *Birth New* is here to give a voice to all of our experiences and empower you on your own journey.

Now more than ever, we need to encourage birthing people to educate themselves on their choices and how to use their voices, and lean on their support crew so that they are prepared for all possibilities. When we feel heard, safe and supported, our nervous systems can relax and we birth better.

In 2012 I did get to experience firsthand what birth can look like when things don't go to *plan*.

I was given the honour and privilege of attending the birth of my niece. I saw with my own eyes just how quickly the *business of birth* seeks to silence a birthing person, and intervene without consent or allowing them to be heard. I will leave it to my sister to share her story in her chapter further into this book. But this is very real, and happening all over the world.

This is why I believe this book is fundamental for anyone stepping into their own parenting journey, or seeking a career in the birth world. Magic happens when women gather. When we take the time to share our stories and listen to the threads of wisdom that run deep in the folds of our collective womb.

It is my hope and intention that each and every reader who comes across these pages finds hope, inspiration and courage in these powerful stories. May you feel held in the knowing that you are not alone, and together we rise and *Birth New*!

Laura Elizabeth

Hi, I'm Laura Elizabeth, a trailblazing changemaker and advocate for women's empowerment. Author of *Loving Herself Whole*, *Back Yourself!*, *Wild Woman Rising*, *Rising Matriarch*, *Heartcentred Leadership*, *The Women Changing The World* and *Birth New*. Director at Maven Press, creatress of Kuntea, and owner of Laura Elizabeth Wellness/Erotic Maven Medicine.

I am dedicated to creating intimate experiences for conscious women ready to step into a deeper layer of understanding of themselves. I assist them to embrace and embody their sensuality, reclaim their voices and own their personal power.

I offer womb and yoni massage therapy, reiki attunements and a catalogue of workshops, education and training events online and in person with a focus on women's health.

I am also the woman behind a steadfast, hand-crafted organic product range topping its 10th year, including the risqué yoni steaming brand Kuntea for reproductive health and wellness.

My love of writing and being a keeper of women's stories has led me

Laura Elizabeth

most recently to create Maven Press Publishing. I am delighted to be able to doula storytellers through the conception, gestation and birth of their books into the world as they step deeper into their truth as changemakers.

A naturally gifted psychic medium born on the east coast of Fife, Scotland, I immigrated to Perth, Western Australia, as a pre-teen in 1999. With 2 decades of experience cultivating my skills as an energy worker and holding space for clients, I offer the safest and most profoundly intimate containers for women to encounter deep transformation.

A boundary-pusher and taboo-smasher, I am best known for my real, quirky and honest guidance, ensuring the deepest empathy, understanding and non-judgement. I believe it is important to keep a healthy sense of humour to stay grounded and authentic.

My service to clients is most definitely a niche I believe is the real missing link in human connection and healing for women. We are programmed to think, feel and do based on the needs of others. But we unleash our real magic when we set aside time to explore honouring, nurturing and loving ourselves back into a belief of radical acceptance and remembering our magnificence.

A passionate solo mother of 3, leading by example, smashing goals and living with purpose, I hope to be a positive influence and for my own children to reach their full potential and inspire others to do the same.

I hold your hand and love you, while you remember how to love yourself.

Website: www.lauraelizabeth.com.au
Facebook: facebook.com/eroticmavenmedicine
Instagram: instagram.com/eroticmaven_medicine
Instagram: instagram.com/kuntea_by_le
Website: www.mavenpress.com.au
Instagram: www.instagram.com/mavenpress

Vicki Hobbs
GIVING BIRTH BACK TO WOMEN

I am a 'feminist' because I am a woman.

There, I said it. And if you don't like it … well, put this book down.

These days I ceremoniously weave my way around the 3rd phase of the Goddess, the *Autumn Maga;* a new season that is not talked about or even known. It's that in-between time after mother but before crone. The menopausal slowing down of my body and the harvest gift before winter sets in. And yet, with the arrival of this Maga phase, there is also a strong call for justice, for the community, and for the celebration and acknowledgment of my long years of mothering and providing, now with a no-nonsense attitude.

I have begun to wonder why I have kept my strong feminist beliefs under wraps for so long.

Perhaps I was afraid to be thought of as a feminist crackpot – you know, what you see on TV and in movies. Those bra-burning, man-hating stereotypical women who would tackle any unsuspecting man down to the ground, with wild eyes and bared teeth, proudly straddling him in order to keep him down whilst raising her placard that says *'women are superior'*. All whilst her plaited underarm hair stands at attention.

Well I no longer plait my underarm hair … Oh stop it! I'm getting carried away now.

What I will say is that I no longer feel I have to be quiet, subdued or a people-pleaser.

The rite of passage into this phase of the feminine Maga can bring with it so many liberating thoughts, feelings and pursuits; I'm all grown up now and I have a plan. I've put on my big-girl pants (quite literally), and I'm not afraid to fight for women and birthing people and their right to choose.

Fortunately, the suffragettes brought us to where we are today with so many more rights and opportunities than we had previously. However, there are still pay gaps and imbalances regarding positions of hierarchy within organisations and businesses. In addition, there are still patriarchal views on so many things, particularly when it comes to birth and women's bodies.

As a feminist and a birth worker, my mission has always been about the rights of women, and with 2021 subjecting us all to an overload of pandemic lockdowns and looming mandates, my beliefs are now even more fierce than they ever have been.

That does not mean that I am an anti-vaxxer; in fact, with full transparency I am fully vaccinated and made that choice long before mandates were enforced. However, I have strong opinions when it comes to the right to choose what is done to our bodies. I believe that we should all ask questions, do our research, and then make informed choices for ourselves and our set of circumstances without being made to feel shame or regret for those choices.

I tell my clients that two women can look at the same information but make different choices, but that doesn't make one woman right and the other wrong. I also ensure that my clients are fully aware that sometimes medical assistance is needed, and it is a blessing to have the medical knowledge and expertise that we have in our maternity system – but not when it comes to unnecessary interventions and caesareans. There is a glaring difference.

When I hear that so many midwives have chosen to lose their jobs over being forced to have the COVID-19 vaccine under the current mandates, I have to wonder where these midwives once fit into the maternity system we currently have. Are any of them the ones that I have seen bully, coerce, and even lie to women to get them to do something so that they can tick their paperwork and move on to the next step in order to speed up the process or maintain hospital policy? I have to wonder if they now understand what women feel when they are told that they have no choice, that this is the policy of the hospital and that they must comply or they will end up with a caesarean, or if they would prefer a 'dead baby' as they have obviously chosen to have an 'experience' rather than be a good patient and follow the rules?

I let out a long sigh … Maybe they get it now.

To me, feminism is not about one thing. It is about educating the community about a woman's right to walk down the street safely. That she has the right to walk alone, she has the right to wear what she wants, and that she has the right to protect her body. Feminism is about protecting the rights of girls and women – to consent, to not consent, and to be able to withdraw consent at any time, including within birth.

Feminism is about us all demanding that NO means NO – the end.

"I do not consent." – four simple words that have enormous power.

The law is not a set of guidelines or policies; the law is mandatory, and NO means NO.

All hospitals have policies and guidelines based on 'recommendations' and many of those policies and guidelines are not evidence-based; they are culture-based, meaning they are assumptions, beliefs and values of a group of people. But just because a hospital has policies, does not mean that these policies are the law, and nor does it mean that the woman has to consent to them. It definitely does not mean that she gives 'implied consent' because she has been admitted to hospital and is now a patient, particularly if she has not been provided with all of the risks and benefits of a recommendation in order to give 'informed consent'.

We know that since the creation of humans, women have always given birth. It was believed that the pain women experience in labour and childbirth was a punishment from God referred to as 'The Curse of Eve' (Genesis 3:16a), because Eve ate the apple from 'The Tree of Knowledge' that she was forbidden to eat. She then convinced Adam to also eat from the apple, therefore implying that she deserved the pain and that it was her duty to surrender to that pain.

To this day I still don't get this story. Why would you be prohibited from eating from a tree of knowledge? How do you learn good and bad if not from knowledge? Seriously, I would be devouring the fruit from that tree, taking cuttings to replant more trees, and savouring the wisdom bestowed upon me and everyone in my community. But if we dissect this a little further, the story is not about the tree.

It is that Eve questioned authority and disobeyed her master.

Eve's punishment also included that men would dominate all women and that future generations of women were to become subservient to men, which is still ingrained in many cultures today. This conditioning is passed down through our lineage; that invisible red thread that binds us to past generations.

But if this is truly the commandment of God, why would he inflict such punishment? And what about the women who don't experience pain in childbirth, or the women who experience orgasmic births or use pain medication?

Tracing back through the lines of red thread, we know that women have suffered.

There were many tears, heart-wrenching sobs of despair, broken hearts from learning of a fate that could not be changed or escaped from, abuse endured, and the witnessing of many deaths of loved ones.

We have been sold by fathers to husbands as a commodity for reproduction to produce heirs to ensure the lineage continued, and for these women their lives depended on producing that heir. Women were stolen from villages and enslaved, and not only raped for pleasure, but also to produce offspring to provide labour in the fields.

Religion also played a huge role in male domination over women, and women had no rights over their body – she was owned by her husband, and she would be subservient or she would be punished, usually with severe beatings, or even death.

We lost traditional midwives, healers, grandmothers, mothers, aunties, sisters and even those who were accused of being witches, who if we were to change our language and perception, were all women.

Yes, those witches were in fact wise women – the sage-femme.

Powerful women, who were incredible healers with knowledge that had been passed down through the generations, that were tortured and executed because men feared their power and demanded that they had to be suppressed or eliminated. When we look at the study of epigenetics, we can hypothesise that the fear, distrust and memories of these events are inherited from previous generations.

Midwives were such a key part of the birthing process for thousands of years. They would watch women, hold space for women, encourage them to trust their body and work with their body to get into different positions, to rest and to do what was needed to get their baby out. They were 'with woman' and their soul was connected beyond measure to holding space for women. They had many different skills, herbs and tonics that would ease the pain of the birthing woman, and she would touch the woman, feeling what she needed and even using her hands to reposition a baby if it was needed. There were no machines to do this, but the midwife was so skilled in her role that she didn't need machines.

Again, it is time for women to rise up, to feel confident in taking back what is rightfully theirs – their bodies, their babies and their births. These days, with our highly medicalised maternity system, the way women give birth has changed so dramatically and has become a patriarchal event (that is pathologised) rather than a physiological one.

Birth is *done* to women rather than women giving birth.

We find that the language around birth is highly masculine, for example, 'the obstetrician delivers the baby' rather than 'the woman gave birth to her baby.' The system and the patriarchy continue to take the glory, the accolades and the power of birth away from the mother and have given it to someone in a white coat with expensive machinery. The mother continues to have less control over her body; she is no longer an active participant but a passive vessel.

We deliver pizzas – not babies.

The patriarchy has always feared powerful women and their strong minds and bodies, particularly during birth. We must ensure that this fear doesn't continue to infect women and their rite of passage into motherhood. We have to go back to our roots and acquire once more the natural ways of birthing, easing our babies into the world in a calm, safe and undisturbed way for a better future.

We have to reconnect with the rituals, the ceremonies and the transition of maiden to mother.

In the sketch 'The Miracle of Birth' in *Monty Python's The Meaning of Life*, the 'machine that goes ping' strikes a cord when you see how relevant it is to the medicalisation of birth today, even though it is meant to be satire. The machines are highly revered, the mother is forgotten, the father is dismissed and there is a room full of spectators whilst the mother asks the obstetricians what she has to do. Their response being, "Nothing, dear, you're not qualified."

My favourite quote by Rosalind in the movie *The Gentlemen*, is "There's fuckery afoot," and yes, indeed, in our maternity system there definitely is fuckery afoot.

But this has been going on for hundreds of years, and it was during the 16th century that men started to look at childbirth as a 'mechanical practice' and men considered themselves more knowledgeable in the mechanics of the human body and how pregnant women worked. With industrialisation came changes in maternity care and hospitals were set up, and poor women were provided with 'free' care so that obstetrical training could be provided for doctors and nurses. These hospitals were unsanitary, and doctors would spread bacteria from sick or dead patients to birthing women. Death due to infection was incredibly high, until washing hands between patients and antibiotics were discovered.

Instead of using natural herbs and remedies from well-known healers and midwives, women were encouraged to take 'over-the-counter' tonics and elixirs that had been made by untrained medical practitioners (also known as quacks), usually barbers, for pain relief or anything to do with pregnancy.

We went from natural, holistic and midwifery-led care, to practices that would make even the patriarchy cringe if they actually sat down and thought about it.

In the 16th century, Dr Eucharius Rösslin wrote the first pregnancy book *The Rose Garden for Pregnant Women and Midwives* which became a bestseller for over 200 years, yet he had never seen or studied childbirth and was a statistician by profession (and we all know how numbers affect birth). By writing this book, he enhanced the belief that men were now the experts when it came to childbirth, even though the book contained ridiculous illustrations of 'adult' humans in various positions in the uterus and he wrote that babies were just small adults floating around in the womb waiting to drop out.

Again, over the years, the patriarchy continued to change the way women gave birth. Scholars believe that the shift from upright birthing to on the back was largely influenced by the French who promoted 'power over women' while they were in these positions, but also for the facilitation of forceps and anaesthesia. Feminists have worked fiercely to claim that power back from men, even in the birth space.

If we look back over history there are so many contraptions that were invented by men to try and make birth easier for women, or perhaps it was more likely for the ease of care providers. For instance, there was one machine that was designed with the idea that they would strap the naked mother onto a frame that spun around at high speed, so that it would create enough force to help the baby shoot out of the vagina into a carefully placed net. Nothing like the fetal ejection reflex transmuted by a machine! Thank goodness this never went past the patent phase, so was never used on pregnant women. I have visuals of seeing adult babies spinning around at time warp speed whilst waiting for the g-force ejection into the net, then jumping up with hands raised above their head and shouting, "SCORE!"

Which prompts me to ask: what do babies and corks have in common?

Well, nothing really, but once again we have a device currently in the study phase which was invented in 2006 by a car mechanic Jorge Odón after he watched a YouTube video showing an easy way to pull out a cork from a wine bottle, giving him a light-bulb moment of, 'Hey, this could work with women giving birth.' Honestly, what the fuck? The idea behind this device is to fold a plastic sleeve around the baby's whole head, while pumping air between the two layers of plastic, and then sucking the baby out. Hell yeah, that sounds like a really calm and holistic way of birthing your baby. So, they believe that the head of a baby and a cork are super similar? Once again I'm left visualising the obstetrician holding the handle of the apparatus with their feet on the edge of the bed, midwife behind holding him around the waist while pulling him backwards like a tug of war, all while the plastic sucker is inside the woman and he is pulling with all of his strength to a sensational popping sound and a free-flowing baby? Here I go again, getting carried away with illogical semantics.

Why don't we just let women give birth the way they have been designed to give birth?

My hope is that we start to move away from the 'paternalistic' pedestal, where everyone thinks the doctor knows best. We are conditioned from a young age that it is inappropriate to question the advice of a doctor, but now it's time to start focusing on the woman, asking her what she wants, what she needs, how she feels and then listening to her, trusting her to tap into her innate wisdom and feel into birth once again.

Women hold the power and have the ability to make informed choices based on their circumstances, recognising that every woman, every pregnancy, and every birth is unique. There is no one size fits all and no one textbook for birth.

The way a woman is treated during childbirth can and does have a life-lasting effect on her future, and the mental wellbeing of a pregnant woman is equally as important as her physical wellbeing.

Just because you are pregnant, in labour or giving birth does not mean you hand over your body autonomy to a medical professional and become just an incubator of your baby without rights. We have seen too many women in the past just fall through the cracks once they leave hospital, having suffered incredible trauma during their birth and then becoming just another number on the conveyor belt … NEXT!

No matter what hospital policies say, you still have legal authority over your body.

Signing a consent form does not mean you have signed away your rights or your ability to decline a procedure, even if they are based on hospital policies.

Find your voice – I want to hear you roar, not only as you push your baby out, but when you want someone to listen to your wants and needs for your birth.

You matter!

Many times I have held space for women who have poured out so much grief around their birth that has been festering under the surface. They haven't wanted to say anything to anyone else, because they didn't want to appear to be ungrateful for having a 'healthy baby'. A lot of the time, it is after their first birth and during debriefing that women start to recognise that they may have been lied to, manipulated or bullied into treatment, and therefore they become more confident in protecting their right to choose for their future births.

A healthy baby is not all that matters.

A healthy mum matters as well.

A healthy mum creates a healthy baby and a healthy family.

But we need you to be prepared and educated before you get pregnant, so that you feel confident and ready for your first birth, because what happens in that first birth will have an influence on your future births.

It is also common that your future pregnancies can bring up deep underlying trauma and fear from your previous birth/s. This may be confronting for you, so it may be a good time to listen to your fears and perhaps even seek out professional birth trauma counselling.

On the other hand, this can also give you a fire in your belly, which makes you do everything in your power to ensure that you don't feel out of control or traumatised again.

This is why I became a childbirth educator and doula and why I also now train doulas.

"Did you say jeweller?"

No, I said *doula*.

Doulas are trained to provide continuous physical, emotional, mental, spiritual and informational support and advocacy to the mother and her partner before, during and after childbirth. A doula's main purpose is to help the mother have a calm, memorable and positive birthing experience, encouraging her to keep breathing, releasing and letting go, surrendering, moving and focusing.

That applies to a homebirth, hospital birth, planned caesarean and even an emergency caesarean – *any* birth.

I liken a doula to a coach: preparing you, pushing you to your limits and supporting you through one of the biggest events of your life with the ultimate trophy at the end. Research shows that doulas help to lower caesarean rates and interventions because they are completely focused on the mums' needs and not the medical environment. A study released in 2012 identified that women who had an independent birth support (specifically a doula, not a midwife or someone from their family or friend network) were:

- *More likely to have a spontaneous labour.*
- *Less likely to have synthetic oxytocin.*
- *Less likely to ask for an epidural or drugs.*
- *Less likely to be dissatisfied with their birth.*
- *More likely to have shorter labours.*
- *Less likely to have a caesarean.*
- *Less likely to have an instrumental birth (forceps & vacuum).*
- *Less likely to have a baby with low Apgar scores.*

Doulas want you to own your birth – we don't make decisions for you, and we *won't* make decisions for you – and we want you to find your power over your own body, your birth and your baby.

As doulas we are not there to save a woman and we are not there to fulfil our own agenda of wanting everyone to have a natural birth *because it will bring peace on earth* or whatever our beliefs are that sets us on this path. We are there to provide education, resources, guidance, support, care, kindness and compassion to each couple, seeing them as individuals and not as one size fits all.

We can be your advocate by reminding you, prompting you and guiding you through your birth plan, but handing over your power to us is the same as handing your power over to your midwife, your obstetrician or the system.

You and your partner can advocate for your own wants and needs and truly own your birth choices, and we will be the conduit that holds it all together.

We are working for you – not the hospital.

It's your birth – not ours.

Now more than ever it is important that the role of the doula also includes helping the couple get back to basics, and embrace birth as a human experience, rather than a medicalised and mechanical one.

We also can't empower you. Nobody can empower anybody else. We can give you tools, techniques and information so that you feel empowered, but you do that – not anybody else. You will feel so much more confident, which means you will start to ask questions to get all of the information you need to make an informed choice.

You cannot make informed choices if you don't have all the information at hand.

Sometimes just having another woman there to connect with can be incredibly nurturing and increase the confidence of the birthing woman by having that female understanding and connection. This is in no way meant to replace the role of the partner who is there to love, support and protect the mother as well.

The way a woman is treated during her pregnancy, labour, birth and immediately after birth can and does have a huge impact on her mental health during the postpartum period. Just because she is pregnant, in labour or giving birth does not mean she hands over her body autonomy to a medical professional and becomes just an incubator of her baby without rights.

Pregnant women have the right to informed consent and refusal of doctor recommendations. I also make it clear to women that they can change their mind at any time – the ball is always in their court – they can consent, not consent or withdraw consent at any time. I also remind my clients that with choice comes responsibility and consequences. You have to own those choices and those consequences.

So with all that said, it's easy to see how feminism, consent, birth and the right to choose, all go hand in hand. We cannot speak of one without the other. It's time to truly give birth back to women and the Autumn Maga in me is ready. To bring in yet another chapter of protecting women, protecting the space of birth, holding space and being loud. And to hell with what anyone else thinks.

Vicki Hobbs

Hi, I'm Vicki Hobbs. I started my business in 2004 and have been working with women and complementary therapies since that time. I am one in a long line of wise and experienced women who bring calm and clarity to the birth space, so that women feel safe, supported and listened to.

I am well-known for sharing my commitment in educating and advocating for women, and fiercely advocate for their rights and choices in pregnancy, birth and during the postpartum period.

I am a national multi-award-winning practitioner and offer an extensive range of services including as a Back to Basics Birthing childbirth educator, Hypnobirthing Australia™ practitioner, birth and postpartum doula, remedial massage therapist specialising in pregnancy massage, mother blessings and placenta encapsulator along with many other services to focus on women's mental, physical and emotional wellbeing.

My mission is to take the fear out of birth and help couples see pregnancy and birth as a normal event, but to also bring them closer together as a couple on all levels as they learn more about themselves, their partners and their role as a parent and the change in dynamics of becoming a family. I help them create a magical moment of love, acceptance, endurance and belief.

I have been training doulas across Australia since 2018, and these doulas are well educated, highly skilled birth workers who honour and protect the birth space while maintaining their scope of practice and being an instrumental part of the birth team.

Back To Basics Birthing

Business email: vicki@vickihobbs.com
Phone: 0435 559 988
Instagram: @backtobasicsbirthing
Facebook: vickihobbschildbirtheducator

Doula Training Academy

Business email: vicki@vickihobbs.com
Phone: 0435 559 988
Instagram: @doulatrainingacademy
Facebook: doulatrainingacademy

Emma Woodham

SHEDDING THE SHAME

It was the right decision, but that didn't make it any easier …

I was 20 at the time. I hadn't noticed anything unusual; I was a serial yo-yo dieter so it wasn't uncommon for my weight to fluctuate 5 or 10 kgs depending on what was going on in my life. Knowing nothing about hormones, I'd been taking the pill continuously to skip my period for over 6 months. It wasn't until a passing comment was made by someone I worked with that I thought that maybe I should do a pregnancy test. So on my way home from work, I went to the chemist and bought a pack of tests, never expecting the result that came next.

POSITIVE. With those two pink lines, my world came crashing down. This could not be happening. Not knowing what to do, I booked myself in to see a GP. Not my normal GP, though – I couldn't bear the thought of going to the same doctor I'd been seeing since I was a newborn baby myself and telling him that I was pregnant. After feeling my stomach, the doctor could already confirm that I was pregnant. Knowing nothing about pregnancy or babies, I thought – *Is this normal? What can he feel? How far along must I be if he can already tell?!* After what felt like an eternity, I was sent for a scan which confirmed that I was quite far along. I was absolutely shattered. This wasn't what it was supposed to feel like.

Emma Woodham

A pregnancy should be a joyous occasion, just like in the movies – the expectant mother unable to contain her excitement. This was not how I pictured my life at all. I had a bright future ahead of me, so many goals and aspirations. I had just started uni, studying psychology; something I'd wanted to do since high school. I had a job that I loved. Having a baby right now just didn't fit into those plans!

I had always been against abortion; I'd never understood how someone could terminate a baby and I just couldn't justify those actions. I'd never understood how anyone could do that to their *own* baby. Well, at least that's what I thought until I was faced with the decision myself. There I was, totally unprepared for what I had just uncovered, and definitely not ready to start that journey.

I didn't want an abortion, but I also didn't want a baby in my circumstances. I didn't feel that I could give a baby the life that it deserved. My life was so full of uncertainty. It seemed less hard to have an abortion than to face months and years of hurdles, known and unknown.

Retrospectively, none of the problems I faced seem insurmountable now. The wonderful power of hindsight is that, in fact, none of these things couldn't have been overcome. But at the time, in my confused and emotional state, I was unable to see a way through them. I wasn't married. Where would we live? How would I earn money if I had to be at home to look after a baby? Because of how far along I was, I didn't have time to think. So, only days after finding out that I was pregnant, I was on a plane to the other side of the country to get an abortion. Naively, I thought, after this I could get back to being me – the pre-pregnant me – not realising that I could never be that same person again.

The day of the abortion was one of the most lonely, terrifying and upsetting days of my life, and I remember every little detail so vividly. I got a taxi from the airport but I got them to drop me up the road from the clinic that I was going to, so the driver didn't know where I was going. The shame encompassed me and was already too much to bear. I walked in

Birth New

the rain with my suitcase to a big car park with a bland medical building, located on a dual carriageway in an outer Melbourne suburb. Croydon is one of those places nobody ever goes to unless they live there. Or, unless, like me, they have to – or feel they have to.

After being shown my room in what looked like a run-down motel, I could see protesters sitting outside the fence from my window. It was like something out of a movie, and something I wasn't expecting. Why did these people think they had the right to do that? A group of complete strangers, gathered there with the sole purpose of judging you at a time that was already so difficult – they clearly had no understanding of the harm they caused. The image burnt into my brain for so long afterwards.

The procedure was done over 3 days, and on the final day I was given a drip of Syntocinon to bring on labour. I was totally unprepared for everything that unfolded. I had no idea that I would be going through labour. But there I was, completely alone in a bed, having contractions to give birth to a baby that I knew I wasn't bringing home. After a whirlwind few days, it was all over. And I felt empty and alone. What had I done? How could I have done this? How had I been so stupid to not even realise that I was pregnant? And what have they done with my baby now?

When I asked the nurse that question, she told me that they cremated all the babies and spread their ashes at a special rose garden at a local cemetery. I don't know whether that was true or not, but I found solace in believing that my baby was among the roses with all of the other babies whose souls weren't yet ready for this earth. I later got a rose tattoo on my foot to remember the baby that I never held and pay tribute to a time in my life that was so undoubtedly difficult but ultimately shaped my life forever.

After a few days, I was back on a flight home. Back to work the next day. I buried it all into the archives, to pretend like none of it had happened. With no-one to speak to and feeling too ashamed to admit what I had done, I kept quiet. I mean, I had made that choice, so I had no right to be upset or grieve, right?

Emma Woodham

Only months later, after trying to pretend like nothing had happened, I received a phone call from the department of health. They told me that during surgery, I may have contracted a serious communicable disease, hepatitis C. I would need to be tested, and if I was unlucky, I would need treatment. Apparently, the anaesthetist was addicted to the drug fentanyl, which was used in procedures at the clinic, and would inject himself before using the drug on his patients. I endured another shameful trip to the doctor to be tested, and the wait for the results was nothing short of traumatic. Thankfully though, I was not one of the 55 women he did infect. This was another extremely distressing event that left me wondering what on earth I had done.

Years went past and I suffered numerous ovary-related problems, including an operation to remove cysts. In my head, this was of course all my fault and had only happened because I'd had the abortion.

After getting married, it finally felt like the right time for me to have a baby. But those voices within made me question was I really worthy of calling myself a mother? I came off the pill and to my absolute delight, I fell pregnant really easily. Just like in the movies, I finally got to feel that uncontrollable, all-encompassing excitement that seeing those two little lines can bring when you're ready to welcome a baby into your life. I was a couple of months pregnant and couldn't contain my elation so I started to tell a few close people, even though I wasn't at the 12-week mark yet, but what could go wrong? I was pregnant and I wanted this baby! Then one night, I started having major pains. Then came the bleeding. There was so much blood, I thought, *There's no way that this baby is okay.* That night lasted forever, curdled over in pain. Hoping for a miracle that this wasn't a miscarriage. I Googled everything, reading stories where other people had gone through the same thing in early pregnancy and now had a happy, healthy toddler. These glimmers of hope in what seemed completely obvious made me think, *It might be okay!* I went straight to the doctor in the morning and was sent for a scan where they confirmed that I had lost the baby. *Well, that's karma*, I told myself. I deserved this. This was what I deserved for having an abortion years earlier, this was my fault. I should have had the baby when I was given the opportunity.

Soon after, we fell pregnant again. We got past the 12 weeks and I breathed a huge sigh of relief, but the anxiety never left throughout the whole pregnancy. Holding my beautiful baby for the first time, I finally felt whole, like everything else could finally be forgotten. Did my previous abortion affect the love and completeness I felt when I held my baby girl for the first time? Absolutely not. I was made to be a mother, when the time was right. The newborn stage was difficult with my daughter having to be medicated for silent reflux, but I wouldn't have changed being a mum for the world. How my 20-year-old self would have coped with this though, I'm not too sure.

As it turned out, that marriage wasn't to last; another chapter of my life that certainly didn't turn out how I'd expected it to. It wasn't long after meeting my new partner that I found out that I was pregnant again. How could I have kids to two different dads? This was not what I had planned for my life! All the while, I was still dealing with the after-effects of a very messy and traumatising separation. Again, I felt ashamed of the way that my life was going. I didn't tell many people that I was pregnant and most people didn't find out until after my beautiful girl was born. I cringed every time questions arose at the hospital around my maiden name, married name and my partner's name, as if I had to explain myself and my circumstances to a stranger. The pregnancy of my second daughter was plagued with stress due to anti-E antibodies, which can cause hemolytic disease in the baby, requiring prenatal intervention. I had to have regular blood tests and weekly scans and was closely monitored throughout my pregnancy.

The prospect that my baby would need an intrauterine transfusion was extremely distressing. The guilt of my previous abortion was haunting me once again, leaving me wondering if these problems were caused by the abortion. My rational side knew that it wasn't, because my previous birth was completely healthy, but that didn't stop those intrusive thoughts. However, the birth, just like my first, was nothing short of empowering. Returning to myself, my inner strength and my primal roots shone through for another drug-free, natural birth. That life-changing, powerful, indescribable experience that is giving birth to your baby. Once again, holding my baby for the first time and feeling that overwhelming love and fierce protectiveness, I knew that motherhood was meant for me.

The journey into motherhood has been a tough one for me, with many hurdles to overcome. These feelings around my abortion seemed to amplify during my pregnancies when I had to come to grasps with what I had been through. I would eagerly check the pregnancy app every day to see how big my baby was today … the size of a pumpkin seed, so exciting! Yet it was an anxious excitement, constantly praying that everything would be okay. Then I would realise just how far along I had been when I'd had my abortion, and I'd feel the guilt, shame and sadness all over again. In this sense, processing my abortion experience was a slow burn. It was still affecting me much later on, in ways that I didn't even realise.

I had failed relationships, low self-confidence and no trust in my decisions or abilities. Had I have dealt with the emotions of the abortion at the time, these patterns may not have manifested. The idea that women who have had an abortion have also forfeited their right to grieve because of the decision they have made is one that kept me stuck for a long time. This concept of disenfranchised grief has been one of the greatest teachers in my life.

While I don't regret my decision, I do hold some regrets around my abortion. The main one being that I didn't take the time to give myself the compassion I so desperately needed, and find the ways to mourn my loss when it was happening.

It wasn't until after the birth of my second daughter that I really dove deep within myself and honoured the grieving process. For me, it was important to personally acknowledge and validate my loss, allowing myself to explore the meaning in that pregnancy, to feel the significance of the connection, and to honour the effect it had on my life. I discovered that the ability to go through such a traumatic experience and to then see the light at the end of a dark tunnel takes a huge amount of courage and strength. I've developed a deep resilience and used my experience as a transformative process. I've unveiled the powerful woman who was buried deep in my soul. I now look back at that 20-year-old me; the me that struggled for so long to come to terms with her journey and I now no longer feel shame or regret. Instead, I offer her compassion and empathy. Only then am I able to incorporate my abortion experience into my life journey.

This journey has brought me here, to serve and support other women going through similar experiences; women who come from all walks of life, who for many different reasons have made the decision to have an abortion. They are mothers, daughters, sisters, nieces, wives, aunties and grandmothers. They are doctors, lawyers, students, teenagers, nurses, women who 'don't believe in abortion', beauticians, politicians, journalists and hairdressers. They come from many different cultural and religious backgrounds. They are single, married, in long-term relationships, divorced or having casual sex. They usually share the belief that while the decision to have an abortion may have been a difficult one, they made the best choice they could at the time.

Because of the societal stigma that is placed on abortion, like myself, many women choose to keep their abortion a secret. Abortion is a decision deeply intertwined with our spiritual, ethical and political belief systems and the emotional aftermath is so impacted by these factors. We are left fearing judgement or believing that no-one else will understand or empathise with our pain.

I didn't share my abortion story until over a decade later. The worst thing about my experience was the shameful secrecy and the heaviness of it. It made me feel so alone and insignificant. The culture of shame and the stigma in our society meant that I felt I had to hide my abortion experience. I didn't know many people who had been through an abortion, but I knew what most people thought about them and a lot of them were never afraid to voice their opinion. It wasn't until much later that I realised that I did, in fact, know people who had had abortions. The problem was, they too were afraid of the stigma and judgment surrounding the topic. So instead of creating a community of compassion, support and understanding, we remained complicit in the shaming and ostracism of one another. If I'd only known that I had someone else with a similar experience to talk to, I don't think the load would have been so heavy.

The potential benefits of talking about our experiences are feeling heard and validated, finding meaning in our experience and being able to process the experience. My work with women encompasses a holistic approach, with the combined use of clinical hypnotherapy, strategic psychotherapy, mindset work, mindfulness and self-compassion. I hope to leave women feeling empowered and more in control of their lives, no longer doubting or questioning themselves by changing their mindset and shifting beliefs that are keeping them stuck. I help them to develop self-love and acceptance of themselves, so they can feel that they are good enough, loveable and worthy of everything they desire.

My abortion has been a dark shadow that held me back for so long and it is my hope that I can hold space for women, so that they too can know that they are not alone in their choice to have an abortion. So they can know they were the best person to make that decision that was best for them at that point in their life.

Stories have power, they help to bridge the gaps. They help us to learn, to recall, to empathise and to provoke. It has, at times, been hard for me to make my story make sense to others, but I know talking about my abortion has helped me make room for the rest of my life. Whether people agree with my decision or not, it is part of my journey and it is what has made me the woman that I am today.

Birth New

It is said that it is often in some of our greatest struggles that we truly find ourselves and I wholeheartedly believe this to be true. I now understand that the word loss is so important to my narrative because it helped me find and accept my own grief. And it is equally important for me to say the word abortion because it is my truth, and that sharing my truth may offer someone else an opening for their own.

Emma Woodham

Hi, I'm Emma.

I am a clinical hypnotherapist and counsellor based in Perth, WA. I help women who are adjusting to the changes of pregnancy and motherhood, birth trauma, antenatal and postnatal anxiety, miscarriages, abortions or the loss of a baby. I hold a Bachelor of Psychology and Addiction Studies, Diploma of Counselling and Diploma of Clinical Hypnotherapy and Strategic Psychotherapy. I am also a HypnoBirthing Australia practitioner.

I am now a mother to two beautiful little girls, a journey that has changed me in ways that I could have never prepared for. But my journey into parenthood has been far from smooth sailing, having experienced the heartbreak of loss, the shock of an unplanned pregnancy and the stress of a pregnancy that had medical issues. Nonetheless, this journey has brought me here, to serve and support women going through similar experiences.

Pregnancy and motherhood, whether intended or unintended, can create challenges to a woman's sense of self and identity, as well as their hopes, dreams and goals, and gaining good non-judgemental support is crucial. My hope is that women leave feeling empowered and more in control of their lives, no longer doubting or questioning themselves by changing their mindset and shifting beliefs that are keeping them stuck. I help them to develop self-love and acceptance of themselves, so that they can feel that they are good enough, loveable and worthy of everything they desire. My work with women encompasses a holistic approach, with the combined use of clinical hypnotherapy, energy work, mindset work, mindfulness and self-compassion.

Love and light.

www.elevatedtherapy.com.au
emma@elevatedtherapy.com.au
Instagram: @elevated_therapy_

Jenna Richards
BEAUTIFUL BEGINNINGS – CONNECTIONS BETWEEN BIRTH AND BREASTFEEDING

"The thoughtful energy we put into our pregnancy educates our birth, which enables our breastfeeding, and all of these communicate love to our parenting."
– Jenna Richards

"In the final days of my pregnancy I was pulled inward, meditating, often when I wasn't even aware of it (especially while cleaning), making space while my body was preparing for birth. Little pulls here or a sensation there, telling me that baby was going to be arriving soon. This time was peppered with small but increasing stretches, pee breaks and sleepless nights pacing back and forth, my womb responding to internal changes that softened me to my baby's coming. 'Are you getting ready, Mommy? I can't wait to meet you,' was constantly in my head and heart. It was as though they were looking for an optimal position to settle before the big marathon of their birthing. As the hours went by, I turned further inward to connect with my baby, to relax, release and open; allowing our bodies to flow and move when needed, rest when needed and work hard when needed. With every breath my baby moved through me, I yelled and moaned, said the same words over and over *in rhythmic meditation: 'I am soft, I am open.' I felt the need to open my hips and place my hand between my legs to feel my baby's head resting at the opening to this world. This is when I surrendered to the inborn reflex that moved baby out of my womb and into my arms."*

It has been said that while birth may have multiple holistic stages, it is within these spaces that there are multiple phases and pivotal steps along the way. Birth, just like the many other important junctures in our life, has times of great growth bookended by periods of pause; these pauses gift us the gaining of energy, learning, education and allow us reflection of our goals. Though at times it may seem like we have 'stalled', it is our body's way of preparing for a powerful burst of movement forward. Breastfeeding is no different, and in fact, I believe acts as the foundation in which all of our parenting is rooted.

Our body's ability to have a physiological birth is also the ability that allows us to nourish and nurture our babies from our breasts. The hormones that support our birthing times are the ones that initiate our milk-making cells, and the emotions that we feel when we hold our freshly born babies for the first time are the same inborn responses that we get every time we bring our baby to our breast. Because of this, breastfeeding is an essential part of meeting your baby's needs and those of your newly postpartum body.

Just as your baby will come, so too is your milk waiting. Our milk comes in stages just like the sensations and tightenings of birth. Not a lot at first; always just enough to keep baby suckling frequently, telling your breasts and your body that baby is saying, "I am here, and I am eager to feed." When we keep our baby at our breasts without the constant interruption of visitors or well-intended interventions, we create a rich environment where our baby's intuitive mechanism communicates their needs. This is picked up and understood by our maternal senses and starts to grow the connections for communication that will develop into instincts as new parents.

"My movement throughout my birth helped my baby navigate our birthing time and my birth canal; it provided me with relief when I got into a position that worked for the both of us. I remembered this while latching my baby for the first time. It makes sense, right? That different positions and ways of latching would be driven by the needs and instincts of me and my baby and not by outside influences. I asked myself: How does my latch feel? How does my body feel holding my baby in this position? Do I find my baby fidgeting or that I want to hold my breast? Following my instincts in birth and breastfeeding was one of the most important factors in having a good experience and reaching my goals."

When we give power to outside 'experts' who tell us to intervene in a way that doesn't speak to our own gut instincts and the inborn instincts of our babies, we neglect our rights and sovereignty as the expert.

Our baby's nervous system is also programmed to connect with our own because we are their protection against disease and infection. Just as the placenta protects our babies in our womb, feeding infants from our breasts grants our babies access to our immune support, and antibodies for bacteria and viruses that we come into contact with. It is our immune system that responds to viruses in baby's saliva making their way through the skin on our nipples to help them prevent serious illnesses.

Hormones

Our pregnancy, birth and breastfeeding journeys are all driven by the same hormones, the first being *oxytocin* which is also well-known as the *love* or *bonding* hormone.

"It was the same feeling after I orgasmed, the feeling I got when I pushed my baby out. The one where I felt at total peace with the world, the same feeling I get from a long and much-needed hug from a close loved one, or when I eat a piece of very yummy chocolate. This is the feeling I get when I smell my newborn baby's head; my body relaxes and knows I am complete. As I latch

my baby I close my eyes and run the tips of my fingers up and down their belly, I playfully circle their knee and wiggle their toes. I open my eyes and make contact with their stare. My loving and gentle touch makes my baby smile, just like holding their hand, singing our favourite song. This is how I connect with my little love, and all of this happens when I feed my babies from my breast."

Progesterone is the hormone that is responsible for continuing our pregnancies and is produced by our placenta. This connection abruptly ends with the birth of the placenta, and it is this distinct drop of progesterone that signals to your body that the baby has been born and that it is time to start increasing the volume of our milk, which takes place over the next couple of days. This is why it is so important to have baby actively suckling at the breast and that your baby is given the opportunity to have unrestricted access to the birthing parent and their milk directly after their birth and in the following early days.

Prolactin (pro=positive, lact=milk, in=increase) is responsible for the increase of milk after the birth of your baby and changes from hormone-driven supply to responding to our baby's needs as demand and supply takes over milk production. This means that the more your baby feeds from your breast, the more milk you will make to match their growth and calorie needs.

Babies are born full; they desire to be at our breast for comfort and to awaken the cells that make and secrete milk.

Emotional stages to breastfeeding

Just as there are the holistic stages of birth, I feel there are emotional stages to breastfeeding:

Baby coming to your chest and nursing for the first time

The first emotional stage of breastfeeding starts when our babies leave our womb and are placed on our bodies. When we reach down and pull our baby from our vulva, we pause and have our first glimpse of the person who has been growing and sharing our body for the past 10 months, as our baby takes their first breath. This is the start of breastfeeding.

This stage is marked by high levels of oxytocin, of fierce emotion and an intensity that has been described as an eternal gratitude.

This stage is linked to our birthing time and should be met with reverence, a dark room, no disruption, the only voices to be heard are the parents. Don't you dare take the baby away from the birthing mother – not for checks (unless there is a medical need), don't wipe away the protective vernix, don't touch the baby, don't interfere. Just don't.

This is a sacred time when baby and parents get their first sense of being together as a family. There will be tears, cries of love, gratitude, and whispers of 'we did it!' along with plenty of kisses. This is a sacred time. When we start to come back to the outside world and from the veil within ourselves, we may start to acknowledge the other persons in the room, start to talk about our birth and maybe ask for something to drink; if we don't, please have someone offer it. We will be protective of our babies and have a strong internal instinct to keep baby close; this should be protected at all costs. Our babies need to be kept with us. Unless there is a medical emergency (a real one), there should be no wiping, weighing, cleaning, checking, poking or prodding, and all health care professionals (really anyone who is not a direct parent of the baby who was just born) should leave the room. Every parent, every family, every baby deserves to be gifted with a period of unhindered and peaceful bonding time directly after their birth that should be continued until the family decides otherwise. It is true that all births – hospital, homebirth or freebirthing families – benefit from this all-encompassing time away from prying eyes and eager hands. It allows for connection and communication to begin directly after our birth. The first person baby should see, hear and feel their touch is their parent. Consideration should be given that while this is true for all families, this is not attainable in most medical settings such as a hospital, surgical or birth centre, and we need to be very honest about this.

If we let them, babies will slowly make their way across our bodies towards our breasts, using their legs to push up and forward. They use their hands to grab and navigate; their senses direct them towards our breasts using a scent that is secreted by our Montgomery glands (bumps that follow the ridge of the areola) that produce an oil which mimics the smell like their amniotic fluid, and the dark colour of our nipples helps our near-sighted babies direct their progress. This 'breast crawl' usually takes around two hours, but it can take longer or shorter and that's okay as well.

Once baby is at the breast they will nuzzle, lick and rest. They will latch and let go, reposition, latch and suckle. There will be no pattern, just trial and error. Our babies may stay latched and have a good feed or be more 'uncoordinated' and practice coming on and off the breast. This is the baby's way of learning to feed from your body and you learning how to support their cues; this is the first step of parenting with love and the foundation for communication.

"I was told that my baby was hungry, that my 'milk has not come in yet', that baby is 'not getting enough from my breast' and that giving them a bottle of formula was needed. I knew this was not true and put up my hand and said, 'No, thank you, my baby and I are learning.' I asked the nurses and doctors to leave our birth space which gave us time to attune ourselves to this new soul. We knew that baby was born full, full of poop! That they were feeding not out of hunger but out of a need to suckle and to be close to me. This helped us stay calm and let their inborn natural reflex speak to my body, that my colostrum was there in the perfect amount that my baby would help my breasts make more milk the longer baby stayed right where they belonged."

All babies lose weight, whether we see it or not.

After a time of quiet awareness, after a good amount of time at the breast, our babies will have a good sleep. This is the end of the first emotional stage of breastfeeding.

Jenna Richards

Getting to know your baby and getting to know breastfeeding

As we nurse our baby over the next couple of days, we may discover that breastfeeding is a talent that we improve with practise. After that first night, and for the majority of the next 6 months, our baby will almost always be happily at your breast.

These are the simple truths of breastfeeding:

- *Most of our babies need to nurse through the night.*
- *Our newborn infants will likely feed up to and past 14 times a day, and this is likely to continue in varying degrees throughout the first year.*
- *Babies nurse from the breast for more reasons than just the need for calories.*
- *No baby weans on their own before the first year.*
- *All babies benefit from being at the breast.*
- *Any amount of human milk is beneficial.*
- *Our babies are always communicating with us.*

"We were told by our friends and family that nursing through the night is important and is to be seen as biologically normal, something that we should plan for during our 4th trimester. Both me and my partner benefitted by planning for our baby to wake often, to sleep next to us and to wake us when they are in need, whether that need was for milk, a nappy change or for comfort and help getting back to a restful sleep. Instead of a nursery we created a postpartum bedroom that was kept warm enough not to need covers, dark enough to sleep but with a light source that allowed us to parent without waking our baby. When we got up to nurse, my partner would get up as well to restore and refill our supplies, refilling my water bottles, bringing the charger for my phone, getting me a snack, bringing diapers, cloths and nipple balm if I needed them, finishing their part of parenting only after they checked in with me and had whispered loving words of pride and support for my hard work. This did not come easy and was hard work, but it was important for me to remember that I can do hard things, I gave birth."

When night-time parenting gets hard, and it will, stay close to home. Nap when baby naps. Have friends and family mother you while you mother your baby. This means having meals made and put into your freezer; laundry cleaned, folded and put away; vacuuming, dusting and tidying with one room a week cleaned fully. You should do NONE of this, and if you cannot afford a postpartum doula then this duty rests on the shoulders of friends and family. Partners can wake early to give you space in the morning to sleep, bath, have quiet time or anything else that replenishes you.

The number of times a baby feeds throughout the day is not a predictor of supply but rather the act of a smart baby. Newborns are not only learning how to transfer milk from the breast, but they are also learning about their own needs and when hunger turns to satiation. Just like adults, infants can desire a quick snack or large meal and it is not our job to control how long or how often baby is at the breast but rather to make sure that they have the opportunity to feed when the need comes to them. You can't overfeed your baby when breastfeeding, but we can offer the breast too little.

"I was not fully prepared for the vast number of reasons my baby would feed; of course because they are hungry, but also because they wanted to keep me close. I knew it made them feel safe. They fed when they were scared and upset, like they were asking me for a hug. As they grew up and we continued to follow their lead and continued to breastfeed, I noticed that they would feed from my breast when they were thoughtful and needed time to pause and think about their environment. I never felt that these reasons were manipulative or unimportant, but that they were a normal part of their developing mind, and there was no safer place than at my breast or on my lap."

During the first year, our babies go from getting all their nutritional needs at our breast to trying new foods. This does not mean that the importance of our milk is less, but rather that we are introducing other foods that speak to our traditions and allowing them to learn about food in a way that is supported by nursing from our breast. Our baby's need for our milk is of the utmost importance for the first 2 years of life and beyond, and it isn't until after 6 months of life that we should start the move towards other foods.

"After our baby turned 6 months, we felt it important to offer breastmilk first before giving any solid foods, to allow our baby to feed from my body when they wanted, and to gently suggest the breast when they played, getting them down for naps and at bedtimes. It was our way to soothe and meet their emotional and physical needs. My husband and I felt this was important to meet our baby's growing physiological and emotional needs as well as to keep my body in sync with our little love. I feel that because of this all 3 of us were connected, responding to and communicating with each other, and this helped us feel confident that baby was getting everything they needed while we started our journey to introducing new and exciting foods."

While this stage of breastfeeding comes with its difficulties and learning complexities, it is also a time for great developmental strides and growth in bonding between us and our babies.

Finding our stride and leading from the breast

This step is a time frame all of its own and is different for all families. This is when the confidence of our interconnected nature and the interdependence between us and our babies comes into its true light, both keeping our babies close with a loving touch while making space for the gift of encouragement and independence. While our baby's inquisitiveness and play take them farther from our sides, the knowledge that they will always have a place at our breast boosts their confidence and chides any thought of affliction from the unknown.

We have grown through our struggles to the knowledge that our body is capable of providing the nurturing environment and nourishment our children need. We trust our instincts and take back our rights to decide what is best when it comes to our family's care.

We *know* that we are the experts in what is best for our babies and ourselves, that we pay little to no heed to naysayers even when they are deemed by society to be experts in their field. We allow our relationship to our babies and theirs to our breast to ebb and flow as it needs without giving thought to the 'what ifs' and 'buts'. When we do seek further knowledge, we do so from others who speak to our own heart and goals as a parent, who want to lead with love and from the breast. Our babies will feed less one day and more the next, they will take food as they see fit, and we won't feel the need to be dictated by numbers or presumed normalcies.

These stages of nursing are flagged by the birth of our baby and their first latch, to learning alongside our newborns as they educate us about their needs, and we cultivate their emotional and communicational intelligence by responding to them with loving and compassionate guidance. While these things can be taught in other ways, there is no better source for security, nourishment and nurturing than what we give our children when they are at our breast.

Jenna Richards

Hello friends, I'm Jenna Richards, an International Board-Certified Lactation Consultant (IBCLC) and radical doula that supports homebirth, family births and families experiencing loss, including miscarriage, stillbirth and abortion. As creator and owner of Logical Lactation, I am passionate about creating dyad-focused support spaces for new families, getting the word out there on the 4th trimester and educating other health care providers about the significant and powerful resources of community care.

Originally from Toronto, Canada, we spent 10 years in Vancouver BC where I had my first daughter M after struggling with fertility for 5 years. She was diagnosed with 'failure to thrive' which moved us to make the decision to give supplemental milks. I worked hard for the next 6 months to build my supply with medications, pumping schedules and still vividly remember feeding at 4am, crying and in pain. Because of my passion and commitment to my parenting goals, I continued to nurse my first daughter until they were 6 years old, through my second pregnancy and am currently breastfeeding my second, now 5 years old, who was born at home with a private practice midwife in Sydney shortly before moving to Perth, WA.

It was such a difficult time. So, I decided I needed to know more ...

My very first lactation course was Breastfeeding Support for Health Care Providers through Douglas College and after that I was HOOKED! Over the next 7 years I became a doula with Wise Woman Way of Birth, a La Leche League breastfeeding counsellor and started working towards my IBCLC, finishing off with the lactation consultant program through the University of California (which I graduated with distinction).

As the owner of Logical Lactation, I am an International Board-Certified Lactation Consultant (IBCLC), lactation educator counsellor and doula who specialises in nutrition and community development, supporting families to birth where and with whom they choose and to reach their nursing goals. I am also currently working towards my degree in counselling. Through my business, I offer lactation support to new and older families, touching on topics such as birthing and its connection to nurturing our babies from our breast, prenatal breastfeeding classes, relactation and induced lactation, new parent nutrition and meal preparation classes for partners, as well as community and family support groups for breastfeeding parents and those planning a homebirth. I also do lectures and love writing articles on topics that I am passionate about.

During my free time you can find me on my SUP or hiking around Yanchep, WA, at my computer with continuing education/ally training, and enjoying beach life. I also work with current lactation consultant students, supporting them through their certification process, and assisting doulas working with nursing/breastfeeding families and creating space for new parents to find like-sminded friends, lifting each other up and sharing their stories so that they can nurture their own communities.

www.logicallactation.com
Instagram: @logicallactation
Facebook: LogicalLactation

Nicole Aly
HONOURING HER

Intuition. We're all born with it. That gut instinct that keeps us safe, the warning bell that rings when we need to pay attention. When did I stop listening? When did I allow other people's opinions or judgements determine how I treat my body? Did I surrender willingly? Expectation of self is rarely unique or authentic. It's carved and moulded by our experiences, our parents, our society and our community. The numbing that comes from surrendering to the flood of the masses, a familiar trust. Insecure safety from a truth that is unreliable and unforgiving. How do we occupy this sacred space to be honoured and revered, and not used for another's ego, purpose or agenda? In a world of artificial intelligence, alternate realities and misguided truths, what is still ours to own, if not our own bodies?

It was a magical night for some: a fairytale. Mary was preparing to walk down the aisle to marry her prince, Prince Frederik of Denmark, and I was about to give birth to my first child. As I walked the corridors of the hospital, I felt a sense of trepidation. The hospital was busy and buzzing with excitement of the royal wedding. My midwife seemed particularly keen to discuss the 'goings-on' of the wedding. Like I gave a shit. Mary's dress was not high on my priority list.

Birth New

It had been more than 24 hours since my water broke. Fatigue and exhaustion occupied every cell of my body. Labour wasn't progressing and I was administered Syntocinon to bring on contractions. A monitor was placed around my abdomen, to pick up any changes in the baby's heartbeat, recording onto a paper printout. External monitoring is often used when there is a risk of complication.

Another examination of my cervix revealed that I was not yet fully dilated. The midwife left the room and returned with an ultrasound machine. While preparing the doppler, she began to explain that the baby may be in a breech position and proceeded to talk me through the birthing process. A hot panic rose in my chest and radiated throughout my body. I asked to see a doctor. I voiced my fears, demanding a caesarean. It had been hours; I was in so much pain and the pethidine given to me earlier had provided no relief. I didn't feel like I was in safe hands. Her refusal to seek outside counsel felt almost dogmatic and self-serving, with no regard for my wellbeing or that of my baby. I was dismissed, my concerns perceived as unnecessary and dramatic. My body was screaming, I didn't feel like I was in control. The ultrasound revealed that the baby was not in a breech position, so I put my intuition to the side, and naively, placed my trust in the midwife.

Needing to go to the bathroom, I pressed the buzzer requesting assistance. The monitor around my abdomen was disconnected and when I returned to my bed it was not put back on. At some point the midwife noticed that the belt was disconnected and reattached it to the monitor. The paper printout began to record and the needle scribble was off the charts. The midwife was visibly alarmed by the reading; however, she quickly recovered and told me that my heartbeat must have been interfering. Another wave of anxiety flooded my body. Why was there so much resistance to call for a doctor? Not at any point in the night had I felt secure, looked after or safe. It was confusing and messy and the midwife was trying to keep it together with sticky tape and words of encouragement. I felt like I was in the in-between, locked in a chasm of pain and fear, with no way to escape, no way to call for help.

It was finally time to push. I don't really remember the specifics. Forceps were used, baby's head was crowning but she wasn't moving forward. My perineum was cut to speed up delivery. Jade entered the world, silent and purple. The medical staff, who were previously unavailable, now filled the room. Time slowed down as they pumped oxygen into her tiny lungs. I held my breath and prayed that my baby girl would take her first one. Eventually I heard a cry. She was breathing! Swaddled in a blanket and in the arms of the midwife, Jade was brought to my side. I looked at my beautiful baby, her jet black hair and her precious blue eyes. She was more beautiful than I could have imagined and then she was gone, whisked away. I didn't even get to hold her.

Jade was taken to special care and I was wheeled to my room for recovery. Sometime during the night I heard a code blue and I sat straight up in bed. I knew it was Jade. I waited for someone to come and get me. I had no idea where special care was. I wasn't even sure I could walk there. I sat in my bed, alone, in the dark, exhausted and scared. Not knowing if my baby was safe.

I was woken early the next morning, the nurse presenting me with a wheelchair, to take me to the special care nursery. Overnight, Jade had experienced several seizures, the doctor explaining how her legs had been cycling throughout the night, indicating seizure activity. The words he used didn't convey the gravity of the situation, but I could feel the urgency and concern in his voice. Jade was being transferred to a bigger hospital with a NICU (neonatal intensive care unit) where she would be put into an induced coma to reduce the swelling on her brain.

I feel so disconnected from this story, I barely remember the sequence of events. I found a photo of Jade laying on her back, her body still – I assume she was asleep. Her head is swollen and cone shaped. My index finger is stroking Jade's tiny left foot, the only visible part of her body not consumed by medical tape, leads or IVs. Next to Jade I notice a handheld resuscitation pump. There is a numbness that comes with this level of overwhelm, a mixture of disbelief and shock. One foot in front of the other, moving to where I'm pointed. There's no room for anything else in this moment.

For weeks I watched Jade in her incubator, touching her tiny hands and feet with my hand, through the hole in the side. Hours spent sitting beside her, wondering what was going on for her, longing to hold her in my arms. To bring her close to my face and smell her delicate baby scent, instead of the pink sanitiser that filled my nostrils.

When they woke Jade from her coma, the swelling on her brain had come down, an MRI was taken and Jade was transferred from NICU back to special care nursery. Jade's care was complex. There were nearly a dozen different medications to administer, feeding was challenging, and it required skill and patience. Jade was unable to breastfeed, so a nurse gave Jade her first bottle and a nurse gave Jade her first bath.

A few days prior to discharge I stayed with Jade to learn her full routine. Our last night at the hospital, Jade managed to wiggle out of her wrap and her little hat had fallen off. The nurse woke me in the middle of the night, to scold me and tell me that Jade was cold. She then took her for the rest of the night. I felt defeated and hopeless, and I hadn't even left the hospital yet. Every interaction with Jade felt clinical. I was told what to do, when to do it and how to do it. And by the time Jade was ready to come home, I felt like I was leaving with the hospital's baby.

We were told that Jade had suffered a brain injury and that we should take her home, enjoy her and wait for her milestones. Life at home was hard. I felt very alone, disconnected and vulnerable. There isn't a word for how sleep deprived I was, how hard it was every minute of every day. Jade wasn't thriving and she never stopped crying. Fingers were pointed at me to do better. I felt like I was drowning. My strong sense of responsibility and the mammoth doses of guilt and shame kept me from running.

Friends just disappeared. I can only assume they didn't know how to support me or thought I was doing fine. Bryan had gone back to work when Jade was in NICU, and he didn't know how to cope any better than I did. Desperate and alone, I rang my mum and asked her to take Jade, to adopt her. I didn't want to be her mum anymore. That was the day I left; I left Jade in her cot. My baby was safer in the house by herself than she was with me. I was screaming for help, and no-one was listening.

A nurse from the hospital came to the house to do a welfare check. We lived on the outskirts of Melbourne and had to travel a fair way to access services and shops. We had so many medical appointments in the city, the long car rides were torturous. Jade felt unsafe in her body when she wasn't being held, so her screaming was unbearable. I remember driving the winding roads, lined with tall trees, and thinking how nice it would be to just keep driving, straight into a gum tree. How peaceful that would be. I was so far removed from reality that I didn't realise this was a confession, until the nurse threatened custody of Jade. I was forced to see the hospital's psychologist.

I had spoken to many professionals about Jade's birth, and their resounding response was the same. "It is just one of those things, you need to get over it and move on." I was still seeking answers, so the psychologist arranged a meeting with the hospital to go over Jade's birth records. I didn't know what I was looking for, I had no medical background or knowledge. We went through the entire folder and recounted the events of the birth. They assured me all protocols and procedures were followed. I then noticed an exchange between the nurses, confirming to me that they were hiding something. I was angry. I felt like the midwife had taken chances with Jade's life but the more questions I asked, the more I was made to feel like it was my fault. Eventually I gave up. It was easier to believe that my intuition was wrong.

I was in a holding pattern, navigating a world of unknowns, trying to keep my head above water, while every wave threatened to engulf me.

Not knowing was an agonising torture. Would Jade talk, would she walk, would she understand the world around her? There was no relief, no respite from the burning questions that I allowed to exist in the quiet of the night. Waiting, watching for a sign, any sign. Something to hold on to, a spark of intelligence, an interaction. One night, after a bath, I gave Jade's chest a little tickle, like I had done many times before, hoping for a response to my playful gesture. This time a tiny giggle escaped her lips and my heart filled with joy. Relief flooded my body and I felt love for the first time. Finally, we made a connection.

Jade was eventually diagnosed with cerebral palsy. The extent of the brain injury was unknown and dependent on new pathways forming. I think of Jade's brain like a map. The CBD represents Jade's cognitive brain, her intellect, and the suburbs are the pathways that carry messages to the country (to the nerves in Jade's body), the area that receives messages and tells the body when and how to move. Imagine that there was a huge fire in the suburbs and the whole ring around the city was destroyed. You're in the city and you want to drive to the country, so you must go through the suburbs to get there but every road you turn down is damaged by fire. The only way to get through is to keep driving down different streets until you find a way. Jade has a high physical disability and is non-verbal, but she is intelligent, switched on and she understands everything.

As I sat opposite Jade's neurologist, I was hit with a reality that I had always known. The bruising on Jade's brain was indicative of a birth-related injury that could have been prevented. Would Jade's outcome have been different had I stood in my power? Isn't this what I had been searching for? Answers to my burning questions? Someone to blame, other than myself and my body? A body that let me down. No amount of money in the world was going to make up for the mistakes made that day. I am still wading through this mess of feelings. Multifaceted layers of healing, stacked high upon one another, waiting to be unravelled. Waiting to forgive.

We began legal proceedings, suing the hospital for negligence. No doctor or medical professional in Australia would speak out against another for fear of retribution. For 6 years I relived the trauma of Jade's birth. I was scrutinised by the hospital's legal team, their specialists, psychologists, therapists and lawyers. We were preparing our case for court, working with an obstetrician in the UK. We were fighting for a better quality of life for Jade.

Jade and I attended early intervention at CPEC (Cerebral Palsy Education Centre) in Melbourne. At 18 months old, Jade was one of the youngest to attend. The first year was brutal and exhausting. Jade cried all day, and I cried all the way home. We repeated the physical routine of body movements and patterning, and the repetition helped Jade's brain find new pathways and Jade began to trust her body. She was fierce and determined, wanting to experience all of life. Jade found her voice through alternative communication, using a PODD book – a complex book of symbols. Jade would use her eyes and nod her head to indicate each word she wanted to communicate. The process was painfully slow but allowed Jade to express herself beyond a simple yes or no head movement. Jade now uses a speech generating device, an electronic version of the PODD book, that she operates with her eyes. Jade is well known in our community for her daredevil qualities and her FOMO (fear of missing out). "I want to do what the others are doing" – a phrase Jade uses regularly. No matter the adventure or the level of inclusion, there is always a way to allow Jade the same opportunities as everyone else.

Jade had her first surgery when she was 9 months old and has had multiple surgeries since. I no longer stay silent; I watch and I listen. I speak up, ask questions, and I challenge belief systems. Jade's doctors and specialist are consultants and I welcome their expertise and allow them to do what they do best but I no longer place Jade completely in their hands. This year Jade had spinal rod surgery. During recovery she wasn't breathing and a MET code was called, bringing in a medical emergency team. In these situations, I don't panic, I stay focused. Medical staff rely heavily on my input of what is 'normal' for Jade. Balancing pain relief and her little body is trial and error. I stand in my power and in my knowing, and I advocate for Jade. Hospital is exhausting but it's no longer a scary place.

Jade loves food and will absolutely throat punch you if you're not feeding her fast enough but she is unable to consume the volume needed to sustain a healthy body weight. A feeding tube goes directly to her stomach and food is administered via a pump. For years the hospital supplied Jade with formula. Jade was quite sick with chest infections and pneumonia, and she regularly vomited up her feeds. I wanted to change Jade's diet and see if that made a difference. The hospital refused to supply Jade's equipment if I didn't order formula, so I began making a wall of formula boxes in my living room, while I worked with a naturopath to produce a nutrient-dense, blended diet that was thin enough to go through her feeding pump without blocking it.

Jade put on 10kg, stopped vomiting and had no chest infections or hospital admissions. The change was extraordinary, and I had enough evidence to confidently approach the hospital again. They continued to hold their position on formula being best practice for patients, based on studies that were funded by the same company that supplied the formula. I asked to see the study on blended diets and there isn't one. Apparently, studies cost millions of dollars, and no-one was interested in funding this one. In the end we agreed to disagree, and I was allowed temporary access to Jade's equipment while they reviewed my case with the hospital board. I never heard from them again and I know many families that have since made the switch to a blended diet, however, I am still advocating for the right to choose while in the care of the hospital, as an inpatient.

As Jade is getting older, I am moving away from my role as primary caregiver. I have more opportunity to simply love her, be her mother and witness her journey. I can now take time to pause, reflect and review my life as a mother and as a woman.

Nicole Aly

The right to choose was taken from me in the most profound of ways, during a time when my value should have been held in the highest regard. I was denied the right to choose my birth plan. I was gaslighted, manipulated and shamed. I was broken. My body was broken. A toxic burden built inside me, twisting and distorting truths, placing blame and punishing accordingly. Deep loss, grief and sorrow filled my body. I was not worthy of love.

I am allowing my body to feel again, massaging my edges, supplying blood flow to parts of my psyche cut from my conscience, numb and forgotten. I tip toe through the technicoloured spectrum of feelings, discovering each new variation with wonder but not always with ease – that rush of blood flow can be painful. As my body lightens and learns to release, to unclench my stomach and relax my shoulders, I am reminded that I am loved. I am worthy. I am perfect and my body is perfect. I honour her.

Nicole Aly

Hi, I'm Nicole Aly and I am the founder of Honouring Her Temple.

I am privileged to reside in both Phillip Island and Melbourne, where I split my time equally with my three children, two incredible girls and one spirited boy.

I spent my whole life never really knowing who I was. Growing up, I felt like something was missing, like I was walking around with a gaping hole at my centre. I rarely gave a thought to my own needs or validated my opinions. I was not in touch with my sexuality, my pleasure or my orgasm. I was not open to receiving in any way.

In 2020, I began a healing journey of self-love, working with powerful healers and powerful medicine. One night, sitting on my couch, I was hit with a thundering wave of desire that rolled and vibrated through my yoni. I felt pure love radiating from my womb to my heart. My whole body was yearning and aching to receive. I had never felt anything so glorious or so powerful in my life.

I could feel what I had been missing. As women we are meant to be connected. We are born to be a powerhouse of creativity and love, desire

Nicole Aly

and passion. To live in our authenticity and rise. I imagine a world where every girl, every woman remembers who she is, remembers her worth and remembers her power. Our love of self can change the world … we just have to remember.

I have experienced the potent alchemy of what is possible when women connect, love and support one another. I have cried from the depths of my womb, released the primal screams of my wild woman, awakened my body to pleasure, reclaimed my voice and reconnected with myself, my powerhouse and my intuition. I can't wait to see all that I will create and birth.

Honouring Her Temple offering yoni massage therapy, reiki massage, woman's circles and self-development workshops.

www.honouringhertemple.com.au
Instagram: @honouring_her_temple
Facebook: Honouring Her Temple

Claire I'n't Veld

YOU AS THE MIRACLE OF BIRTH

Do you ever wonder how we each came to be here? Where we uniquely began in the lands and time and space before we were conceived, when we were the seeds of creation ourselves?

Have you ever considered the importance of such a question? The point or intention to understand what is your unique origin and essence of your truth and self – the source and life force which ignites the soul and lifts within you the wellspring of your spirit?

Pretty big questions to open with, I know, yet the miracle of birth is not lost on me, nor is the magic of birth lost within you.

Whether you believe you came from an egg or star or seed or a zygote fusion from cellular divisions, the words you choose to describe the origin of you, form the language of the lands that weave the world within and forge the mother tongue that sings the songs of home in your heart.

Birth is where we each begin the embodiment of our origin. It is the debut of our artistry, our mystery and our mastery. Birth activates our mission, grounds the passion and colours the shape, frequency and framework which anchors the canvas of what and who and how we are and why we create the many masterpieces that emit from our being, into being here.

Birth has always captivated and fascinated me. My favourite part-time job as a teen was at a dairy tending cows in calving where I was blessed to witness birth each day and each cow with her own way. I had a visceral longing to be with everything. Even pregnancy testing and the process of entering the void beyond the fecal matter to hold hand in hoof with a life not yet seen, touched me so deeply. It built for me the recognition of the bridge that we each are between worlds and what links us in life to every other living being in this realm and beyond.

Before I share my story with you, I wish for you to know more of your own.

For if we are to talk about birth and the deep ways it connects us all to the core of who we are, I would love for you to know more about you.

I invite you now to travel back to your birth. To sense in your own way your arrival for the first time in this body. To ponder the ways in which you were received and how you were welcomed. To discover what it was for you and you alone, to be born here. What it meant for you to come and bring your essence and light and truth and to be seen and it shared through you, as you were then and as you are now, in your fullness and in all of your potential.

I wrap these words around you now and implore you to explore how it really was for you. What it felt like in those first moments as you calibrated the outer world from the one within you. What you drew as the imprint of life itself as you in turn gifted yourself here and breathed those first breaths of your essence into the atmosphere.

The opening to and the recognition of the process for each of us, and the bliss and challenge and every myriad of sensation and emotion along the way is important, vital in fact to the whole of ourselves as humans and as a collective humanity.

This is our untapped resource – birth. The birth of ourselves and what we open to in the birth of others. Many of us do not experience the magnitude of our power, possibility and potential in our own births, yet we are offered again the doorways and opportunity in the experience of birthing another. Whatever the pathway or process of birth, we are a miracle to it. Yes, we are gifting ourselves as the miracle to birth. You. You as the one who said yes. Yes to coming here and yes to bringing another and more of yourself through you. Birth does not exist without us.

We are each created as the individual essence of our energetic signature, drawn from every reach of the cosmos and beyond, yet unique to the field in which we draw on as our sense of source and beacon of home. For all that you are and all that you believe yourself to be, in the moment that you availed yourself to the seeds of creation that wished to come here, you sent out the song of your heart. Like a siren of vibration and signature symphony, you made it known that you were open.

Every moment from that intention sent out the sonic waves of your heart to not just call them here but find the echo of their energy intending to find their home in you. It was this initial resonance that not only did magnetise you in to the planetary particles of all possibilities and sparks of potential to find your form, but it so too creates a vortex of light so bright it would propel a wormhole from the void to form that which would hold and swirl a new life and all their source to travel the distance from their timeline in space and their world and dimension to be here.

Each journey, each step of the way from conception is built by the recognition of your hearts beating in unison to a drum and song that synchronises these worlds and realities as one. Through the stages of gestation and cycles of growth, expansion, death, renewal and integration you pave the way for an entirely new consciousness to come through, both that of the babe in the womb and of you.

A bridge is formed, in every sense, threading its way as a web between you and them and each field that will resource you. As you collect and gather and grow the codes that will be sown into the future to support the birth and beyond of both of you, you embody the cellular templates and genetic expression that will inspire the inquiry of remembering again and again.

Every day, each breath and activation is an initiation. A milestone and a magnificent mastery of how you meet the differences of your energy and assimilate together as one to innately know and integrate within you the alchemy of meeting and embracing your individual signatures without bounds or separation.

As you build and serve this communion, a foundation of energy grows within you. One which holds all worlds and dimensions. You open and embody the unlimited source to be available to everything that is asked of you whether you dare to know it in that moment or not. You become the gateway not just to pass through it, but to be continually served, resourced and fulfilled by it. The innate trust that those worlds hold in you, as you, as the keeper and the door, exists beyond your belief of it, not needing your approval or recognition of the divinity of you because it innately knows you already are it.

In the process of birth, the unique energetic signature that we are calibrates from the womb of the mother to tessellate with the ever-evolving dynamic of the earth's energetic field and find a place here and home in her heart. For each of us, the passage of birth and the dance of finding our alchemical fit is different. It is not a process which only travels hand in hand with the physical birth. It continues on in the sacred time and daily unfolding of the ever-present expansion of postpartum and parenthood. Grounding our energy as far into the heart field as possible and expanding the bridge and new partnership with the earth, akin to the one of warmth, nourishment and safety that we found in the womb with the one that grew us.

In the understanding of this uniqueness, we wish for you to know that all is sacred. And by this we do not mean that it is not challenging or harrowing or healing or heartbreaking or horrendous or ecstatic or blissful or surprisingly enjoyable and every fullness you may ever find of yourself in it. What we wish for you to know is that however you experience birth, it is a divine expression of you and you are celebrated no more or less from the experience of it but from the fact and pure existence that you gifted yourself to it. That your presence in birth is always honoured as the miracle of you as birth itself.

For it takes all potentials to create the infinite ways available to us all as a template for possibility and to carve on the halls of the heart the records for potentiality. Birth becomes our blueprint that we use each day to bring and become more and more of ourselves here.

So a little bit about my own birth journey. I was born on a Sunday afternoon in March under a new moon amidst a solar eclipse in Aries. A brand-new starseed so excited to be here, my mum described to me that I 'pretty much birthed myself' which does no justice or service to what I have asked of her in being here.

Fresh, exquisitely sensitive, open and full of fire, my enthusiasm to experience this planetary creation soon wore off as I landed in my body and felt the reality of what it actually meant to be a human. The sensations, emotions, temperature, taste, noise and hunger overwhelmed me. The act of having to fit my enormous pre-sense of myself into this teeny body felt excruciating. This, along with the heartache of being separated into a tiny form from the truth of love as I had known it, whilst still receiving the thoughts and feelings of everyone and everything beyond my bodily bounds, made for a very challenging time. I was labelled colicky, fussy, unsettled and intense with a set of lungs that I was not afraid to use.

I was not at all comfortable until I got on the move and could put all my will into action. Between the age of 18 months and 2 years, I had 3 close calls with death. Two drownings and one big leap off a very large wall onto very hard concrete. Each of these experiences were my own orchestrations of attempting to return to my home before birth. I was intending to get a ticket out of here and take my human suit back to the workshop for a different model, though it would seem that my body and soul contracts had other plans.

These experiences in my early life were the beginning of many rebirths into this body of multiple incarnation experiences. Some were soul exchanges and energetic upgrades and some are what you may refer to as walk-ins and higher self embodiments. In each experience, a new part of me was born into this body and a new template of incarnation was activated. Without the guidance and support to ground these births into the earth, I struggled to integrate these exchanges and the mismatches of my energy signatures in my body. This would see me passing out and abandoning ship any time the energy within me was activated and pushed me over the limit level of my calibration.

It was not until I was in my early 20s that I began to really explore and gain understanding of what it was for me to be here and started investigating my galactic lineage and pursuing the 'gifts' and abilities that had been giving me so much grief in my childhood. I began study in self-mastery and training as a channel which gave me such an understanding of myself, though it wasn't until facing my death again on a spiritual pilgrimage in Egypt that I anchored more deeply into this incarnation and skin with a reckoning of choosing myself to be married soul, spirit and body, and I resolved wanting to leave and really committed to being here.

As the timing would have it, exactly 9 months after that rebirth in the Temple of Edfu and the day after returning from a quantum field higher self-embodiment retreat, I conceived our son.

I knew instantly the moment he dropped into my womb and the excitement I felt was reminiscent of my own time in gestation. I felt so high and alive with light in his pregnancy. His energy signature was piercing, clear and so high frequency, that I became averse to the density and heaviness of anything grounding here whilst becoming home for him for that time.

His birth was earlier than I anticipated. He came strong and fast with a force of will that remains to be seen. It was a lightning-quick change of plans for me from intending to be birthing at home to going to the hospital with sudden PIH from my own reaction to my differing expectations. With the courage of his defiance to fitting a mould, we broke so many rules of the system we were in and he lent me the strength of will to fight to birth him into my own hands. I felt victorious, invincible and that anything was possible, but in the company keeping me, I was not welcomed with a warrior's return from the bowels of birth. My golden moments were ones I experienced as trauma and a closure to the openness of my heart and celebration of myself, and in turn narrowing to the portals seeding, feeding and supporting me here to mother us both.

It was difficult for each of us to integrate in this realm. His reactivity, his intensity, his unwavering will and ferocious insistence to master life beyond his physical capabilities of infancy reflected everything about my own experience of my first years of being born. The postpartum and my death of the maiden was deep, dark, lonely and long as I steadfastly built the bond for him to be here amidst the scrambling of humility and self-compassion to again open the gates of what I had closed to protect myself. It was hard to find community and connection because of the lostness I felt within myself.

My second, Sunny, was conceived whilst still in this season. It was a year and a half on and I so wanted her here even though the reality of her pregnancy for me felt like I was holding the sun in a cauldron made of ice. She was not meant to be here to put down feet, but revealed to me then, and still to this day, that she held the power to alter the passage of time to gift grace to me in the growth and compassion in my own recognition. She taught me about forgiveness as she would give forward her love to me so that in time, I could again open and receive the gifts of her presence and grow it into the love I would hold for myself. Her birth was one in which I gave my body over yet without a sense of safety, surrender and permission so that I could indeed be held. I resisted the surgery and woke within it as, despite the anaesthetic, I struggled to leave my body to give passage for her to leave mine. She taught me so much of what I held within myself and she birthed early so I could birth myself. Through the grief, loss and confusion of postpartum, I returned to the void within me and within all, again and again and again. Going home to the spaces between what was and what is, and letting the nothingness of everything fill me. Each visit of meeting the feeling and opening to it yielded a sense of peace and relief which eventually opened the way for clarity, acceptance and gratitude. She reminds me now of how much we gift to one another through co-creation, no matter whether our energy resides in the physical planes or the ones within our heart.

It was only a couple of moons and cycles after the birth of Sunny that I conceived again. My 3rd, a daughter, was the gift of pure love. From conception and gestation she asked of me the deep, unwavering, unconditional love of everything I had withheld my heart from. There were certain milestones where I was asked to commit to this in order to continue. Her love and the intimate way that only she could see me, lent me the wings to say yes, and from this, a beauty of every human flavour blossomed. I could have held her in my womb forever. Her presence, her love, was like a golden sun bigger than my body as she held me in my highest vision whilst I grew around her. Her birth was long, slow and deep. A degustation of sensation where nothing was left off the smorgasbord and I had time to be with it in the space of my own home. She was patient and gentle as I traversed the depths and realms of records within me that I was invited to let go, to again decide if I would return to a new mission.

It was one of the deepest initiations and invitations of my life to bring her here, and to continue in postpartum and beyond to embody each day the truth in me that nothing is unloveable. This one vow took me right back through each birth and each experience to gift recognition, love and grounding to all my children and myself as a child. It reconnected me to my time in the womb and to the restoration of my own original source blueprints to anchor a new mission and co-creation for the future.

All of my births, of myself and of my children, have been the most cherished and challenging experiences of expansion. Birth, like death, is one of the pinnacles and pillars of the precipice of transformation. It is the tipping point in our state of being and the consciousness we are. All of my children and the child I am have each offered me healing and wholeness that I would not have found without them as the catalyst.

As I invite you again to consider the power and potential of birth and the gift that is each divine child that comes here to be with us, I want you too to acknowledge the divine child that you are.

For us to truly see and receive all children in the fullness of all they came to be, we must also recognise and receive ourselves in our divinity. To know that each child that is born is a unique frequency that comes to co-create with the earth. To celebrate and support another to ground and be their fullness here is to offer that to our own hearts.

The ways we are received in conception, gestation, birth and postpartum, gifts our innate sense of connection to being here. It is a template for how we bring more and more of ourselves through our being to ground and anchor and become a part of this earth with the same sense of home and belonging that we experience being held in the womb.

It is never too late to be received in birth. To ground, anchor, activate and restore the templates of our divine blueprints. You are never too old to be honoured and recognised and celebrated with love, tenderness and adoration just for being you.

Whatever is held from birth, stored in any body, time, space or dimension, deserves freedom and love and recognition. I want to know how you came to be here and why and the celebration of you choosing to do so. I want to know what it took for you to descend and inhabit this body and all the doubts and despair and challenges and surrender that it asked of you along the way. I want to know what it was for you and honour what it took to say yes then and what it asks of you again and again to continue to be you here, being all of what and who you are.

Birth is the passage of all into one. The milestone and initiation we each enter through to be here. It is the observance of such, and the knowing of all of humanity as divinity, that fills me with the greatest sense of hope,

Claire In 't Veld

excitement and wonder for all of life and what we will create here. The receiving of the ceremony and sacredness of each of our births is one that yields for me the potential, purpose and gratitude for what it means for me personally to be here also, for we are all born on this earth.

Claire In't Veld

Hi, I am Claire and it is my pleasure and heart's gifting to be here with you.

I am a mother, lover, divine channel, starseed, human being and everything in-between.

I reside now on Whadjuk Country in Bedfordale, Western Australia, where we chose to put down roots not far from where I was born in Armadale and where I first began my life. I share the land with my partner, children, horses and chooks and the many other beings of creation we live alongside.

Sensitive, strong willed, deeply feeling and open, I was driven as a child to get to the heart and truth of everything no matter how uncomfortable or embarrassing it was, and could often be found cornering adults and interrogating them with prying questions on the purpose of life, what they were really doing here and why.

My search to understand this world and my own humanity led me to study the science and art of our body, our being and that of the planet.

I have lived many lives here, energetically and physically, including but not limited to a koala handler, geologist, Muay Thai fighter, yoga teacher, cattle hand, personal trainer, reflexologist, landscape labourer, remedial massage therapist and many more. I may be a jack-of-all-trades and yet I am also a master at the embodiment of embracing all parts of us as one.

The gift and teaching of my being here is the deep knowing that we are each an ever-present, evolving and infinite source of creation not bound by what we do, how we experience it or who we perceive ourselves to be. Anything is possible and nothing is unloveable.

During the pregnancy, birth and postpartum of my youngest daughter, I trained as a doula whilst simultaneously receiving the gift that it is to be seen, witnessed, celebrated and received by my own doula.

It is so deeply sacred to me to be in communion with others and entrusted with holding them in the ever-unfolding transformation that is the embodiment and birthing of a whole new being and consciousness here.

It is my heart work and service to support humanity to feel at home here, within their heart, fully integrated and embodied and deeply grounded into the heart of the earth as our place of belonging, so that we can be fully here to be all that we are.

I offer ceremony, guidance, support and services as a light and energy worker, channel, body worker and caretaker of creation in the processes, initiations and transformation that reveals and reflects the innate wisdom and power that we each are. My niche is supporting the new humans and galactic star beings to birth, integrate and embody the new earth frequencies in their being and with the planetary energy body.

I'm not just here to love what is enjoyable and easy but to reclaim and honour the whole spectrum of our human experience as divine so that nothing need be seperate from the love of our own infinite and eternal heart.

Facebook: Claire In't Veld
Instagram: claireintveld
www.claireintveld.com

Laura Van Der Meulen
BIRTHING WITH WISDOM AND POWER

Did you know that birth can be amazing, powerful and awesome? Ina May Gaskin, our spiritual homebirthing heroine, says that, "If a woman doesn't look like a goddess during labour, then someone isn't treating her right." When you are ready to give birth, I want you to feel this statement to be true; but at the start, most of us are filled with thoughts quite far from this.

My pregnancy journey began as a bit of a surprise. I was 30 and married for only a few months. As far as being prepared goes, all I had was private health insurance to cover maternity care to be sure that I could have my baby in a private room with a specialist of my choice. But when I went to my first doctor's appointment at 6 weeks to confirm my pregnancy, I suddenly had a doubt as to whether I even wanted to give birth in a private hospital. Having a baby was suddenly real and decisions had to be made.

I was divided. I felt like I should take up the option of a private hospital because I had a professional career, and it was what people in those privileged positions were able to access. But deep down inside, I didn't feel connected to a private hospital for the elite. I grew up in the hills and I had never been to a private hospital.

Laura Van Der Meulen

Where You Birth Matters

At the time, I had no clue that where you birth matters (it really matters!). I just thought it was a question of public or private, based on whether you had private health insurance or not. Now I know, it is actually a decision which can have an overwhelming impact on how your birth will play out. In fact, it is perhaps the most important decision you will make, yet it is often one of the least thought-out decisions made. I went with my gut feeling. I decided to have my baby at the Family Birth Centre at King Edward Memorial Hospital.

The Family Birth Centre was a place I'd known from many years before. When I was just 13 years old, I was with my sister when she birthed my nephew there. Me being at the birth was not something we had questioned at all, I was always going to be there. I was so young but mature having had a sister 7 years older than me. My nephew's birth was one of the most amazing experiences I had ever witnessed. My sister and her partner just trusted in the birth process. They had Tim Buckley playing, soft lighting, used the pool, and the birthing room was more like a holiday home than a hospital. In the end, my sister was transferred up to the hospital but birthed my nephew powerfully on her own with no complications. I was in awe as I watched my nephew's head inch out. It took so long that I was totally dumbstruck, when, after a further pause and final push, the rest of his body came flying out. The midwife yelled at me, "TIME!" and I stood there looking at the old school analogue clock for quite a few seconds until I could actually register what it said! Adrenalin surging, my little auburn-haired nephew was born and I was able to call my dad to tell him he was right; it was a boy. The rest of us were convinced that he would be a girl. He also had red hair like my dad.

Looking back now, I realise that without intention, my sister had fulfilled an ancient tradition and wisdom of passing down from sister to sister, generation to generation, the secret of women's power – birth. My sister allowed me to witness the magic, strength and beauty that is created in the birthing room. She channelled a birthing goddess and this is what birth should and can be like. And those that are involved in this mystic, spiritual, underground world of natural birth, forever know and trust it to be possible.

Over the years the power of birth has been taken away from women and turned into medicalised birthing experiences where women have been subjected to little information and maximum rules and procedures. These experiences are often traumatic and whilst often shared, they limit us by reiterating a negative connotation drilled into our subconscious that birth is horrendous. So as a result, most people have no idea that birth can be positive. More often than not, they even seem to go out of their way to convince you that it is anything but.

Our ignorance of positive birth surrounds us every day, in every way. My husband's nana first birthed in Australia in the early 1950s. This was a time when you were told nothing of birth. You went into labour not knowing anything that was going on and then when your baby was about to be born you were knocked out with anaesthesia. You woke up hours later in a bed without your baby. Your baby would then be presented to you. You would freshen up so that when you were at your best, your husband could come to meet you and the baby. That generation of women birthed our mothers or grandmothers so for the majority there is very little to pass on to the next generation about positive birth.

This is changing. One informed birth and one informed family at a time. I know in my children's future, birth will again be known as positive and powerful. Until then, for my friends and for those reading this, I hope that we will learn to see birth as it should be; positive and powerful. And education is the key.

For my birth, I knew I wanted to have a vaginal birth without an epidural. I blindly trusted that I would be supported in hospital to do this. I believed that only those women who wanted or needed a cesarean had one. I now know that this is absolutely not true. We are unnecessarily medicalising birth, increasing cesarean rates to over double of the World Health Organization's recommendations with no better outcomes for babies or mothers. To avoid this you must ensure you have a birthing team and environment that supports the type of birth you want. Private hospitals have far less chance of natural births than birth centres, and again birth centres have far less chance of natural birth than homebirths. For me, I wanted the assurance of being close to the hospital in case I needed it but I didn't want to labour in a hospital because I had spent traumatic times in them when my brother suffered a severe head injury years before. There is no way I could relax and birth in a hospital that gave me surges of fear from trauma and loss. Where you birth must be where you feel most comfortable, most relaxed and most at home. For every woman that is different. Take the time to consider what safety and security means for you. This should then form your basis of where you want to birth.

Continuity of Care

The best standard of care is to have a continuous care provider that you connect with. Connection is so important. When I think about my midwife, I feel like I am remembering a great love in my life. I felt heard, valued and respected at all times by her. If you do not have this type of relationship with your care provider, you have to move on. Ask and find someone else. There is always another option. My midwife discreetly but skilfully built up a rapport with me over our monthly appointments so that by the time I was ready to birth my baby she knew what I wanted and how I felt, without having to ask me in a contrived or superficial setting. If you don't feel such a connection, tune in and move on. You cannot give birth well with a care provider who does not create feelings of trust and security.

Fears

As my pregnancy went on, I still felt confident that I could birth naturally but I had two niggling thoughts pop up. Firstly, I was scared of failing. What if I can't birth naturally and I have to tell people 'I couldn't do it'? I couldn't do it even though I had prepared for it and everyone else in my family and my husband's family had. I actually started to think that perhaps it would be better to birth alone, like nana had done. I was always independent and did not rely on anyone else. Why start now? I was also scared that I wouldn't be able to make it past the 'crisis point' of transition, that I remembered my sister going through and how tough it was to watch her in pain and unable to cope. I watched helplessly and wiped away my tears. Her midwife came in and helped her with a guided meditation and visualisation to get her through it. What was I going to do when that happened to me? I figured that there was nothing I could do about it; it was just a rite of passage.

Childbirth Education

As I hit the 3rd trimester, I began to think more and more about the actual birth. I still wasn't scared of birth but my husband was; he faints at the sight of blood. My nephew's father had repartnered and had another child, and he had told us all about hypnobirthing and the difference it had made to how he was able to contribute to the birth with his new partner compared to how he was at my nephew's birth. I was a little surprised because I thought he had done a fantastic job at the birth, so I started to look into it. The course was quite long and cost a bit of money and no-one else I knew had done it. The more I looked into it though, the more I liked the idea of it, and mainly I felt it would help my husband. After the first class, I could not believe what I had learnt. It changed my life forever. Hypnobirthing isn't for everyone but childbirth education is a non-negotiable. I am not talking about the hospital ones where they explain the process of induction and C-sections, but the actual childbirth education where you learn how to navigate the hospital systems and how to allow your body to birth naturally.

A lot of my friends were skeptical of hypnobirthing but I have realised that this was mostly because they had no idea about what it was. Generally, people who have negative birth experiences have often not prepared at all or hold onto some fear surrounding it. Education and preparation is fundamental to getting the birth you want. You must prepare, plan and prioritise. Childbirth education classes not only teach you how to physically promote natural birth, but they also teach you how to navigate our modern birthing world.

My mother was a midwife, trained in medicalised birth. She was sceptical too but then I asked her to recall how her mother birthed in India. My mother then remembered as a small child being invited into the mud hut to see her baby brother freshly born onto the dirt floors with women surrounding her and the local midwife. She was witness to the proof that birth is natural and woman centred, but in our modern world she had forgotten about it. Few women today can say that they have had the privilege of having had or seen a natural birth, but it is not because women can't do this anymore. It is because our medicalisation of birth has increased and we no longer have a village of women sharing natural birthing wisdoms and power.

Preparation

Preparation for any big event is necessary for success. Birth is no exception. Some people like to simply say that you can't plan for birth as you never know what will happen. But a proper planning of your birth is a process of preparing yourself for all outcomes of birth. You will make a plan A, a plan B and a plan C. You will run through all of the options so that if something unexpected does arise you will have already thought about it. This will mean that if things don't go to plan, which is often the case, you will have prepared for it and you will know what to do. Most women have had a traumatic birth experience because they felt like they were not given options, they were not heard and they were not respected during labour.

For me, I was most afraid of epidurals, inductions and caesarean sections. Even now, when I think of surgery for birth it brings me back to my brother's traumatic emergency brain surgeries. I just could not cope with that. I had to confront those fears and plan for how I would tackle them if they had to happen. I had to plan for a caesarean birth and once I did I realised they could be magical too. They could dim the lights, not reveal the sex, I could have essential oils on a cloth to take away the surgical smell, I could listen to music. Once I embraced this, I was able to let it go, relax and accept any turn my birthing journey would take me. If I had had a caesarean, whilst it may not have been what I wanted, I had acknowledged it as a possible outcome and so I made peace with it before I birthed. In the birthing world we often say, "If you don't know your options, you don't have any."

Being Informed

The important part of preparation is using your BRAINS for each step of the way. Looking at the benefits, risks, alternatives, intuition, nothing and space. At every appointment and care decision you need to consider this. You need to ask the questions. It is your baby and your body. If you ask the questions, giving yourself some space to consider the responses, then you can be the most comfortable in making your decision, including difficult ones. Towards the end of my pregnancy I was seen by a different midwife on one occasion. At the appointment, this midwife tried to book me in for a future induction even though I was many weeks off my estimated due date. I wanted to know why, given my baby and I were both healthy, but she just said it was better to book it now rather than try and get a place later. She pushed me for a date but I held strong and said I would like time to think about it and would talk to my usual midwife at the next appointment. This midwife made me feel so horrible that I cried. I told my midwife to ensure that I did not have that midwife again. My midwife also said it was a preference to pre-book induction but it was not necessary. If I had not used my BRAINS, I could have been induced unnecessarily and a flow of interventions could have followed.

Surrender

Once the logistics are planned, you can surrender and let go. Uninterrupted birth is a mystical and magical event but the chances of it being that way without education are slim to none. What I love about hypnobirthing classes versus other childbirth education classes is that it provides tools to harness your subconscious so that your mind can relax to allow your body to relax and birth your baby. Surrender to your emotions, expectations, thoughts and feelings; let them out. Often, until we really tune in and sink into our feelings, we don't realise that we're holding onto something that we need to let go of. Most people readily accept that when people die there is a massive amount of subconscious control that comes with being able to let go and cross over. The same is of birth. You are bringing yourself to the brink of the in-between worlds where your subconscious has a part to play. If you don't give your mind time and space to address any hesitations you have about bringing a baby into the world, then it can be a barrier to your body letting go and allowing your baby to be born. As a point of survival, your brain must be convinced that it is the right time to birth.

The biggest problem women face in birthing is our over-advanced minds, in comparison to other mammals. I had a spirit animal to tune into for strength and power in birth. My horse! How did she birth in nature? It was in the green grass without anyone to coax her through it. On the days leading up to it, her teats would become waxy and swollen, she would become restless and be creating a little nest on the ground. Then when the dark night came, she would birth and in the morning there would be a foal.

Women need to tune into themselves and nature when it comes time to birth. Switch off when it gets closer to your due date. In fact, forget the due date. Consider it as an approximate time. Don't let people know when the time is. Turn off Facebook, TV and the news. Go into nature. Feel the sun, the moon and the fresh air. If you give yourself time and space, you will be able to feel the subtleties of your hormone changes when you are about to give birth. The surge of feelings will make you wonder whether it is true but you need to trust your body and know it to be. Embrace those feelings. Don't move away from them.

Dr Sarah Buckley provides great insight into how our natural hormones interact in the lead up, during and following birth. Hormones either promote or hinder labour. Fear creates cortisol and triggers the fight, flight or freeze reaction. It is the enemy of the birthing room. Oxytocin is the love hormone and that's what causes the surge of contractions to start and progress. Oxygen helps us stay calm and boost the blood flow to your womb so that the muscles there can work effectively. Oxytocin also synchronises with melatonin, the sleepy hormone, so that as night falls with the shelter of darkness, labour can progress.

When my due date neared I felt like something may be happening but there was a small crisis with the care arrangements of my brother. It was internally overwhelming and emotional for me having to worry about this and the birth of my baby. As soon as it was resolved, the next day I started to feel the sensations. I wasn't sure how intense things would get but I stayed calmly relaxed and used my breath to steady me in and out of rising surges. I stayed at home for as long as possible so I could feel safe and secure (away from the hospital's bright lights and intervention). After about 6 hours I got in the shower and hit the 'crisis point' of that intensity of transition. I visualised my horse in a mist of green. I then felt like I was about to push and I wanted to get to the hospital as I didn't want to birth at home, but I really didn't feel like I could get up and go. Just then that little seed planted all of those years ago came up and I remembered my sister. *If she could do it, then so can I.* I got up, walked outside and took a moment to stare up at the shining stars and feel the warmth of the still autumn air. When I got to the hospital, the first thing the nurse asked me was, "What drugs do you want?" I didn't answer her. Then, my waters broke. The nurse checked me and said I was crowning. It was time to deliver. I couldn't believe it. I was so happy. I had done it. My midwife arrived and we all relaxed knowing that she knew what I wanted.

One hour later, I was standing opposite my husband, holding his hands tightly. He was smiling and I was laughing. You could feel the love and excitement. I was taking the final stage slowly as I did not want to tear. I told my husband not to look as I was sure it would look like I was trying to squeeze a watermelon out. Then I felt another surge come … I put my head down, leaned forward, breathed in and out and on the tips of my toes, bearing down with a yell, my baby was born into the arms of my beautiful midwife crouched beneath me. I received my baby into my arms. A baby girl. She didn't cry straight away. There was a moment of peace and connection between us. She was so precious and I felt so alert and so capable. I did it! I birthed my baby without any interventions or drugs, just as I had worked and hoped for.

Sixteen months after the birth of my daughter, I was expecting the birth of my second baby. I was in tune with my baby and my body. As my birthing day neared I felt my body change and I knew my baby was coming a little earlier than expected. I went about my day as planned and made little fuss. Second time around, my mind knew that I could do it. I breezed into the birth centre and met with the same midwife. I breathed my baby boy out in the pool so calmly 40 minutes after I arrived. My midwife said it was amazing to watch. My mother could not believe I was in labour even though she was a midwife. I arrived home just 4 hours later, under the light of the spring moon to tuck my new baby and my little girl into bed. I still remember the shocked look of the neighbours when they saw me a week later riding my bike down the road.

Imagine if you could tell everyone that your birth was amazing, powerful and graceful. Imagine it, visualise it, prepare for all options and you will. "When you change the way you view birth, the way you birth will change." – Marie Mongan, founder of HypnoBirthing International.

Laura Van Der Meulen

Hi, I'm Laura and I am a childbirth educator who is in love with everything to do with birth. I am married and have 2 children who are somehow now 5 and 6.5 years old. I am a lawyer and often people are surprised when they discover my passion for birth. I guess they consider that the 2 worlds cannot align and maybe usually they can't. But I am a very down-to-earth person and grew up in humble surroundings with immigrant parents from India and Slovenia.

When I was pregnant with my first baby in 2015 I did hypnobirthing classes. The classes changed my life. I had the most amazing birth with my daughter and I told everyone about how positive it was. I then had an even more amazing waterbirth with my son in 2016. I was so inspired that I began to teach the course in 2017 and have taught childbirth education ever since.

The course made me aware of my birthing options so that I felt informed and empowered. My husband also had a clear role and a sense of purpose in the birth which is a total contrast to how he felt before he did the course.

I love to teach families now how to navigate the pitfalls of the modern birthing world and how to take back their power. To see families start their parenting journeys on a high is priceless. Hypnobirthing is a wonderful way to become fully informed and educated so that you can have the best possible chance of a positive birth without fear.

Written in loving honour of Nichola – who was so proud to have birthed her three beautiful girls into this world naturally.

Facebook: HypnoBirth Zone - Laura Van Der Meulen
Instagram: @hypnobirth_zone

Emily Schoeman
MY JOURNEY THROUGH MATRESCENCE

One thing that I have learnt, both from my own personal experience but especially since becoming a doula, is that while women and their partners are taking classes and researching labour and birth, most of the time this education stops at exactly that. To the minute the baby is born seems to be the extent of what we know and research. Yet this is only just the beginning. This is not only the birth of a whole new human being, but it is also the rebirth of the woman into a mother.

This transition is called matrescence and it encompasses all of the changes we go through as we enter this new journey. It is psychological and emotional, it is physical and it is hormonal. How do we learn to love this new body we have? Why has my body not bounced back like I see other people's doing? How do I keep this small human alive now? Just like any other transition in our life, it is not a smooth road nor one without struggles, and everyone's transition looks very different.

We are learning a whole new set of skills; we learn how to communicate with our child without words, we can learn what each of their little cries mean, and what they need by their facial expressions. Even breastfeeding; quite often we are told, "Oh, breastfeeding is so natural, it comes so easy." Yeah right! That is a whole different skill that you and your baby both need to learn. There's also the hormonal shifts that cause changes in our brains. And then we swing the door wide open to motherhood guilt! And honestly, I still don't feel like that door is ever going to change.

I am a mother of 2 and am currently pregnant with my 3rd child. I have 2 very different children and I have had 3 very different pregnancies. I fell pregnant with my first not long after I got married at 19 and so I found this pregnancy very isolating, and when combined with a lot of other difficulties including dislocating my hip at 32 weeks pregnant, it wasn't a horrible pregnancy but it was a challenge. I went in knowing 'enough'; I knew what I had watched on TV and what other family members had gone through, but in reality I knew nothing. And I knew even less about postpartum, matrescence and the 4th trimester, along with the overall changes that my husband and I were in for let alone just how much these changes and challenges would change and impact our relationship. I never expected in my wildest dreams to be having a C-section at 20 years old and the long-term effects that that would have going forwards, especially on my body image and mental health.

I really felt the weight of the world on my shoulders. I carried so many unrealistic expectations plus the judgment from 'health professionals' for being such a young mum all at the same time; a time where I found that I needed more support than I ever did previously in my life. During this time, I found myself more alone than ever before. I was trying to recover from major abdominal surgery and I was also trying to mentally come to terms with everything – all of these physical, mental and hormonal changes. And the whole 'the only thing that matters is a healthy mum and a healthy baby' is garbage because a physically healthy person and a mentally healthy person are two very different things. But that didn't seem to matter at the time, as I had people wanting to come and hold the baby for the first few weeks and then it was almost like the novelty wore off. And when people did come to see my new baby they would also expect to be waited on hand and foot. No-one was there to truly hold me. I felt so alone. During this time, again due to the lack of support and education, I ended up with full-blown mastitis and was back in hospital for very strong antibiotics. It wasn't exactly the start to motherhood that I had envisioned.

I fell pregnant for a second time nearly 2 years later, and this time I knew that I wanted a different experience and I had started to explore the options that were available to achieve a vaginal birth after C-section (VBAC). At 12 weeks things changed; I noticed blood on my knickers and rather than going into work, I headed to the hospital with my mum and then 2-year-old. Whilst waiting at the hospital, I got a call from my boss (who hadn't been told I'd called in sick) and I had to say the words, "I am in hospital with a potential miscarriage." The line went silent and I got back, "Oh, okay, well keep me posted and let me know when you might be back to work." Now it's important to note that I worked at a large baby store, where we sold everything you could possibly need for a baby. After a long wait in the hospital, all I was told was, "Well, we can't do an ultrasound now because we only do those in life-or-death moments and your blood work is inconclusive, so you may be pregnant or you may not be. We can book you for a scan in 4 days." I had my 12-week scan booked 2 days later and so I chose to stick with that. I was, in fact, not pregnant and I had lost our baby at about 7 weeks. My husband and I just started to cry; to this day, it is the only time that I have ever seen him cry.

We then had to go to King Edward Memorial Hospital where they explained our options and I elected a D&C to remove the remaining tissue, yet the worst was not over. My husband made the choice that he was needed more at work than what I needed him for and yet I couldn't verbalise why I needed him to be there. Due to a string of emergencies, my surgery kept being pushed and pushed, even after I started to pass large clots and had a significant bleed. It was then requested that I get an IV due to being dehydrated and in the process they managed to go straight through my vein; cue another bleed. I was at the hospital from 10 in the morning and didn't have surgery until 9 that night, after which point my blood pressure was so low from blood loss that I was made to stay the night. Alone and empty in a hospital bed, separated from my husband and child, and yet I still couldn't tell him how much I needed him, so at 7 the next morning my dad picked me up (it was also his birthday … Happy birthday, Dad!) and took me out to treat me. No-one quite prepares you to be the one in 5. People don't like to talk about miscarriage or stillbirth. The loneliness and emptiness that follows, and then 1 week later I had to walk into this baby shop where I worked and put on my fake happy smile as I served all these pregnant women, and everyone around me – family, friends, co-workers – none of them ever acknowledged my loss or my baby, not even my husband.

It took 5 months for us to fall pregnant again and I did use this time to research even more into my options, choices and care providers. Nothing quite prepared me for the anxiety-ridden pregnancy that would follow a loss; I would find myself so sick every time we prepared to go for a scan. Overthinking every time I wouldn't feel him moving much, yet no-one seemed to understand why I felt the way I did. Although, aside from this anxiety, I had a wonderfully easy pregnancy! No aches or pains, no issues at all. I even catered my husband's 30th whilst in labour.

This time though I was so much more prepared; I was confident in my choices, I had done the research and knew all the facts about pregnancy and birth. Yet I still hadn't learnt to prepare for the post-birth, nor had I learnt that I needed to share all my research with my husband. Whilst we had done some work together, once again there were some things that just weren't communicated (he did do a lot better this time though).

I achieved my VBAC with my son and I was now a second-time mum who had had an 'easy birth'. He was the second child, so no shiny for you, sorry, buddy. There I was, trying to deal with severely engorged boobs (because apparently I am a great overproducer), sleep deprived and with a husband who was in the middle of a busy season … What the fuck was going on? I craved a community of people, even if it was just someone who was there to check in and ask me how my day was. Someone who wanted to come around and have a cuppa but was happy to make it themselves. But I felt like I had even fallen into the expectations set by society on how to be the 'perfect mother'. HA! But it also made me doubt that this was even a thing, and that this community didn't exist. I found myself apologising all the time about the messy state of my house. It was a whole new experience though; I had 2 children now and I was learning how to be a mother to these 2 humans, one who was going through her own changes as she was learning to share everything and the other – well, he was a stranger. I grew him and I birthed him but I didn't know him. He was still a stranger and we had to get to know each other.

It wasn't all negative Nancy; there were so many positive moments. I achieved my vaginal birth, I was also more educated so I was able to work through the breastfeeding issues and avoid mastitis again, and I eventually found some sort of a routine that worked for us and our lives ended up finding a new normal. But that is what I find seems to be the problem – society, media and social media all portray this ideology of what things should be like after you've had a baby and that very quickly you should get your life back to a new normal. Your body should look the exact same, and look, let's be real here … Even if you don't breastfeed, pregnancy does a right number on everything, including your boobs. I am not sure how they are ever supposed to look the same again. You are told breastfeeding is natural and easy and you'll both know exactly what to do, yet if you are struggling, just give up and use formula. Oh, but then you'll be judged as to why you aren't formula feeding! Ah, but don't breastfeed in public either because that's indecent and you are sexualising yourself and your baby. Like, who the hell comes up with this absolute shit! We are also told that the mother and baby bond will be instant, that as soon as you see your baby you will fall in love and everything will be perfect, but what happens when it doesn't happen that way?

Birth New

This transition into motherhood is given its own name for a reason. It is no different to childhood, adolescence and adulthood; it's a change in growth, hormones, appearance and our abilities. Matrescence is very real and it is a time that we need to give more appreciation and respect to however you gave birth: vaginal, belly birth, surrogacy, even adoption. This transition will occur at some point. It is a hormonal response to an outside stimulus which basically means that eventually as your hormones shift you will start to feel a change, just as our bodies change and grow during pregnancy. I do wish that I had done so much more research into this during my other 2 pregnancies. But now I am here hoping to impart just a small piece of my knowledge to you, so that I can help make even the smallest difference to your birthing journey, but more importantly, to your postpartum journey.

The best piece of advice I can give you is that the more education you gain and the more research you do, the easier this transition can be, and whilst there will always be ups and downs, some days will be a lot harder than others. Being prepared for these situations can help you understand them when they do arise. Working through everything with your partner can also help you both understand the changes that you are both going through. In what feels like a different lifetime, I once worked at a baby store, remember, and we would see all the types of people and parents coming in that you can imagine. But what would stand out to me is the difference in how much research some people would put into *every single baby item!* From the full nursery set-up, the pram, the car seat, even down to the toys. Yet nearly none of them had spoken about what happens if they face issues with breastfeeding. Who do you call? What are you going to do about overnight feeds? How do you share the load? As a couple, what are your expectations going into being new parents?

All of these are equally as important as what pram you use or what car seat is safest, and yet 9 times out of 10 they are not asked. Nine months after Connor was born my husband had a vasectomy and whilst I was so angry with his decision and we were so close to separating, neither of us were prepared for this journey and we weren't coping or functioning as parents or as a couple. So whilst my heart longed for another baby, I knew that if an accident did happen, it would quite possibly break us, so I agreed. Eventually, as life got easier and the kids got older, we went through a fair amount of counselling together and individually we learnt how to improve our communication, which meant that we started to tackle our expectations. Fast-forward and we ended up discussing in-depth what we each expected of one another, which turned into what it would mean to have another baby and what that would mean for our family. And spoiler alert, he ended up having his vasectomy reversed and now we are expecting number 3. So whilst I can't comment on what life after baby number 3 is like, I do know that so far everything has been very different and these conversations happen many times, even now. We still very much have open discussions about everything and we have both been able to shift our expectations and work within the reality of our situation which has made a world of difference. It has even had an extremely positive impact through this pregnancy as we are able to have an open-heart conversation before shit hits that fan. In this time we've learnt to heal through communication and have since had the most in-depth conversations that we've ever had in the lead-up to our previous births.

We've also learnt along this messy road of parenthood that we are still a couple, and that we were a couple first and that taking time to focus on going on a date is so important. Even if it's dinner at home by candlelight. It's made it easier to listen to each other and the more we listen, the more we are able to understand the other person's needs at that time. During these moments, we remember why we got married, we laugh and have fun like before we had kids and sometimes we fall in love all over again.

In saying that, my next piece of advice is that your journey through motherhood will be riddled with guilt. The dreaded 'mum guilt' is very real and as yet, I still haven't found that it has gone away and sometimes it is over the most random and silly things. The most important thing is to try and not let this get you too down or get in the way of you doing the things that light you up in life, as this is what gives you all of the opportunities to fill up your own cup.

One of the biggest triggers for myself, however, is when I prioritise myself or my needs over those around me, or I do something for myself at the expense of my children. Now I am not talking about anything big or anything that means my children go without, although at the time it does feel like I am a horrible mother for making myself the priority. Yet through this journey I have found myself on over the last 2 years, I have discovered that for me to be the best mum I can possibly be, I need to make time for these small things. That my needs are equally, if not more important, than of those around me. Why? Simple, I cannot fill their cup if my own cup is empty. So taking the time to remember that I am so very much more than a wife and a mother has meant that finding things that are important to me and things that I enjoy doing on my own has allowed me this opportunity to fully embrace motherhood and all the ups and downs that come along with it. And with this, I have been able to connect with some amazing humans who have helped me find my place in this world, and have helped me understand the true meaning of surrounding yourself with community. The support I receive from these amazing humans is just indescribable; they have made me feel like I am safe and supported no matter what and I always have someone to talk to, even if all I need is just to have a whinge.

I feel like I have jumped from here to there and back again, but the point I want to make is that there are so many changes going on in the time after you have given birth (and this just isn't after your first baby either, it is after each and every one) and everyone has a very different journey and experiences. But by taking the time to learn and understand the process our bodies and our brains go through, not to mention the transition our babies make during this time as well, we are better able to prepare ourselves for the mystery that lies ahead. We may never be truly prepared for the roller-coaster that is parenthood but the more informed we allow ourselves to be, the more we are able to communicate with those around us who are supporting us, and if we can find ourselves a community in which we feel truly safe, then we can make these adjustments that little bit easier. We can also learn to be kinder to ourselves and appreciate ourselves as the goddesses we are.

I also believe we can begin to learn about how strong and powerful we are as human beings, as mothers and women. And my goal in my career now is to help women see and believe this too. As a photographer, I am there to capture the lioness that lies within, to help you see your true power, to see how absolutely beautiful you are and how amazingly fierce you can be. And as a doula, I'm there to hold you and hear you, to unconditionally support you on this roller-coaster ride we can embark upon together. I will help you find your path and if you need, I'll also be your community.

Emily Schoeman

My name is Emily Schoeman but please call me Em. I am a doula and photographer, and my main drivers are helping to encourage and support women and their partners as they navigate this new journey of birth together. Through my photography, I love to tell a story, capturing the raw emotions, the love, the power, the fun and everything that happens in-between.

My journey started in 2014 when, at 19 years old, I fell pregnant with my first child. I knew the stories of my family members and what had always been drilled into me – "Doctor knows best and trust the doctor!" Plus you add into that what you see on mainstream media, and essentially I let my pregnancy follow that same logic and mindset. I suffered horrific pelvic pain which resulted in a dislocated hip at 32 weeks pregnant. I also believed that from 38 weeks you were basically good to go and that babies come around then … Cue asking for an induction at 37 weeks and 6 days! After a horrific induction, a failed epidural and being told I couldn't get off the bed for labour (15 hours), an emergency C-section was called. But, healthy mum, healthy baby, right? I was led to believe that my body had

Emily Schoeman

failed me and I was very clearly incapable of birthing even an average-size baby; therefore any future pregnancies should just be an elective C-section.

After an extremely traumatic miscarriage in 2017, it fuelled my desire to have a vaginal birth and to research the fuck out of absolutely everything I could to achieve a VBAC.

We decided that due to extra anxiety caused by the miscarriage it would be best to see a private OB again. This time I stayed active and mobile and saw a chiropractor and had none of the same issues I had with my daughter. I went into spontaneous labour at 38 weeks and 2 days, I had a fantastic midwife who was a huge encouragement and never once mentioned the 'C-word'. However, I was still in the private system and ended up with a very hands-on birth and there was a lack of communication between hubby and myself. I did, however, successfully birth my son via VBAC! Although my main takeaway from that birth was that I want to be that support and encouragement for other women.

This led me on my path to become a doula and following on to be a photographer. As I provide emotional, physical, spiritual and energetic support to couples through their own journeys, I capture their moments at the same time to help them cherish each and every moment.

I am now pregnant with my 3rd child and attempting a HBAC with the care of a private midwife. I have an incredible birth team made up of the midwives, a doula, a photographer and my husband, and I look forward to documenting and sharing that story later!

www.thelionessdoula.com
Instagram: @thelionessdoula
Facebook: Em Schoeman – The Lioness Doula and Photographer

Ashley Rose
THE VILLAGE

Birth is such an expansive topic. I have honestly started my chapter a few times now not knowing which way I wanted to take it. There is an endless depth and complexity that surrounds birth. And there are conversations that continue on for hours unpacking various perspectives. It isn't just birth. It is pregnancy, labour, birth and postpartum that really transforms a woman from maiden to mother. Birth is the one true chemical transformation that is so pivotal in a woman's lifespan. It is during this period that a woman should receive the utmost respect and support throughout her journey. My name is Ashley. I am the mother to 2 sweet and divinely unique souls. Each of their births took me on unexpected journeys that have ultimately taken me back home to myself. They have taught me some of the greatest lessons in life and that is to surrender and take accountability when control is no longer an option.

My journeys with both of my children were vastly different from pregnancy to postpartum. This time period creates space and the opportunity to connect with different women. Throughout the journey from maiden to mother, the road is a little bumpy. I thought I knew what I wanted and it wasn't until I had my own experiences and I listened to my intuition that I found what I really wanted. My experience with my first baby transformed me, but my experience with my second baby took me home. In my first pregnancy in 2017, I wanted a homebirth, but I was honestly scared. I knew I wanted a homebirth, but there was some fear around it that I had to work through based off of my conditioned beliefs around birth. Several women I knew had successful homebirths with the Community Midwifery Program (CMP). The midwives that work for the CMP do support homebirth, but are also very much tied to the hospital system. Needless to say, I went with the CMP. I had regular appointments with my midwife, but she wasn't guaranteed to be at my birth. At the time, I had no idea that the CMP didn't support homebirth beyond 42 weeks and I also had no idea that I would go beyond 42 weeks. Since induction is so common, babies are 'typically' born between 38-40 weeks. When people hear 42 weeks they generally gasp in alarm. The stress that I felt and the pressure that I felt to go into spontaneous labor by 42 weeks was beyond immense. Plus, when you tell people your due date and you go over, the nonstop calls and text messages become very overwhelming. I had 2 stretch and sweeps. I felt desperate. I wasn't aware of the cascade of interventions, and I thought I was playing it safe by having them. Firstly, they are unnecessarily painful. I found the midwife that carried out my stretch and sweeps to be very aggressive and rough. And secondly, they are just plain unnecessary since a baby will come when a baby is ready. Babies don't care about time. The stretch and sweeps did not work and a week later, on the day of being '42 weeks' I went into spontaneous labour. I was so excited I let my midwife know right away, oops! First-time mums – there is time, bask in it before letting your midwife know. In the system, homebirth or not, women are put on the clock. In Australia, it is a 24-hour clock. If labour goes longer than 24 hours, the pressure of more and more intervention will be present. My midwife came over early. She fell asleep on my couch as I laboured, scared as hell in the dark. I thought I was ready and prepared but I wasn't. My husband, Tim, stayed up with me. We had a TENS machine and a birthing pool. Labouring in warm water can stall labour and I jumped in pretty early. There was a lot of poking at my belly. There were a bunch of unnecessary vaginal exams. I thought the stretch and sweeps were painful until I had vaginal exams mid-contraction upon request of my midwife.

I had hit the 24-hour mark. There was now a different midwife with me than the one that started with me. Her claim was that I was 8cm dilated, but that I wasn't progressing. At the time I believed her. I was naive and I wasn't listening to my body. I was feeling like I needed some relief, the same feeling I felt when I was in transition with my second baby. The feeling that I couldn't do it anymore and the feeling that I needed something to give. Again, the feeling of transition. I'm going to really hit this point home, because I feel a bit robbed and this is where things spiralled. I was in transition with my first baby when we transferred to my local hospital. Anyone that knows me knows I am not a fan of hospitals. My labour naturally stalled because I was out of my comfort zone. I was given pain relief and they let me go for another 2 hours. My biggest fear throughout my first pregnancy was that I would end up with a C-section. I never spoke about this fear out of fear that I would manifest it into a reality. The nurses at the hospital informed me that I needed to start mentally preparing for a C-section as I was 'failing to progress'. They need to throw that phrase out the window. The failure to progress is actually the failure to wait. The quick action of interventions inhibits ever seeing how a woman's body navigates birth. The surgeon came and spoke with me about how the birth of my baby was going to play out. I lost all control at this point and I was hysterical. They wheeled me into theatre in a horrible, brightly lit room. They ran a popsicle up my body to see how numb I was. There were more people around me than I had planned to have in my birth space. The energy of who was coming in and out of my space didn't matter anymore. The amount of people meeting my perfect baby was more than I had planned for. I asked for vaginal seeding and that was dismissed. They did not have time for that – that was evident. I had to surrender. The cascade of interventions had caught up with me and at 5:01pm, my big, beautiful, Libra boy was born. He had a pronounced cone-shaped head. His cone head confirmed that I was in transition at home. My emergency C-section baby had a cone. The surgeon commented on how far my baby was down in my pelvis. That thought may haunt me for a long time. I asked for delayed cord clamping, and they gave my baby a minute. My entire journey I felt like my voice wasn't being heard. I kept giving my power away by not standing up for myself and it was a hard lesson I needed to learn. The midwife commented on how big he was and how thankful I should feel for not giving birth to him vaginally. I couldn't hold him; my arms were shaking violently from the drugs they gave me, but he sat on my chest. I remember just wanting to sit up and to hold my fucking baby. After sewing the gaping hole in my body back together, they wheeled me to another room where I was surrounded by 3 nurses. Thankfully my son was hungry and knew how to breastfeed immediately. It was our one true victory. I was so proud of us for knowing what to do. We got to the room and not long after we got there they told me that Tim would have to go home because in the public system they don't allow anyone to stay the night. This was prior to COVID-19. I felt sideswiped again. After a C-section, you are not meant to carry anything over 10lbs. My son was 9.6lbs at birth. He was in a plastic container on the side of my bed and I couldn't reach him from where I was laying. When he cried, I stood up and walked around my bed to get him only 3 hours after major surgery. I pressed the call button countless unanswered times. It's supposed to be the best time of my life welcoming my perfect new baby into this world and it could have easily been the scariest and most unsettling night of my life. I needed help.

Welcome to motherhood! The drugs wore off. Labouring for over 24 hours followed by a C-section and the pain that followed was something I wasn't prepared for either. I used to have this mindset that taking everything on means you're strong and that if you asked for help it makes you weak. I've had that story for as long as I can remember and it took until after my second baby's birth to fully accept and ask for help. My postpartum journey with my son was okay. The transition is just really out of this world. On my 4th day postpartum, the hormone drop hit hard, primarily because of the strong repercussions from the drugs I had received at the hospital. Thankfully I had my placenta encapsulated and I was adamant about taking the capsules. The 'blues' only lasted about 24 hours. I was trying to continue with my normal day-to-day life with my baby and a giant wound. Everything was sore. I didn't know how to ask for help. It was a really challenging time and everything felt stressful, except for breastfeeding. I heard countless 'at least the baby is okay' comments after my son Westin's birth. The midwife told me I wouldn't be able to have a vaginal birth with their program if I was planning on having another baby. And in the moment, all of those comments don't really sink in. They tried to convince me that they saved me. They didn't save me; my birth didn't end in a caesarean because I failed to progress, and it certainly was not an emergency, despite what they write down on paper.

In July of 2019, we found out that we were having another baby. This pregnancy was a true surprise! My brain instantly went into plan mode of how I thought things would go and how they should go. The joy was there and then as time carried on the fear started to creep in. I definitely doubted if my body was capable of having a vaginal birth and I initially thought I wanted a hospital birth. I started to look around for independent midwives that supported homebirth with admitting rights to hospitals. I called around and spoke to a woman who gave me a list of four independent midwives with hospital admitting rights which means they work independently and that they support homebirth. That's what they say, anyway. If a transfer into hospital was needed, they would be accepted to the hospital with no issues. I met with two midwives and the first midwife I met with I didn't feel was going to be a good fit. The second midwife I met, I felt confident after meeting her and that she would support me. She said she would support me through anything initially, which I later found out towards the end of my pregnancy wasn't the case. Our first couple of appointments were great. I had one scan at 20 weeks throughout my entire pregnancy by choice and I declined all other testing. I started to listen to my body and my baby. I started to trust my body. I found the Free Birth Society (FBS) podcast halfway through my second pregnancy and it really blew me away. Hearing how women were birthing with confidence with supportive people around them sounded so appealing to me. Even VBAC freebirth women were explaining physiological birth so beautifully. I was starting to understand and to really turn inward. I moved through my own fears and I felt so inspired by these women. I understood physiological birth; the challenge was trusting that I could do it. A lot of inner turmoil came up for me throughout this pregnancy and I spoke with my midwife about the Free Birth Society podcast. I was feeling confident in my body and my baby. I could tell she was instantly not okay with the FBS and I feel that's when our dynamic shifted. At this point I was certain I wanted a homebirth. My midwife had asked me to go to the hospital for an appointment and to play along that I was going to transfer in and that that was my plan. It was not my plan. Going to the hospital to play along was her plan and it was to cover her because I was considered high-risk from my previous C-section. I was so confused by this entire experience. I had to meet with a woman who was high up in maternity. This appointment was mind-blowing, I wish I could've recorded it. She insisted that I would have to come into the hospital because I was considered high-risk. I was not high-risk. She sat there, belittled me and drew diagrams for me. I then declined the rhesus shot. I asked her questions she didn't have answers for. She insisted that she needed to palpate my swollen belly; I said absolutely not. By this time, she was very annoyed with me. The tension in the room was thick. She was adamant that I come back with my midwife and she booked me an appointment. I called my midwife afterwards and I told her I would never be going back there. And I never did.

Weeks later, around the 36-week mark, the back-up midwife came to my house. The second I opened the door I felt like the energy was so dense and heavy that my gut was saying, "This feels so wrong." She was abrupt. She was rude. She brought fear, fear, fear into my house. She palpated my belly and said that my baby was breech. I told her I had plenty of time before baby would turn and that my son came at 42+1 and even then, I had stretch and sweeps prior to him coming. I wasn't worried about having a breech baby at home. My midwife later told me that if I didn't get a scan to confirm that my baby wasn't breech that she would have to discontinue her care with me. I was totally confused as to why someone would palpate my belly and confirm baby was breech, but they couldn't confirm by palpating and feeling that baby was head down. I knew my baby would turn and even if my baby didn't turn, again, it wasn't a fear of mine. I sat with it for a couple of days, though I knew I definitely wouldn't get a scan. The moment I paid her in full a couple of weeks earlier, I knew I had made a mistake. I spoke to my husband about it and said I couldn't continue my care with her and that I would rather freebirth than have her there. She had said some condescending things to me prior to cancelling my care, but once I cancelled my care with her she said things like, "You're the type of woman that sabotages her birth," "You have your blinders on," and, "I've never had a woman decline so many things." She seemed a bit contradictory to the woman I met in the beginning of my pregnancy who said that she would support me through everything. She said that I would never find someone to support me and that she's never had anyone cancel care with her before. I know that I'm not the only woman that has cancelled their care with her and I actually ended up finding a midwife shortly after I fired her. She made those last weeks of my pregnancy deliberately stressful. I'll never forget the way she treated me and I sincerely hope she doesn't put any other pregnant woman through the same gruelling process.

I found a new independent midwife at 37 weeks. She happened to have an opening right when I needed her. When I called her for the first time, I was in tears. She sat and listened to me with the most gentle and kind voice for over an hour. I knew she was something special and we are still friends to this day. She showed up and came into our house with respect and took the time to honour our wishes while we brought our baby into this world. There is truly something magical about her and her name is Norafiah. We had a doula as well who was extremely supportive throughout my entire pregnancy and labour. They both respected us and our decisions throughout our entire time with them. All women deserve to be heard and respected through their journey. This time I did not want anything to kick my labour off. I honoured that my baby would come when they were ready and I went into spontaneous labour at 42+1. I laboured for 28 hours and like I had envisioned through the majority of my pregnancy, I got down on all fours next to my bed and roared until my baby was out. I felt her head in my birth canal before she fully emerged, and man, there is nothing more magical. It wasn't until I felt her head that it became totally real that my body was capable of a vaginal birth. When I saw my baby, I instantly thought my baby was a boy. My entire life I saw myself with boys and boys only. After about five minutes my husband asked me what the gender of our baby was and I pulled the cord back. I saw that our baby was in fact a girl and still to this very day I cannot believe how blessed we are to have a baby girl. We were so connected throughout my pregnancy. We stayed in communication with one another. We both wanted a homebirth. We went on countless walks together and rode the highs and lows of pregnancy. I listened to my intuition when it came to the first midwife – thankfully. I know if I didn't, my birth would have ended up looking very different. I had to fully surrender and trust the process and that certainly wasn't easy to do.

Pregnancy and birth have taught me how to find my way back to myself. It has stripped back all of the layers to show me what is still standing. It tested me in the most unexpected ways. It set a new standard of what I will allow energetically into my space. My sincere hope is that women start to lead with their gut and their intuition. I want women to know that they have options and that they don't have to settle. Women deserve respect and support, not fear and to feel inferior. I was in charge of my birth. I was responsible for my birth. It is time that we change the way that women experience pregnancy, birth and postpartum.

Ten months into Liv's postpartum I started a business called Ten Moons Postpartum Services in hopes to create that village and provide women with postpartum meals. I found cooking and grocery shopping incredibly stressful after having both of my babies. When my friends would have babies, I started to take them meals afterwards and I realised how helpful even one meal is. Shortly after creating Ten Moons, I went through a very transformational phase; a rebirth. I was looking around and noticing how much I was missing community and connection. I contacted a friend of mine that used to hold circles. The first circle I ever went to was hers, and it was magical. I asked her if she wanted to start a circle with me and I decided to open up the doors of my own home. We have been running circles for women to connect and communicate and share food fortnightly since June 2021. It has been one of my greatest accomplishments and brings me pure joy and I feel nothing but love. We laugh and share stories. We cry and hug, but mostly we know we aren't alone and that we can count on one another. We run our circle with two other women and together we have created The Mumma Village Circle.

I sincerely hope to see women taking control of their pregnancy and birth by discovering their options and finding their power. I hope that women can start gathering and supporting each other and not to talk about their babies, but to talk about them and how they're navigating through this time. I hope that women find their village and can feel comfortable to ask for help. We were never meant to do this alone, and in a very isolated society, it is time that women start to find their village. It is time women support women and not from a space of fear, but from a space of love.

Ashley Rose

Hello! My name is Ashley Rose. I have been living in Perth for the last 10 years, but I am originally from Pennsylvania in the United States. I met my husband in the US and moved to Perth shortly after. I'm a mother to 2 beautiful babies; ages 4 and one. And I am a wife to my very dry-witted and terribly attractive husband whom I have been married to for over 8 years.

It was not until my own journey with each of my babies and navigating pregnancy, labour, birth and postpartum that I understood the absolute magnitude of birth and all of its symbolisation that mirrors life. The concept of trusting one's innate intuition and the ability to surrender are both played out daily.

In February 2021, I started a business called Ten Moons Postpartum Services with the aim to provide meals for mothers in their early stages of postpartum. Entering motherhood, even for a second or 3rd time, is very challenging and to relieve the stresses of shopping and cooking in those early days was something I treasured. The transition into motherhood is something we shouldn't take on solo. It is a time when the people around us should rally together to make it as relaxing for mother and baby as possible.

Shortly after Ten Moons, I was really craving to have that village of women around me. I was missing connection, particularly with women. Given the current state of the world and the rapid descent of one-on-one human interactions, I decided to do the opposite and open the doors of my home and call women into my space to sit in circle with me. Three other women have helped me achieve this and we have been gathering fortnightly ever since. We talk, we sit, we laugh, we cry, and most importantly, we eat.

Recently I have been focusing on my babies and being a stay-at-home mum. Before I started my business, I kept feeling like I had to be doing something. Currently, I have come to realise that all I need to be doing is showing up for myself and my family. Birth changed me. Motherhood has changed me and is continuing to show me a mirror of all the inner work that needs to unfold. Birth and motherhood allow women to ultimately step into their power. It allows women to return home to themselves. I am returning home to myself.

www.tenmoonspostpartum.com
Instagram: @tenmoonspostpartum & @mummavillagecircle

Tara Caetano
MY BIRTH, MY BECOMING

As I sit here writing this chapter at almost 6 months pregnant, it's hard to really know where to begin …

Do I let you in on the 10-month preconception journey my future daughter took me on, complete with family relocations, nude nature ceremonies, teeth being pulled and reacquainting myself with my mother tongue?

Or do I dive into how everything about this pregnancy feels like the complete opposite to how I approached my son's birth 4 years ago and how everything that ever went 'wrong' in that birth is what led me to ensuring that this one feels ever so 'right' for me?

No matter what stories I choose to share or what seasons of the journey come through, I know deep down that it's always going to come down to the same core message. That one underlying truth that has never failed to escape me, through all 4 years of being a mother …

That when it comes to birth, and all creation for that matter, it's who you become along the way that truly enriches you to your core.

Yep, not the baby. Not your perfect birth. Not the dream team in postpartum, nor the ideal pregnancy circumstances. All of that is wonderful (and your birthright) and incredibly vital for new mamas to thrive in this season.

But what we fail to really acknowledge is that for many mamas that have had all of this and more, feeling truly enriched by their conception, pregnancy, birth and postpartum is something left to chance and seen as something more connected to the outcome than the process. It's left to the roulette of their external world somehow lining up perfectly without any expectations falling short or people letting them down. And when we come to understand that birth is in fact a huge rite of passage designed to see your old self die in order for the new mother to be reborn, I'm going to go out on a limb and say that 10 times out of 10, throwing the dice on your enrichment based on having control over every outcome almost always turns into an absolute flop.

So, what do I mean by enrichment?

I love to think of it in terms of the way we might enrich the soil of our garden. The way we can actually see our actions and approach making the soil more fertile, more abundant, more full of life and nutrient dense than before. To be left enriched by an experience is to not only walk away feeling richer, enhanced or even better than before, but to have access to all of that whilst it's happening … during its becoming. To literally let every layer of that experience, every moment of that process expand you into deeper, fuller, elevated levels of whatever it is you truly value. Pleasure, satisfaction, joy, meaning, love, connection … Whatever you're here to live and breathe, your becoming becomes your very own way there. And yes, no matter what we've been taught, birthing a whole new world should 100% be a becoming that we get to associate with an enriched state of being.

Now, don't get me wrong. This doesn't mean everything has to look peachy or cruise along without any hiccups. In fact, that's the whole point. That even when it doesn't go 'right' (not 'if'), you have chosen to see every single element of this wild, primal becoming as a vessel into your deepest enrichment possible. You're in full-bodied agreement; there is no direction, no roadblock, no reason why any element of this journey might be designed for anything else but your highest, most enriched experience. Wild, right?

Do you even realise how revolutionary it is to claim something like this and to claim one's undeniable right to enrichment, whilst we're all here living in this pandemic-riddled world? To even own this choice and declare it for oneself is enough to ensure your very existence makes most people wildly uncomfortable. Most people will see this as setting the standard too high. That we should be focused on just getting by unscathed and keep putting one foot in front of the other. But to that I say – this is not a game to me. This is not me just aimlessly shooting for the stars, and seeing if this lands. This is for our survival. This is for our preservation.

The way I see it – with the direction this world is taking – I *must* condition myself to feel enriched by what is present in the *now*, if I am going to have any hope of meeting what's to come in the future, with my nervous system intact. It's no longer a 'luxury' to choose to rest my resistance towards 'what is' and open-heartedly devote myself to the acceptance and receivership of the life I have unfolding in front of me. It's no longer okay for me to settle into a state of complacency when bringing a child into this ever-changing world (nor really was it ever).

Because these babies we are holding, they are something else … And they need us to feel different to how we've ever felt before. They need us to go first in letting the ecstasy of this time and this season penetrate us, so they too can hold that same imprint in their cells as they meet the wild unknown.

So to the mamas who are pregnant and embarking on their birth journey at this point in time, I want to ask you:

Do you know how powerful you are right now? How on-tap you have the voice of this new world, with its desires, demands and deeply delicious visions?

Do you know how privileged you are to birth at this time, amidst a grand rising of sovereign self-reclamation?

Do you know how catalysing this season is for every dream, vision, hope and buried desire your family has?

Do you know how much enrichment, sustenance and soothing relief is available to you right now, through every movement, niggle and full-bodied sensation?

If not, then please keep reading and let me pour my overflow out onto your delicious experience, because if there's one thing I want you to walk away knowing it's that you are safe to live in the overflow – of enrichment, of love, of peace – of anything you damn choose.

In order to claim my desire, my right and my need for enrichment at every stage of creating and birthing life onto this planet, I had to do one huge thing – I had to cut my own umbilical cord to so much of the outside world. I had to stop feeding off societal expectations and approval, I had to learn to breathe on my own and I had to finally accept that all I had control over was this world of my own that I was creating moment by moment. And I had to be prepared to live there, more often than not.

For most people, taking full responsibility for their life, their baby's life and their experiences just feels too much. Many would rather deal with the side effects and consequences of a choice made by someone else, than face the side effects and consequences of one they made themselves. We fear the worst-case scenario, but we also fear the most ecstatic, best-case scenario too. We fear it's bigger than we can really hold. We doubt our capacity to hold 'too much' of either enrichment or suffering. We're threatened by what we haven't yet attuned to or allowed ourselves to become changed by. Yet nothing is more of a threat to us than our own perceptions. And if you know anything about pain (especially in birth), it's that it increases in relation to how under threat you feel.

I personally felt petrified and threatened by the level of intensity I experienced in my first birth. I was completely unprepared for it. It took me by surprise and I immediately felt like I was in danger. I knew nothing about birth going into it (besides the standard hospital classes) and was completely naive to the whole process. Alongside that I had zero support, aside from my amazing partner, who too was completely blindsided, and I left that birth experience with a subconscious fear of any kind of intensity whatsoever. I saw intensity as my kryptonite, and feared birthing again because of it. It led me on the path of trying to understand birth and learning about other people's birthing experiences, because I initially just couldn't understand how someone would choose to do that twice! No matter how much I loved our son and the incredible gift of being his mother, I just couldn't fathom how what I experienced could be considered normal. It just felt … too much. And so I did what my curiosity led me to do, and I studied to become a doula. As they say, keep your friends close and your enemies even closer. And if birth felt like my enemy, I needed to get under its skin and learn everything about it that I could. And here's what I learnt …

That birth was not bigger than me. That intensity was just another form of intimacy, and when embraced, welcomed and cherished, it could be a flavour of potent ecstasy that most chase their entire lives. I realised that I wasn't afraid of what the intensity could do to me; I was afraid of who I might become if I actually became attuned to the intensity I feared and I let it all in. Who was that woman who could handle such power coursing through her body? Who was that woman who went all-in on such an intimate embodied experience?

Whenever we're afraid of something, it's usually who we'll become on the other side that we fear the most. And when this part is actually the becoming that serves us the most potent source of enrichment, we're missing out on so much that our birth has to offer us when we steer clear of letting ourselves change and evolve in such a way. We live in a world that adds glitter to every transformation with highlight reels and before and afters, and we've been conditioned to desire and expect only the shiny side of 'becoming'. So when we're actually faced with the full-spectrum experience of our becoming, especially the parts that are so subtle or internal that others can't see, acknowledge or validate for us, it can crush us and send us straight into resistance. But here's what you need to do instead …

Let yourself crumble.

Let yourself submerge into the chaos and the messiness that wants to be embodied. Let yourself feel the fullness of the crisis as it's presenting itself to you at that fulcrum of your transformative becoming. Because I promise you that your crisis point is often the very initiation you're being asked to meet in order to taste and enjoy that very next layer of your deepest enrichment.

When we first cut our own umbilical cord to the disempowered way of life we've led to date, especially when we really want to do so after finally realising how much it hasn't been serving us, there's this subtle expectation that were going to feel instantly empowered, or it's going to be like a switch we turn on and feel instant release and relief. But that's just not the case. Just like birth, there's this ring of fire, this initiation; the very real aspect of any rite of passage that requires us to burn, to grieve, to fall to our knees in the deepest embodied surrender and pretty much say, "I give up." And in that process, we reach that tipping point, that crisis of confidence. And like birth, it's usually not until we feel that intensity and reach that tipping point where our body just lets go and we surrender our mind and say, "I'm out," that we really know that we're at transition. That we're becoming someone new. And like with any rite of passage, we need to have reverence for the way it's going to break us before it's going to make us. And it's that reverence that enriches us and has us going back for more, time and time again. So, cut the cord. Go through fire, meet yourself in flames, and then birth new. Rinse and repeat.

I want to just pause here and remind you that I don't share any of this without deep acknowledgement and understanding of what I'm really asking. I get that it's BIG work. I see you in the bigness of this work and your becoming. I live it daily, but here's the thing … Birth is big work.

Which is why it's even more important to let yourself welcome in whatever you need to sustain yourself through the bigness. To finally let yourself reconcile any thoughts or beliefs around how worthy you are being someone who chooses to feel enriched by life, and birth, and death – moment to moment.

Every day we get closer to death. Birth has taught me more about death than any other area of life. The intensity and chaos of death is something most of us run from because we don't know who we are in it all and we lack reverence for its role in our lives. We feel like it's something that happens to us, something we aren't a part of – so we disassociate and avoid. And yet, we are just as much made of death as we are birth. And when you really regard your own becoming as *for* you, a part of you and something you are here to be a participant in during this lifetime, you can also begin to see how not separate you are from death.

I've had to learn how to stop creating separation between me and such key elements of life, both the dark and hard stuff and the big lofty dreams and desires too. The fastest way for us to slow down our own becoming is to remain separate from it. To see it as something outside of us, something not for us or something sitting on some kind of pedestal. But even when you can't 'see' yourself in something 'yet', it's important you don't skip the chance to pull up a seat at the table and simply join the conversation. Claim your role as a human being for whom nothing human is unavailable. Only then when you've truly let it be something that you're allowed to participate in, will you begin to see how very much 'for you' something is.

I've had to do this in so many ways during pregnancy and birth alone. When I first felt my daughter in my womb calling for her own conception, I felt so detached from my desire to have a daughter, despite it feeling so strong. Her energy felt big and full, and as a 'boy mum' I felt so separate from being someone who had a daughter. So much so that I would play this detached game of putting all my desire into the hands of the universe and really standing back from owning my longing. To be honest, it wasn't until I was already in my first trimester where I really looked at this separation and detachment in the eyes and faced off with how 'too much' my love and desire really felt. It was safer to keep us separate, to keep us as souls intertwined vs. mother and child, sharing blood, living as one full and interdependent ecosystem.

It happened again when I received a strong and powerful message within a visualisation that she wanted me to have a freebirth. At first, I was deeply intimidated. Feeling absolutely inadequate for this request I'd received, purely because I always saw people who freebirthed as being very different to me, in a sort of pedestalled way. They knew more than me, they were wired differently, I didn't seem to have that level of in-built trust that they embodied. But I soon realised that this separation was the only thing standing in the way of me actually listening and honouring my child's requests for the very first time in her life. And so I stopped making myself separate from something so human, so real and so available to anyone who walks this planet. I immersed myself in it, I took a seat at the table, I let myself participate in the conversation and eventually it became the biggest no-brainer of my whole pregnancy. Now? Of course I will freebirth, I can't believe I ever considered anything else. THIS is the power of letting yourself experience your own becoming.

Dropping this idea of being separate to both the pain and the pleasure of birth and life is also what ultimately helped me move past so much of my birth trauma following my son's birth. Yes, becoming a doula and becoming educated and normalising birth for myself was a huge part of my process. But none of that would really have 'stuck' and let me embrace this next birth if I hadn't decided that birth was no longer separate to me and the life I live on the daily.

You see, for years, I longed to see birth as beautiful. I longed to find enough peace, enough healing, enough information, enough understanding to effortlessly say that birth was exquisite, extraordinary and a masterpiece of human nature that I couldn't help but be totally in love with.

Because underneath that longing lived anything but love. Birth had broken me and in my recovery I had not one person in my field that could help me see its beauty. I didn't yet know the true magnificence and astonishing art of what it meant to die and be reborn. To crumble at the altar of one's heart and never really know who would return.

Birth felt like the enemy; this part of life that I would need to just accept and endure. And this deeply saddened me. I felt somehow less worthy of my humanness. Less worthy of my womanhood and motherhood, and this body I'd obviously failed to figure out. Until I decided … No. This will not be my story. I refuse. So I befriended the enemy. I forced myself to sit in the heat of her flames and I let her burn my skin until we spoke the same language. I let her intimidate me and overwhelm me, and make me all kinds of uncomfortable.

I refused to give up something so innately mine to own as a womb-led human being. I refused to just tap out of something so obviously meant for me to grow and learn from. I refused to not claim my inherent humanness – my human nature. The wisdom that supersedes all. I decided I would rather die in the flames of birth, than live my life trying to avoid the heat. And what I discovered was the kind of life I'd die for time and time again.

I'm now no longer afraid of the dark. *I am the dark.* And in all honesty, I'm more afraid of forgetting how utterly beautiful the dark is than the living and being with the dark itself. And in all its contrast, I can now say that birth is undoubtedly the most beautiful experience in the world. One that is mine to live and own and experience. One that I can't wait to do again.

So I want to ask you – who are you being asked to become in the process of creating your baby?

Who are you resisting becoming, and what are you keeping yourself separate from?

Where we feel most wobbly is usually where the wisdom lies. Go there. And when it all feels too big to hold or handle, surrender that bigness into the earth. Let Mother Earth hold it for you. Root who you are – as a creator, a mother, a birthing human being – into the earth at your feet. Either energetically, or do as I did and literally dig a hole! Whatever you need to do to let yourself be held in this becoming, so you are free to be wild in your adoration for it. Because the true fullness and enrichment that is available to you at this time? It's incredibly infectious, for you, the world and everyone around you. It's time for you to begin feasting on it for yourself and letting it flavour your whole world.

You deserve to be so undeniably available to the potency you're being asked to channel right now. And yet your capacity to feel enriched by that potency is connected to how deeply you can let yourself rest into the life you've already created and what's available to hold you. We can't hold a vision for the collective or for our own children that we cannot hold for ourselves. We must start there first. You are safe to make this all about you. Whatever you're carrying that keeps you from going all in – bury it into the earth.

Your becoming is a spiritual, emotional and energetic transformation that happens daily, guided by the unseen and yet commands that you change in ways so visible and visceral that they can intimidate you. Let them. Let this be the part of pregnancy and birth that you live for. And then commemorate and celebrate yourself for it as much as you can. Every inch of you and your world deserves to be commemorated. Every opening, every closing, every moment of intimate expansion ordained with a reverence that not only says 'thank you', but 'more please'. Ordinary milestones seen for their extraordinary impact, because YOU decided that they are inherently worthy of celebration. If there is one secret I can share to sustaining oneself through the mess and magic of metamorphosis, it's to never stop celebrating. Never stop making it all sacred. Your season of self-honour has no start or end date. Take yourself there every chance you get. *That* is what I call an enriched becoming.

Tara Caetano

Hi, I'm Tara Caetano. Spoken word poet, writer, entrepreneur, mother and mentor, and if there's one thing I know I'm here for on this planet, it's to let love alter me. To let it change me, mould me, move me and make me weak at the knees, time and time again, as I create life, create worlds, create art and create myself.

Obsessed with connecting women with their own stories and leading them back into a world of their own, I've been on a wild journey of creative expression, self-empowerment and undoubtedly my favourite part, embodying the divine mother that I know lives within the walls of my heart. Leaning into all the ways that we are designed to be fed and nurtured by our own innate nature of creation feels like such a deep soul calling to me, and getting to play with that in the realms of motherhood, art, business and sisterhood is the greatest gift.

I choose to do life here in Australia with my partner of 11 years, my 4-year-old son and the beautiful being currently in my womb, and it brings me to life every single day to know that the adventure we're here to have together is only just beginning. I'm also the proud nurturer of my

Birth New

art as a poet, and my business Bold Heart Creative – a creative agency that weaves intimacy, intentionality and embodied expression into the creative process of artists, entrepreneurs and bold-hearted humans.

Website: www.taracaetano.com & www.boldheartcreative.com
Instagram: @taracaetano & @boldheartcreative

Tania Henderson
JUST PERFECT

When I became pregnant for the first time, I dutifully went to see a GP. For many reasons, the allopathic medical system is *not* my first port of call in pretty much any circumstance. She asked me which obstetrician I wanted to be referred to. Despite working in senior management at a large private hospital (yes, I appreciate the irony) for nearly 5 years, I was confused by that question. Why did I need a surgeon?

Fatefully, I ended up not long after at the Community Midwifery Library in Leederville before they closed, and a delightful midwife queried me about my plans. I still had no idea. So, she asked, "Why don't you have your baby at home?" I voiced my only resistance with, "Isn't that a bit messy?" and she laughed. We chatted more and I happily applied for the program.

I will be forever grateful to my very first midwife and beautiful space holder, who I had only very few appointments with. She asked all of those initial questions and opened my mind in regards to honouring or using the placenta, options in regards to immediate vaccinations, delayed cord clamping – all the things now so innate to me, but that had not even crossed my mind, still fresh on this motherhood journey.

My first and second babies were born uneventfully and with ease at home through that wonderful program. Because of my incredible personal experience of encapsulating and using my own placenta postpartum, I spent 3-4 years serving women and mamas by providing them with that same service. It was such an honour and privilege every single time. I only stopped because I started to feel unreliable with having my kids with me – as a homeschooling family, we had a multitude of activities during a week as well as naps to ensure for a long time, and the juggle started to feel unfair on everyone involved.

When I became pregnant for the 3rd time, I was tandem nursing my 2 little ones and hadn't had a return of my cycle. I guessed that I had put on a little bit of weight around the tummy, noticed only when wearing my youngest on my back in a carrier. Finally, I was complaining on Facebook in the Tandem Nursing for Conscious, Gentle Parents group about my super sore nipples, and a friend subtly asked if I was pregnant. Haha, of course not! But guess what, I peed on a stick and it is the only time I have told my husband that I was pregnant via text message – I was lost for words as I was so shocked.

With me having no clue about dates, I assumed I needed a scan to give us some idea, so went again to a GP for a referral. At the ultrasound, the poor student who was meant to be developing their skills had to hand over to the senior radiographer as the little peanut he was expecting to see ended up being a 17-week-old baby. I had missed my whole first trimester!

We received a phone call from the GP asking us to come in later that afternoon after the scan and we were blindsided by the information that our baby was suspected to have 'chromosomal abnormalities'. Subsequently we were rushed for a blood test and scan at the local specialist women's hospital. Once those were done and we were sitting in the private little conference room where bad news is delivered, I understood why we had been rushed through so quickly … so that we could have an abortion easily before 20 weeks.

No. It was unanimous, my husband and I didn't even need to look at each other when asked the question – the first time of many, as apparently it is unacceptable to bring anything deemed less than perfect (by society's standards, anyway) into our world.

So this 'bad news' (we eventually found out) was that our baby may have Down syndrome. What a freaking relief. Honestly, language is so powerful – the fear that was projected onto me by the GP's wording was enormous. We were 'managed' as if we had a definite diagnosis, with many appointments at the hospital, monitoring growth, checking for this, that and the other. We had an initial cardiology scan – the results from this were the hardest to process for me – and at that point we thought our little one may need urgent surgery after birth. This meant a hospital birth as well as immediate separation – both of which I couldn't fathom and didn't feel right about. Every single time I had to go in for another scan and the nurse asked where the baby was being born, I would say, "At home unless there is a reason not to." But my voice wasn't being heard – they kept asking, and they kept offering the option to terminate (which can be done until full term for babies with Down syndrome).

Fortunately, after the Community Midwifery Program as well as the hospital's Birthing Centre program blessedly declined me as a patient, we invited our amazing private midwife onboard with us. She really helped me to unravel all of the fear that I was getting drawn into; the energy was exhausting and not positive for a pregnant mama. She had been our back-up midwife for our first baby and primary for number 2, so it was a very easy and right decision for us to make.

Around this time, my amazingly gifted friend and naturopath was able to check in with my little growing babe – directly connecting to him to ask him if there was anything we needed to be worrying about. She blissfully disconnected the energetic cords from the fearful medical staff that were attached to me and reported back – "He just says that he is perfect." That's the moment I found out we were having a little boy, and I was able to block out the medical negativity more easily.

Another beautiful friend – who was a doula-in-training at that stage – offered an amazing ear, shoulder to cry on, very wise words as well as hypnobirthing resources which I really enjoyed using and ended up being super valuable. I had listened to a different variation of hypnobirthing meditations when I was pregnant with my first, but these really gave me a focal point of positivity each day that I really needed whilst feeling so enmeshed with the medical system.

At no point in time were we given information about Down syndrome, referred on to speak to anyone with actual lived experience in the Down syndrome community or offered anything positive by anyone associated with the hospital. However, I do still remember our midwife letting me know that her sister has always wanted to adopt a little one with Down syndrome … so naively – I responded with, "Why?" – I thought that was very interesting but a little confusing at the time!

There was another heart scan at about 32 weeks. I saw a wonderful cardiologist at this appointment and he explained that he could now see the heart better and that the concerns from what was seen previously were simply a heart that was wired a bit atypically. So, totally within the realms of normal, though not uncommon in babies with Down syndrome (keeping in mind we didn't have an official diagnosis). He was very considerate and respectful in how he spoke to me; I have to say it is a theme that has continued to this day, that all of the cardiologists I have spoken to have a certain way and energy about them that I guess comes from working with such a beautiful and powerful part of our body, both physically and metaphysically. However, I digress. Most importantly, after this scan, I pointedly asked whether he could see any reason that urgent medical attention would be needed after birth, as my preference was still to birth at home, but I needed to know cerebrally (I already knew intuitively) that it was okay. He gave his blessing, which was amazing.

Just before 37 weeks, we were out at a playgroup with friends, with my compact tummy noticeably looking as if there were plenty of cooking time left for babe. A friend gave me a tummy rub and commented as such, as I sat resting on my butt watching my other 2 play.

Hubby came home that night a little later than usual – it was a Thursday evening and it was a public holiday the next day, Good Friday – so he had had 'last drinks before baby' with mates, squeezing them in with plenty of time before we expected babe to arrive. He was in good form once he was home and I was sitting on our outdoor chair in our lounge room (everything else sucked to sit on by then) just laughing and laughing. I couldn't even tell you why, but the kids were in hysterics at his antics. We all eventually went to bed; I nursed the kids to sleep as I had continued to do during pregnancy but then couldn't sleep. I put a hypnobirthing track on to listen to; it usually sent me straight to sleep, but I was uncomfortable with Braxton Hicks which had been extremely normal throughout every one of my pregnancies, but more so when I was breastfeeding. Eventually I hopped up to walk them off, doing a few laps inside the house. I messaged my midwife letting her know I was having trouble getting to sleep so I was just going to have a shower then go back to bed. The water felt amazing, and my shower and bathroom were pristine from the nesting that had been happening for at least 2 weeks, only in that space.

My little guy woke up probably around midnight, so I got into bed and nursed him back to sleep, thinking I too would go to sleep. But no. I don't fully recall exactly what I was doing at this stage – it was a combination of swaying against my bookcase, walking around and getting into the shower – all with the intention of going to sleep once I felt comfortable.

Little guy woke again around 3am, and by then I had got hubby up to complain that I couldn't sleep. I laid down to try to nurse him back to sleep but then got hubby to grab him to walk him around to help him sleep. At just before 3:30am I sat on the lounge and I offered to nurse him again to help him settle. About 30 seconds after he latched on, a massive contraction crashed through me. I roared and almost threw him to his dad who was sitting next to me. I told him that I needed him there and am pretty sure I damaged his hand, squeezing it as I roared through what apparently was a sudden transition.

I messaged my midwife something to the effect of 'I think I need you here now', put my phone on the bathroom bench and hopped straight into the shower. Intuitively, I knew what was happening, and I felt to check for a head whilst I had baby resuscitation techniques flying through my head, acutely aware that I was alone in the bathroom with a baby about to arrive. I worked with the next contraction, not sure even after 2 homebirths whether I was doing it right, and the next moment I knew, I instinctively crouched down to catch my little guy, en caul, and absolutely perfect.

Immediately upon setting eyes on him, I simultaneously felt 'you're here' and I knew he had Down syndrome. And all was as it should be.

I eventually called out for hubby; he was reluctant to come to me as he had almost gotten the new big brother to sleep. But he finally walked into the bathroom with him to see me sitting on the floor with our new babe in my arms. At that point I asked for a towel to cover him, I had turned the shower off but couldn't reach anything else. I still laugh at the (clean) bath mat he passed me. I am not sure what he thought was going on, I am not sure how sober he felt before walking in, but he was instantly besotted.

Our oldest woke also and both got to meet him as he happily, sleepily but beautifully nursed.

Our wonderful midwife arrived about 40 minutes later after speaking with hubby on the phone; my big girl helped cut the cord, daddy got to have first skin-on-skin cuddles while I birthed the placenta, cleaned up and got ready for snuggles. She stayed for a few hours, just sitting with us after checking him over, watching our newest little one settle into the world. She finally went home, promising to come back late in the morning.

Once she returned, we somehow had one set of grandparents already excitedly present – they stayed and played with the big kids as our midwife gently took us to the side to speak with us privately. She explained that she saw features of Down syndrome in our little one, and whilst all seemed okay, she had needed to find out if there was anything we needed to do. So she had called the local women's hospital to speak to a paediatrician there. It seems that he responded to her much in the way I observed the obstetrician behave at the same facility when she attended an appointment with me; the defences and hackles blatantly went up and there was no respect for the incredible knowledge that she has. He threatened her with removal of her licence and us as parents with removal of our kids if we did not attend the hospital immediately. She did bravely try to buy us some time – she had thoroughly assessed our little one and knew that there wasn't any urgency – but her professional expertise was extraordinarily poorly received.

So instead of staying in our little bubble of bliss just hours after giving birth, we had to go to the hospital, where I had to walk to every department to have the scans and tests done on him that they insisted on. Then they wanted to admit us. We declined but the paediatrician was insisting. Eventually I just asked, "Why … why did we need to be there?" None of the testing showed any cause for concern. Eventually he admitted that most families just want to be in hospital if they think their child has a Down syndrome (or whatever else) diagnosis. Thank goodness my big, intimidating husband was there, backing me up all the way; I truly don't believe they would otherwise have let us leave to go home and just enjoy being with our new family.

I am so blessed with beautiful friends – we had one wait around near home for us with her family until we were able to come home, then gave us some congratulatory cuddles (all we were needing and wanting that day), put food in the oven for us all, made sure the dog was fed, gifted us a beautiful handmade blanket, fussed around for a bit and then left us to it. I still don't know if to this day she realises how special and important that was to us, it meant so much to all of us.

Becoming the parent of a child with a disability is a strange world to be thrust into. Even though I didn't personally experience it – my husband did deeply – there is usually a stage of profound grieving. From what I can tell, it's not because you don't want your child (you fiercely want to protect them) but it's the adjustment in expectations of what your child is likely to be able to do and not do. And that is being said whilst *also* not putting any limits on him. We have incredibly accepting friends and family, but our experience is unusual. With over 90% of babies with Down syndrome aborted because of (I believe) the pushiness of the medical system – who do not even remotely offer informed consent, just a pile of fear – our society is not designed to be accepting of differences. The prejudice and fear of the unknown runs deep, and as a world we are missing out on the blessing and light that is brought to us by trying to avoid diversity and difference.

I have learnt more about love than I already thought was possible through having Blake join our family, and I know with all my heart and soul that he was meant to be here. I get told regularly that I am an inspiration to others; but I really need to say that whilst I appreciate the sentiment, I am not. The road can be hard, it can be isolating, exhausting to the deepest core. But in the end, I do what any mother does for their child – seek the best for them. I do this for all my kids and I know that everyone else does this too, it just looks different for each family.

As hard as this journey was and is to navigate, I wouldn't change it for the world. I feel so honoured that my children chose me to be their mama, I know we are all on this journey together and I am just doing my best to be present and appreciate precious moments when I can. In saying that, there is nothing quite like celebrating the achievements of a child who develops at a slower pace than others. They can be celebrated with so much joy and so much more often as each increment is obvious. Blake makes us all proud and he loves the cheer squad he has in his siblings.

Today, he is 6.5 years old – he is a hilarious and fun little boy. He doesn't yet speak with words, but he is a powerful, clear and effective communicator; there is no mistaking what he is wanting you to do or know. He adores dinosaurs, balls, swings and trampolines. He loves his doll house, playing chasey and swimming with his big brother and sister. He has a special bond with our dog, they often hang out next to each other, squished closely together and he is incredibly gentle with anyone smaller than him. He teaches us all so much every day and I know that he has a positive impact on all of those that take the time to get to know him. I don't feel like the words I have used are enough to explain the experience of bringing him into our lives and having him as part of our family, but I hope you get just an inkling of how special it all has been.

Tania Henderson

Hello! I am Tania Henderson. Passionate disability rights advocate. Believer in the strengths within neurodiversity. Sacral generator. Owner of Rainbow Knots. Holistic occupational therapist. Deeply intuitive, heart-led, homeschooling and homebirthing mama of 3.

As the owner and designer of Rainbow Knots since 2013, my business quickly flourished and earned a reputation in offering energetically powerful support for mamas and their babes – initially with unique handcrafted gemstone and Baltic amber pieces, evolving over time with the addition of beautiful essential oil alchemy and magic.

I am naturally drawn to helping people. One of my greatest strengths is as a problem-solver, hence, I experience deep satisfaction and validation in supporting mamas. Leaning in hard and diving deep to resolve problems and challenges has always made my heart happy. This year I have finally now returned to what seems to be a much more profoundly important identity to me than I previously realised, as a paediatric occupational therapist.

Working with kids was always something I knew I would do, ever since graduating as an OT in 2000. Having my own 3 has now gifted me experience and tools to offer as an additional layer to standard therapeutic offerings. The birth of my youngest with Down syndrome lit a new fire of disability advocacy that has naturally overflowed into my work. My desire to work holistically and with the strengths of each child and their family is being achieved as I empower the parents in understanding how to guide their children towards their optimal and most joyful experiences in life.

I truly believe that all kids do well when they can. I believe strongly in informed consent in all aspects of life – this was a lesson learnt from my very first birth. That life-changing transition into mamahood, and the evolution since, has strongly consolidated my position.

As an innately veracious lifelong learner, I am constantly learning, evolving and integrating knowledge and experiences into all aspects of my life. I seek, absorb and digest all there is on the subjects that I am passionate about. Those subjects benefit not only my family but those I work alongside. I have the courage and strength to stand up to anything if it means that I maintain alignment with my core beliefs and values.

Instagram: @taniahenderson_ot
Facebook: Tania Henderson – Conscious Motherhood
Facebook: Tandem Nursing for Conscious, Gentle Parents

Hayley Leonard
CLAIMING YOUR POWER IN THE BIRTH SPACE

Why should we Birth New?

Call me a jaded ex-midwife, but I have seen and heard pretty much everything after studying and working in a load of different hospitals and settings. Why does this make me so angry and also motivated? Because I know firsthand how bloody *amazing* birth can be. The potential is there and I want you to feel how I did, after experiencing 4 powerful and life-affirming births and supporting many families to feel the same way. Birth has immense power and potential and yet fear often becomes the driving force behind our approach to it. The predominant notion is that your body is either capable of birthing or not, when in fact it is often the system of care and intervention that begins the chain of events which commonly leads to a birthing shitshow. When there are complications it is often blamed on your inadequate pelvis or an uncooperative cervix – not the fact that your body or baby may not have been ready. The idea of birthing *new* should actually see us shifting back to the *old* ways, when birth was seen as a normal life event. In looking forward we also need to look back, so let's consider the origins of the medical system we have today.

Historically, and for centuries, women were supported by other wise women, and birthing was secret women's business. Women were the experts. During the middle ages, midwives would call upon the local barber surgeon if there was any difficulty during labour. These barber surgeons were the first informal obstetricians, who would conduct all manner of random surgery and healing in their shops, along with the obligatory shave and haircut.

Around this time, Frenchman François Mauriceau became one of the most prominent foundation obstetricians whose early work inspired many modern-day practices. He is probably the reason that you are conditioned to lay on your back to birth, which he documented in his 1668 book entitled *The Diseases of Women with Child, and in Child-bed*. He explains that the bed should be designed so that the woman is laying back with her head slightly higher than her pelvis in a 'convenient figure'. He also claimed that this would be a better position for her to push and for her pain. I wonder if he actually asked any of the women how they felt about that? And isn't it interesting that the majority of birthing today happens in this 'semi-recumbent' position? It is certainly the only image that is shown in any TV show or movie, further normalising and perpetuating this bullshit recommendation. From experience, when you leave a labouring person to move around undisturbed, laying back on a bed is the *last* position they would assume!

The decades that followed began the dominance of physician-led births and the comparatively recent rejection of birthing at home, to birthing in hospital. It became normalised for women to be instructed to lay on their backs, be shaved and be given an enema, wear hospital gowns, be routinely knocked out with chloroform and babies to be extracted with 'prophylactic forceps' in an effort to 'save' them from having to endure the stress of labour. This is how birth has evolved into the 'medicalised' version that is promoted by mainstream society and experienced by the majority of women today. Having a doctor was seen as a status symbol, and midwives were only for the poor buggers who couldn't afford a doctor. Crazy how this theme from the 1700s and 1800s still rings true.

It is what we allow and accept that continues. What you need to know about birthing today is that you *can* have a great birth if that is what you desire, but you need to know what you are up against when you meet with the medical model of birth. Yes we are very fortunate to have amazing technology and facilities for emergencies, but it seems as though everyone is treated like they are an emergency waiting to happen. So now what?

How do we Birth New?

We *Birth New* by returning to our roots and changing our mindset. We learn to trust our bodies again, we decide that birth is a normal life event and you surround yourself with people who also believe that you are totally capable. You *Birth New* by learning all that you can through independent birth education classes so you know about many of the common interventions you may be offered. Then you can have a clear idea of what they involve and any potential impacts that these interventions may have upon your birth and your options. Just knowing that you have choices is one of the first major steps to having an empowering birth. You *Birth New* by choosing a care provider and model of care that truly aligns with your view of birth (hint: you may have to look outside of the hospital system to find these care providers). This care provider should support you as the central decision-maker of your pregnancy and birth.

Your first crucial decision: Choosing your care provider

When you first confirm that you are pregnant, your GP will present you with your options for care. The first question is usually, "Do you have private health insurance?" as if this is the best and standard option and anything else is inferior. A client said to me once that they went with a private obstetrician because they figured that they must provide the best care considering they were experts and also very expensive. It was only when they went on the obligatory hospital tour and asked where the birth pool was, that they were told that the hospital does not support waterbirth. It was then that they realised their choice of care provider did not align with their desired birth experience. She and her partner figured that surely the most expensive place would have *all* of the options. What many people do not realise is that an obstetrician is an expert in obstetric surgery, not experts in normal birth and most would have never seen a waterbirth in their entire career – they probably couldn't even make it through a waterbirth video without having to sit on their hands!

With all of this in mind, and taking into account your own beliefs around birth, here are the options available for your consideration:

- *Public hospital through their antenatal clinic.*
- *Public birthing centre with midwives, usually attached to a major hospital.*
- *Public hospital with a midwifery group practice where you have a known team of midwives (not offered at every hospital).*
- *Public hospital with shared GP obstetric care.*
- *Private hospital with a private obstetrician.*
- *Community Midwifery Program – government funded, hospital and homebirth options.*
- *Homebirth with an independent/private midwife, who can come into hospital with you in the event of a transfer.*
- *Independent midwifery for antenatal and postpartum care (so for all of your appointments, then birthing at whichever hospital you choose – random hospital staff attend your labour).*
- *Birth at home unattended though with antenatal and postpartum*

care through one of the abovementioned care providers (who may or may not have any idea of your plans for what is known as a 'freebirth').
- Birth at home unattended with no formal booking or antenatal care known as a 'wild pregnancy and freebirth'.

I bet most of you were not given that list of options by your GP! The foundation of your birth was set in motion the minute you chose your care provider, so please carefully consider this vital step in your journey to *Birth New*.

If you look at the latest statistics at the Australian Institute of Health and Welfare **www.aihw.gov.au/reports/mothers-babies/australias-mothers-babies/contents/summary** you will see that there has been a huge increase in intervention over the last decade, but with no conveyed benefit. There has been no change in the maternal or perinatal mortality rate to justify this rise, in fact, it is slightly worse. You can also compare rates between the public and the private sector. Here you will see the dramatic increase in intervention that occurs in private hospitals. In general:

- *Less people are going into spontaneous labour down from 56% to 42.5%.*
- *More are having their perineum cut (episiotomy) now 1 in 4!*
- *More are having caesareans, up from 32% to 36%.*
- *Induction of labour has gone up from 25% to 35%.*

A healthy baby should be the bare minimum standard for your birth care and every care provider has this central to their mission – and so they should! Everyone should emerge from their birth feeling respected, dignified, valued and honoured as the giver and creator of life; this can apply in any circumstance, however your baby needs to be born. You can still have an elective caesarean and feel the power of owning your birth.

I was 24 when I had my first baby. I was fit and healthy and chose to give birth where my friend was having her baby, at a small hospital with a midwifery clinic. I don't think I saw the same midwife twice and didn't know either of the 2 on shift when I was in labour. I ended up needing to be assisted with the ventouse or vacuum, and yet my midwife waited until I was completely ready as they knew I wanted as little intervention as possible. They had watched me actively labour all night, in the bath, on the Fitball, no drugs and I really felt as though they were right behind me. Eventually I had nothing left in the tank and welcomed the assistance, which was behind the door and waiting for me to give the green light. My daughter had her arm across her chest and her hand up by her face, so after hours of intense pushing I was absolutely exhausted. I remained autonomous in declining an episiotomy; the doctor was about to get the scissors out and I only ended up with a minor 1st degree tear (an episiotomy would have guaranteed a 2nd degree tear, through skin and muscle). I emerged from this birth feeling incredible! I was respected, I was heard and I made informed decisions all along the way, including declining an induction of labour that would have commenced the day before I spontaneously went into labour. I have no doubt in my mind that if I had agreed to that induction, I would have ended up with a caesarean. A baby in an awkward position tends to need more contractions to get into the right position and being induced puts you 'on the clock'. My time would have well and truly run out!

Some care providers will want to do all of the thinking for you, and others will help you think for yourself, but at the end of the day, birth is a big business and profit and convenience can be a strong influence upon your care. In the private system, every intervention has an item number that is individually billed and that includes breaking your waters, incidental ultrasounds, induction of labour, urinary catheters, cannula, drips, forceps or vacuum-assisted births, caesarean section, etc. … This is one of the main differences between public and private care; the public system does not profit from intervention and they are also held accountable for care that is provided so it needs to be evidence based. This does not mean that unnecessary intervention does not happen in the public system, it totally does. Though it is just motivated by ass covering, instead of ass covering, convenience *and* profit.

We are conditioned to see doctors as experts on our body, when in reality, they are experts on illness and surgery, who deal in population-based statistics and policy. They don't see *you*; they look at your vital stats and demographics and then apply that filter to all of their recommendations. It is then *your* job to look at the information, look for *more* information and then apply that to your own personal circumstances when considering your options.

The system is not designed for you to have questions, in fact, I remember being told as a student midwife to, "Never ask the woman how she is – you don't have time for them to start talking …" Which also translates to you not having time to ask for clarification or being able to ask a load of questions – just the obligatory pee test, BP, fundal measurement, palpation, unnecessary ultrasound and 'see you in 4 weeks'.

It is much easier for the system if you proceed along the conveyor belt where you turn up to the 15-minute appointments (usually after waiting for an hour or more) and drink in what they want to spoonfeed you, accept and comply with what they convey as 'routine', and be a 'good patient'. You deserve better than that. What can we do?

Plan your birth

Birth plans have such a bad reputation, and in my mind it is totally undeserved! They don't have to be a concrete blueprint for exactly how things should progress, nor should they be something that you either pass or fail. All plans, be it a building plan, a recipe or a battle plan can be subject to change, but the important part is that plans are made through careful consideration of all relevant information. It is this fact finding and knowledge gathering that is the most powerful part! Here is the time to use your thinking-brain to learn what you need to know and understand concepts, decision points and potential outcomes, so that if you come across any of these while you are deep in your primal labour brain, you don't have to process a whole load of new information. Better yet, if it is written in a plan or map, your care provider should be able to easily refer to it without disturbing you when you need to remain focused.

The majority of people who have debriefed their birth experience with me have all said the same things. Many have been coerced by what I refer to as #birthbullshit such as:

- *If I had known xyz, I would never have agreed to it ...*
- *I wish I knew that xyz was a possibility ...*
- *Why didn't they tell me that ...*
- *I didn't realise xyz would increase my chances of a surgical birth ...*

Whether you have a plan or not, you will have decisions to make. When it comes to birth plans there is a spectrum of approaches:

- *My doctor is the expert so I'm happy to go with the flow.*
- *Nothing ever goes to plan so why bother, I am only going to end up disappointed.*
- *A plan is essential and will be bound and covered in gold leaf and 7 pages long.*
- *I want to have the most natural birth possible, so I have a minimal birth plan.*
- *I know what I want but haven't written anything down.*

Loads of people I have come across in the labour ward have not had any kind of formalised plan or ideas. This can be interpreted as if you are open to *anything* and quite often everything will be thrown at you.

Without some idea of what you want, you will be vulnerable to being misled and manipulated. Fair enough if you *are* open to anything – just be prepared for that!

If you choose to go with the flow, your doctor will have their own flow (usually cashflow) and often they won't tell you what their flow is early on. They usually start out saying how they are really supportive of natural birth *blah, blah, blah* but then as your guesstimated date draws closer they will begin to dredge up your mother's/grandmother's terrible birth history, a marginal blood pressure or amniotic fluid level or perhaps your pelvis looking a bit small or your baby looking a bit big. Then comes the induction or CS talk, and then you are too afraid to do anything other than what they recommend. Not to mention, if you *do* go against their advice, you can bet your bottom dollar that they won't want to be proven wrong. If I had a dollar for the amount of times I have heard the 'you would never have been able to have that baby naturally …' speech after a dodgy caesarean, I would be in Fiji sipping a cocktail on my superyacht.

Another way to look at birth planning is to think of creating a kind of map. You map out your labour journey with all potential routes (common interventions, etc.) identified, familiar and ready for you to utilise if the need arises. As with a road trip, you know where you want to go, you've looked ahead at potential condition changes, you know what to expect on each road, you have the information to know which detours you want to take and can make informed decisions at each detour. At the end of the day, each decision should be yours! Even in the event of an emergency birth, you still need to legally consent. Thankfully this situation is not too common and in most cases there will be adequate time for you to discuss your options and thoughts with your partner and doula or midwife, to formulate your own risk/benefit analysis. For more on this concept, check out the work of Catherine Bell at **www.birthmap.life**

You can also plan how you want your birth environment to look and feel, how your partner can help you to remain calm, active and relaxed and how your care provider can serve you best.

Your birth plan or map also gives your care providers a good idea of how much you have prepared and educated yourself for your baby's birth. I used to love greeting people in the labour ward and finding out that they had a thoughtful birth plan; this told me that they were informed and ready. Any care provider who scoffs at a birth plan is revealing that they do not support you having a voice, they do not trust birth and they intend on disregarding it. This will tell you pretty much everything you need to know about them, and that you should run – not walk – out of their office.

Making sure that your support people have a solid understanding of your plan is a key part of preparing for your birth and making sure that your support people are the right people in your birth space is equally as important.

Choosing birth allies

A huge part of your birth environment are those who you choose to have as your support people. It is crucial that they know what to expect, what is important to you and how they can assist you during labour. Your support person/people become somewhat of a surrogate for your 'thinking' brain, so you can sink into that primal brain who needs your attention for birthing. Your support people are the go-between and the watcher of the birth environment to keep your space sacred. These are people who you trust and who are dedicated to you and your needs. They should attend any birth education classes with you and be aligned with your desires. Some people feel that their intimate partner or family members may bring fear into the birth space so sometimes you need to bring in an expert!

A doula is a non-medically trained expert in normal birth who is devoted to you and whatever you need during labour. They believe that *you* should have the power over your birth and strive to give you the confidence to take it! This is why having a doula as your birth ally is almost essential if you want to have an empowering and positive experience. They are there to tell you, "Hey! You have a choice here!" "Have you thought about this …?" "Are you aware of the impact of *this* decision …?" "Have you looked at the latest systematic review about *this* …?" or simply, "How are you?"

When midwives change shifts, your doula will be constant. You will always feel as though you have someone protecting your space and energy. There is a beautiful worldwide community of doulas, each one bringing their own knowledge base, gifts and connection. You won't have to look too far to find the right one for you!

I would love to tell you that birth is always incredible, always flowers and rainbows and overpriced muslin swaddles, but in reality **you need to prepare** if you want the kind of birth that you don't need to emotionally recover from. Choices in childbirth have never been more critical. Choosing the right care provider, being aware of #birthbullshit, knowing your options (and that you *have* options) and having the right support people gives you the best opportunity to *Birth New*.

Hayley Leonard

I started writing this bio convinced that I needed to weave all sorts of creative, magical and descriptive language that is more commonly used to describe a more spiritual approach to birthing/our existence/the world. I then realised that this, in fact, is just me trying to write what I think I should write – not what is actually in my brain. This probably provides a good insight into me as the person who wrote what you have just read (or are about to read). I hate to be predictable, I am quirky, I like things that make sense and I hate hypocrisy. I am a systematic thinker and love it when people are authentic with me – I tend to know when someone is not showing their true self to me. I don't have time to fluff about and I don't tend to mince my words – probably a strength and a shortcoming, but that's me. If my words don't say it, my face sure will! You will never wonder what I am thinking, I give you my authentic self at all times. So let's begin again.

Here's the raw data … Hi, I'm Hayley. Mother of 4 amazing and unique girls ranging from a one-year-old to teenagers. I am married to Sam who has been in the Defence Force for over 22 years, 19 of which we have been together. I coach junior cricket and have been known to earn a crust riding and educating horses.

I was a registered midwife up until May of 2021 and worked at Kaleeya (now sadly closed) and then Armadale Health Service. I am now a certified birth and postpartum doula, independent childbirth and early parenting educator, Hypnobirthing Australia supportive caregiver and optimal maternal positioning ambassador. There, phew. That feels better.

My journey through birth over the last 25 years has woven a story, revealing lessons along the way that have shaped the birth worker that I am today. Witnessing birth as a teen, experiencing pregnancy loss myself and within my family, meeting a doula during my first pregnancy (when there weren't many around), studying to become a midwife, having both hospital and homebirths, becoming a hospital midwife and birth educator, constantly fighting the system, and having a 4th baby who has tested every ounce of my mettle and gifted me a new path certifying as a doula. This evolution – whilst also throughout a pandemic – has been powerful. I view birthing and maternity care through an entirely new lens and am constantly learning and evolving my ideas. I want to help emerging and new parents discover the potential of birth and how it can transcend their own life with their new baby.

www.ritualbirthco.com.au
Instagram: @ritualbirthco
Facebook: ritualbirthco

Melissa Arnott
MY FIRST BIRTH AND MY REBIRTH

The birth of my first daughter was a powerful initiation into motherhood, where I learnt to transform pain into power, and fear into courage, love and gratitude. The deep dive I took into my womb during my pregnancy and birth gifted me the most divine pearls of wisdom. I learnt how much magic and power we hold in this *sacred cup*, our wombs.

I begin my story at the time when I conceived my first child that I birthed as a single mama. The unplanned conception of my first child ignited something so powerful inside of me. I was called to remember all of the embodied knowledge and wisdom I carried inside of me. My sensuality and intuition was now heightened. My relationship with my body was changing. I was falling in love with this body that was growing a new life. I was in awe of the transformation that was happening. I recalled the stories that I had heard 7 years earlier from beautiful Aboriginal women, who spoke about birthing on Country. I took from those stories they shared that birth was natural, not to be feared and was an initiation into motherhood. These stories imprinted on me in such a profound way! It was a massive download.

I was excited about what was unfolding within me. At the same time I was living in a scary situation. A violent ex-partner would not leave me alone and was making my external world chaotic. It was such a contrast to the sense of peace and divine power that I felt inside of me.

I had to look at this external world as a reflection of the unresolved and unhealed parts of myself that I needed to excavate through in preparation to birth my baby. It was clear to me that for my life to change around me, I would have to do the work within myself so that all of this beauty that I was feeling and growing could unfold into my external world. I had no idea at the time how much this healing was going to be such powerful preparation for my birth.

The father of my baby had left when I was 9 weeks pregnant. The day he left I had to become a warrior mama and totally rock this pregnancy and birth. I filled my mind with information and stories that were empowering. I was well aware of the mountain in front of me that I had to climb to receive my baby, and I was going to do everything I needed to do to be strong, fearless and well-informed about all of my choices and options. I consciously chose to fill my days with things that would support me on my journey to becoming a mother. What did I need to feel confident and calm? What did I need to feel safe to be vulnerable? To be able to cope and adapt? As a single mum alone, I had to love myself fiercely and tenderly, in the same way that I was going to love my baby when she was in my arms.

When I fell pregnant, I was teaching yoga and belly dance. My body was supple and strong and in so many ways was ready to grow and birth my baby. Belly dance is 'the dance of the womb' and prepares the pelvis and birth muscles in such a beautiful way to birth our babies. Each time I danced I felt sensual and strong, I had greater vitality, felt lighter and really empowered! The dance drew me into my womb with my baby. Breath and movement helped my body to relax and expand, creating the exact state I needed to be in for birth.

As I danced, I imagined myself birthing, breathing, rocking and swaying my body with fluidity. My yoga practice allowed me to go into that place of self-inquiry, observing the ways that I responded to discomfort as

I stretched out tension. I practiced releasing thoughts that would invade my mind and create distortion between the messages I was receiving from my womb. This was a beautiful practice for giving birth.

I learnt to respond to all feelings of intensity with a calm, slow, deep, belly breath. This ritual of rhythm and repetition would keep that channel of communication clear and open from my womb, to my head, via my heart. This keeps the cascade of birth hormones flowing, being in a state of flow. I saw my body as a portal of new life. When the heart portal opens, so does the birth portal! If I was carrying stress, grief or fear in my heart and mind, my body would send stress hormones to my baby and I didn't want that, it didn't feel good. I had to find a way every day to come back to that place where I felt safe, loved and in my power. That is how I wanted to feel birthing. My tears flow as I remember just how hard that was. But again, that was such a powerful and potent practice for my birth. When we are in labour, feelings of intensity move through us like big waves. We cannot run from these waves, we need to know how to rise up and ride them out. For me, that was all about finding my breath, moving down into my womb where all of my power, wisdom and intuition is, then breathing that into my heart with love and gratitude. Then my brain could release the hormones my baby and I needed.

When you have someone threaten you and the life of your child whilst pregnant, a fight or flight response is triggered. I reflect on this now with disbelief that I was even in that situation. How did I find the strength to get through that? How the fuck did I get through that and go on to birth my baby the way that I did? The answer is this … We women have more strength and more resilience inside of us than we know! Motherhood takes us into the place where we summon up that power, we harness it and we use it. This is innate in every single one of us. The pain we experience in birth is there with such great purpose. It awakens a strength and a fierceness within us that prepares us to take care of our babies. I call on the strength and courage that I found in my womb during my pregnancy and my first birth every single day of my life. This gets me through all of the challenges that I face. This is why I am now a passionate doula, supporting other women to connect to their innate power, harness it and use it in their own unique way.

Seven months pregnant with my first child, I found myself suddenly homeless. My rental fell through. I had 3 dogs and nowhere to live. I had a 1977 Toyota LandCruiser with a swag on the roof rack. I slept on the roof of my car out at the beach with my 3 dogs. Although this may sound harsh, it was actually a beautiful way for me to feel safe in my vulnerability. I taught myself to overcome some fears in that space of being alone. As I slept with the sound of the waves and woke up during the night under the massive star-filled sky, I remembered the stories I'd heard about mothers leaving their bodies during birth to collect their babies from the stars and bring them earthside. I wondered if I would have that experience too. As the waves serenaded me to sleep each night, I imagined that when I was in labour my body was the ocean and each powerful wave that my body created was going to bring my baby into my arms. How very true this is.

So what seemed like a misfortune by having no home was actually a gift because I had some experiences that woke me up to even more power that I held in my body, heart and mind. Nature is a wonderful teacher.

As the wet season descended upon me, sleeping on the roof of my car was no longer a good idea or comfortable. I stayed with friends here and there and then managed to get a house-sit while I was waiting for a long-term rental to become available. Six weeks before I gave birth, I secured some permanent accommodation and I began to create a nest for myself, my 3 dogs and my baby. I continued my practice of yoga and belly dance. I walked and swam every day. Nature helped me to keep it real. Something I didn't know before I became pregnant is that sometimes a woman's libido goes through the roof. Hooley dooley, was that true for me. An orgasm a day kept the blues away! I think perhaps that practice toned my uterine muscles. I had read about the birth hormones being the same as the hormones we release when making love, and being single and pregnant meant I had to be my own lover. So I loved myself fiercely, passionately and tenderly. I was having a relationship not just with this baby that was growing in my womb, but with this new version of myself that was unfolding in front of me. I had to trust myself to be able to hold space for me and my baby to get through whatever unfolded. I was transforming, I was shedding layers and revealing someone that I had never met before.

This journey of self excavation called me to look into my life experiences that had brought me to this time where I was going to become a mother. With curiosity I looked into how I felt during different rites of passage in my life as a girl. My first bleed at the age of 14 came unexpectedly at a sleepover, and I woke to find myself saturated in blood. This moment could have taken me into a place of embarrassment and shame, but instead I was excited that this time had finally come. That same day I had to compete in a dance competition in a high-cut leotard singing a song called 'Everything Old Is New Again'. Oh the irony! It was my first bleed and I had to jump straight into using tampons. I was suddenly getting to know my body in a new way and then celebrated this new experience with dancing and singing. I reflect on that now and wonder if that experience of moving, dancing and singing as I bled really set me up to have a healthy, uncomplicated, pain-free menstrual cycle, pregnancy and birth. Feeling joy in my body with dancing, using my breath to stay grounded, feel my power, releasing tension and expanding my physical body became my superpower! I would use these simple superpowers to move through all of the rites of passage in my life.

I also began learning about how our own mother's birth stories could help us to heal things that we may be carrying in our cellular memory. I wrote a letter to my mum asking her to share her birth stories with me. She told me that her first birth with my brother was long and traumatic. It was 1966, and she was made to stay on the bed during her labour. Then 3 years later she birthed me with a different doctor who told her that she should be upright and moving around as she laboured. So her birth with me was very different from my brother's. It was not complicated, or stressful. I guess that imprinted on me; my mum moving around during labour was how I came into this world.

With every birth story that I heard, I always looked for the pearls of wisdom in those stories. Each birth is unique to that mother and that baby. I would speak these words to myself during my pregnancy:

"This pregnancy and this birth is unique to me and my baby."

"I am creating my birth story."

Daily, I would visualise myself in labour, breathing, moving, dancing, singing my baby down. I focused on how I wanted to feel and what I needed to feel that way. What did I need to feel safe to be vulnerable? What did I need to feel like I could be wild and primal?

For me I always saw myself in a quiet, dark, private space. I imagined birth would be like climbing a mountain, with many pathways up that mountain. I looked at all the ways that I could adapt and cope if I needed to change my pathway to reach my baby. I gathered all of the empowering information I could so that I would always make a well-informed choice if my path had to change. This was going to be the biggest adventure of my life and I was prepared for all conditions and all terrains by trusting my instincts and my ability to adapt. Then I focused on what I needed to do within myself to climb that mountain MY way. Where the mind goes, the energy flows, so I kept my mind present in my womb and my heart, with my breath.

I learnt that the way I used my voice could either create tension in my body or make me feel really soft and relaxed. I walked the beach during my pregnancy and I sang. I felt the resonance move through my whole body down into my womb and then my belly would relax. I wondered what my birth song would sound like! That beautiful resonance that comes from the surging uterine muscles, with the breath, through the vocal cords. It is the most incredible sound. I wrote a lot during my pregnancy too. It was a way for me to get out anything that I was holding in my mind and in my heart so that I could look at it clearly and then hold space for myself to work through those things that were troubling me. Towards the end of my 3rd trimester I wrote a letter to my daughter. I didn't know for sure that I was having a girl, but I had been dreaming about this little girl long before I fell pregnant with her. I had already named her 'Melody of Joy' because when I conceived her there was a bird singing a beautiful song outside my bedroom window.

This is a poem that I wrote as I gazed in awe of my belly:

This sacred cup I call my belly,
It is a mountain, a river, a valley.
As the seeds of life burst into flower,
My child grows hour by hour.
The sacred place of life-bearing source,
Is no less, my womb of course.
So it is a dance, I circle to honour this place,
For soon will emerge my baby's face.
A new life, a soul, a spirit from me,
With pain, joy and ecstasy.
The wonders of nature my body has shown,
As a girl into a woman I have grown.
I hold no fear as baby and I are one,
She will whisper to me when the time has come.
Gently she whispers into my ear,
Be not afraid, there is nothing to fear.
Pain is your power,
An unrealised love.
Breathe it all in,
And you'll rise above.
I'm healing my heart,
And my trauma too.

Birth New

I'm finding a strength,
That I never knew.
From maiden to mother,
Unfolding each day,
I listen to my body
And it shows me the way.
My breath is an alchemy,
Transforms pain into power.
Surrender resistance,
Open up like a flower.
New life unfolding,
A rebirthing of you,
There is sacredness,
In all that you do.

The night I went into labour I was eating a tub of chocolate ice cream watching a documentary on the big bang theory. I felt a big clunk in my pelvis, then my waters released in a full gush. I stood up and straight away began to rock and sway my hips just as I had imagined that I would. I went into the hospital to just check all was well, and when I walked into maternity I was overjoyed to see the midwife that I had gotten to know during a prenatal class. I felt a connection with her that made me feel an immediate sense of relief and comfort. I didn't have a vaginal examination; I was still chatty and excited and clearly not in active labour. I went home, got in the bath with some candles and sang to my baby. As I relaxed, I felt the surges building in intensity. By midnight I was in active labour and made my way back to the hospital. I got into the bath straight away. I had that quiet dark space that I had visualised. I was really glad that I had only eaten chocolate ice cream, because when I threw up, it was the most pleasant spew I could ask for.

As I laboured in that bath and I held onto the bars that were attached

Melissa Arnott

to the wall, I was in squat position and I imagined I was out in the bush holding onto a tree, and all of those beautiful women that had shared stories of birthing on Country, were standing around me, keeping me safe, reminding me that I was now in this powerful initiation and that I was not alone. I remember thinking, *Next time I'm going to birth my baby at home.* My midwife did one vaginal examination while I was in the bath on my hands and knees without disturbing me, so quick that I hardly even noticed. I'm so deeply grateful that she held space for me to have an undisturbed birth. Soon after that I began to feel like I needed to sit on the toilet and do a big poo, but that was my baby girl making her way down in my pelvis. I moved into transition pretty quickly from there. I took myself onto the bed with my head down and my bottom up where I buried my face into my forearms and with every exhalation, I let out a sustained note with, "Fuuuuuuuuuu uuuuuuuuuuuuuuuuuck!" followed by a deep inward breath! My jaw was relaxed and my throat still soft. I repeated this until I felt an uncontrollable urge to move into a squat and push. My body took over and my baby was crowning! And there was that ring of fire that I'd heard about! I remember my midwife asking me to slow down and take it easy, but my body just took over and out she came. At 4:30 am, my beautiful baby girl from my dreams was in my arms after 4.5 hours of labour. Straight onto my breast where she fed as I waited for my body to birth my placenta. It took a good hour for the physiological birth of the placenta.

My birth showed me how powerful my mind and breath really are. In any moment where I felt like the intensity was too much, I realised that I was holding tension in my body by not breathing properly. As soon as I refocused my mind into my breath, softening and expanding my body, I alchemised pain into power. The other powerful alchemy was using my voice to release tension and pain, and transform that into power. There, my fear became courage! I felt like the vocalisation was a massive release of all of the hurt, trauma and fear that I had been holding in my body. It was a cry of release and a cry to summon up all the power that I held in my womb. Perhaps a call to all of the women birthing at that time. I had visions of a circle of women around me as I laboured. Those endorphins that our bodies create are awesome, and I absolutely harnessed that power and intensity and used it to bring my baby down.

My first birth also showed me that who is in your space can either hinder or enhance the way your body is birthing. My birth experience led me into having 2 beautiful home waterbirths 8 years later. The work I did on myself through all of these births has led me onto a path to support other women to connect with that innate power. The present system where women are birthing is predominantly lacking in the acknowledgement that how women feel in the space they birth in, affects the way her body works in labour and birth. The dissecting of women's sexuality, sensuality and spirituality away from birth is really impacting on women's birth and postpartum experiences. The whole woman is birthing her baby and the space that she is in needs to hold her with love.

Birth is a journey and space that is a sacred rite of passage. It calls anyone that is present to be intuitive and allow the birthing mother to lead the way as she finds her power and feels what is happening in her body. I have birthed as a single mum and I have birthed with a partner. In all 3 of my births, I was called to go into the deepest parts of myself and do the inner work as preparation for birthing my babies.

Holding space for a birthing woman means being deeply intuitive and to never assume anything. To be a presence of love, light and calm strength. This enables her and her partner to be in the fullness of each moment. This is what I have witnessed in the births that I have attended as a doula.

WOMAN, I see you! You are a phenomenal force of life that is unstoppable. I see you dig so deep and respond to the call of your womb as it sings out with deep resonate tones and ethereal light, "Send me more breath, fill me with life force."

I see you move beyond every single threshold you thought you had and rise to heights where you find strength that you never knew existed.

Melissa Arnott

I see you feel your power with every fibre of your being and witness every muscle in your body work to move your baby down.

I see you surrender to the love that pulses through your veins from your beautiful mothering heart.

I see you cry tears and break down all resistance to find the powerful and life-changing breakthrough.

Mountain after mountain, valley after valley, you explore and just keep moving forward, leaving the fears behind you as you rise up, again and again.

Every powerful wave rippling through your body asks you to rise up because you are the ocean, a powerful body of water, bringing your baby to shore.

I see your light fill the room and change everyone in your presence. They stand in awe of your beauty and strength.

I see your courage, strength and love keeping you going. Even when you are tired and want to give up, you don't.

I see you refuse to give up because you are rebirthing yourself into this new life with your baby.

I see you being born as you birth your baby. Letting go of the maiden to become the mother.

I see you talk to yourself as a mother would a child, with such love, tenderness and patience.

I see you open this portal of new life with such power, beauty and passion, as you move, sing and dance through this initiation.

I see your courage come as it whispers or roars and allows new life to move through you, connecting to your primal power that could move mountains.

This magical, mystical, *womb wisdom* that you hold. Woman, you are a light in this world!

Carry this always and it will guide you through the rest of your life.

With the deepest of respect and love for all the women I have met and shared this powerful rite of passage with, thank you.

Melissa Arnott

I am a mother of 3 children aged 12, 13 and 21 years old. I am a birth doula, a belly dance and yoga teacher. I live in Broome, a remote coastal town in the north west of Australia. I moved here from Melbourne 29 years ago. Landing here in this place that was wild and free, I began a journey of true innerstanding of myself as nature and the elements connected me with embodied knowledge and something much bigger than me. I arrived in Broome as a 22-year-old hairdresser and soon found my way back to my roots of dancing and playing in nature, just as I had when I was a child. As a child, I learnt through dancing, the power of breath, movement, balance, rhythm and repetition. I learnt how being present in my body enabled me to feel my power and joy in so many ways that would transform any pain into power and joy. To feel the fear and do it anyway, I found courage. This alchemy would later support me through all rites of passage.

As I explored Broome, I met some Aboriginal women who shared with me their birthing on Country stories. These stories imprinted on me in such a profound way, that they stayed with me and I recalled them when I

Melissa Arnott

became pregnant with my first child. I didn't realise at the time that those powerful stories were downloads for me. When I surprisingly conceived my first child, something was ignited inside of me. I began a journey of remembrance. I was called to remember and feel the embodied wisdom I held within me. To dive deep and find pearls of wisdom.

My first pregnancy and birth was a powerful initiation into motherhood. As a single mother with no family here in Broome, I became my own doula. The way I loved and cared for myself prepared me for my birth. This was where I learnt to be a doula. I had to give myself all the love, knowledge and support I needed to birth with confidence in an empowered way. I had to be my own lover and best friend as well. This was the beginning of my journey as a doula, even though I didn't know what a doula was at that time.

When my daughter was 2 years of age, a friend asked me to support her through her birth. Sadly, her baby was sleeping in her womb as she gave birth at 8 months pregnant. This was the first birth that I attended. I learnt so much through that experience; how to hold space for someone through birth and death and grief, and how it all came down to love. This is how I organically grew into becoming a doula for other women and their families. I bring into my service all my life experiences, intuition, embodiment work and a deep passion and love for connecting women to the divine wisdom, love and power that we hold within us.

Facebook: Melissa Arnott
Womb Wisdom Doula Broome
Instagram: Womb Wisdom Doula Broome
Email: DoulaMel@protonmail.com

Rachelli Yaafe
WE HAVE THE BIRTH WE NEED TO HAVE

All my life, I have wanted to tell my story. I thought at some stage I would write a book about all the craziness my family and I have overcome together; there is a lot. When I decided to contribute this chapter to this book, I thought I knew what I wanted to say. I'd write these stories in my mind every day, my mind constantly adding a new chapter or a new way to start it.

I was going to address this chapter to my daughters and tell them about their incredible and challenging journeys earthside. I have started to write this multiple times but when I sit back down and revisit what I wrote the last time, I can't move forward. To be honest, that's how I feel in my life right now. Stuck and trapped. It's not a new feeling; it seems to be a circular thing that I have to continually revisit and every time I think, *This time, I am truly healed* – BOOM! It's like walking into a door over and over again.

You are probably reading this thinking, *What the fuck does this have to do with birth?* I don't actually know yet but I am sure by the end of this we both will.

At about the age of 16, I was struggling with chronic pain; I was pushed from pillar to post by this doctor and that doctor. Told I was 'too small' to have sex, and tested for STIs over and over again. I was questioned if I was anorexic, told all the pain was in my head, that it was IBS and I had pelvic congestion. The list went on and on but the big thing was that I felt like none of these doctors cared and I was left to struggle with this pain by myself with no relief. I was physically really unwell and needed some help but I wasn't getting anywhere.

One gynaecologist put me on a course of treatment that put me into a false menopause and suggested that if I had a boyfriend then I should try for a baby. After that, they had to stop the treatment due to my bone density decreasing.

Being 16 years old and being told these things really rocked me. I had experienced years of sexual trauma without fully understanding it and then years of evasive treatments and exploratory examinations, only to be continuously told that it was in my head. It was in my head but the pain in my body was very very real and something was causing it. Some days were debilitating and I could not function. Other days were better. After a while I just lived with the pain for many years.

Being told at 16 years old to try for a baby and that I probably wouldn't be able to conceive naturally led me on a destructive path of not practicing safe sex and hoping that every time I had unprotected sex I would fall pregnant. I didn't. Not until I consciously called my babies in.

In 2015, I returned to Perth to continue my travels around Australia. The day I landed I met a man on Tinder, and after a whirlwind romance, we flew to Las Vegas and got married. It was only 2 months after meeting. I had been searching for my soulmate my whole life. That Hollywood romance, 'when you know, you know' kinda thing. I would fall hot and heavy for a guy, thinking this one would save me. The truth was, I didn't need a man to save me, nor anyone, for that matter. I didn't need saving at all, I needed to learn to love myself like I deserved to be loved. The first 6 months of marriage were amazing. Both madly in love and intoxicated with each other. After that, things started to turn sour. My mental health was deteriorating and our differences were shining through more than anything else. We were toxic for each other. I stayed; I was too weak to admit to anyone, let alone myself, that my marriage wasn't right.

In 2017, I was truly contemplating leaving my husband. I had spent 3 weeks with my family in Greece and when my dad dropped me at the airport to return to Perth, in my head I was screaming, *Don't get on the plane, you aren't happy, it is abusive, tell Dad what is happening, don't go back.* But none of those words came out, no matter how much I knew it was the truth when I returned to Perth. I was miserable in my marriage and so isolated in Perth but couldn't open up about it to anyone.

A week after returning to Perth I had my 5th laparoscopy to look for the cause of my years of pain, and this time the gynaecologist found something. She found endometriosis. I remember crying, thinking, *I am not crazy; this pain is real.* My pain didn't vanish though and it was still there, so I spent a few months searching for other causes of this pain. Still, it had to be something in this physical realm otherwise I was crazy, and I didn't want to be crazy.

One evening I was out with some friends when all of a sudden, I knew I had to go home. I told everyone that I needed to go home to see my husband. As I was rushing out of the door of the club, someone asked me where I was going. I replied, "I am going to make a baby." And make a baby I did! With the help of my husband, of course; us women aren't quite that advanced just yet.

After all of those years of not being safe and hoping for a baby, knowing that I had so much love to give, and praying that one day it would happen and thinking it never would, I was finally pregnant. It wasn't the big celebration that I had hoped for. It felt like an anticlimax telling my husband over the phone and feeling like he wasn't that happy.

I suffered throughout my pregnancy in an emotionally abusive relationship, being gaslit by my husband and doctors. I struggled with pain constantly through my pregnancy. I was treated for bipolar (a diagnosis I later challenged) and I had a high-risk pregnancy that needed lots of attention from the hospital and a body that was constantly painful.

I couldn't sit down. I couldn't lay down. Every time I did, the pain in my back, on the left side around my kidney, grew. It was like there was no room in my body and the pressure was so intense. No-one could tell me what the pain was. They dosed me on strong painkillers. I didn't feel supported in my marriage. I felt so alone. My best friend ghosted me and just vanished. I still to this day have no idea why.

At 36 weeks, at one of my many appointments, the obstetrician and psychiatrist offered me an induction. I was in so much pain. I wanted someone else to save me, and to make the decision for me so I didn't have to be the strong one. It was easy to convince me an induction at this stage was the right thing to do.

"You are in so much pain, how will you cope?"

"You are so tired, you need to birth now before you are too tired for your baby."

I was exhausted, and I wanted to be in the hospital so I didn't have to be with my husband. I wanted someone to look after me and make the decisions for me. I couldn't do it anymore. I was physically and mentally drained.

The OB booked the induction for the very next day. She then tried to perform a stretch and sweep but my cervix wasn't favourable, which she totally failed to mention at this point. After the appointment, my husband dropped me at the train station. Again, I was alone. I was terrified but also relieved; I thought it was all going to be over and my baby would be in my arms within the next day or so.

My mum wasn't due to arrive in Perth for another 2 weeks, but it was okay, I had done hypnobirthing so I thought I had the power to advocate for myself. After the birth, I would stay in the mother and baby unit for 2 weeks for 'prophylactic' care. I was told daily that I was at such a risk

Birth New

of mania that I had to be somewhere safe. The mother and baby unit is a psychiatric ward for mothers and their babies.

At 36+1 weeks, I went in to be induced to have my baby; a baby I had no name for yet and wasn't ready to be born. My baby and my body were not ready. I had no idea what to expect and no-one clearly discussed the process with me. Every vaginal exam had me in tears. All the language used by the staff put the blame on me and my body for things not progressing as they should, and that the pain I was experiencing through every vaginal exam, again, was my body's fault. I was conditioned and downtrodden by the patriarchal system. I was submissive to the doctors and midwives; I was a good girl that did as she was told, that didn't talk back and didn't say no. I remember being called a good girl repeatedly, which only seemed to make me more submissive, as if trying to please the medical team.

I was trapped in victim mode, swinging from victim to full responsibility, actually, not knowing if I was coming or going, feeling like a child trying to give birth. I was 31 years old and married. Yet in that hospital room, I felt like I was 10 years old, doing as I was told.

After 20 hours and still at only 2cm dilated, they suggested an epidural as I wasn't coping with the examinations. The OB on duty said it was likely that I would need a caesarean anyway. I managed to get them to wait but I was exhausted. I have never felt so alone. I tried to have conversations with the midwife in the room as my husband had gone home to rest. I wanted my mum. I wanted to go home. I did not feel prepared to become a mother at that moment. I agreed to the epidural, so that I could rest. I needed sleep.

At around midnight on the second night in hospital, an OB woke me up to rupture my waters. The midwife told me to call my husband back to the hospital. At 6am the midwife told me that I was fully dilated and that it was time to push. I pushed for one whole hour, falling asleep between contractions, unable to keep my eyes open. The room filled – 2 midwives, 2 obstetricians, 2 paediatricians and my student midwife. They started to tell me that my baby's heart rate was decreasing and they needed to get her out. First they tried the ventouse but it didn't work. Next, the forceps. The obstetrician shouted at me to hold my breath and push. I was practicing my hypnobirthing breathing, which apparently wasn't good enough.

Forty hours after entering the hospital, with the help of forceps, my baby was placed on my chest just long enough for me to look down at her head with tears in my eyes. The cord was cut and my baby was gone. I didn't even know if it was a girl or a boy. After what felt like the longest time, I found my voice to ask what it was. My husband walked over to where the paediatricians were and told me that it was a girl. I was numb. I had nothing inside me at that point, just pure exhaustion. It had not been anything like I had planned, hoped for or knew that birth could and should be.

They then whisked my baby away and I told my husband to follow. I was alone again, my baby was in NICU, my husband was with her, I had been stitched up and everyone had left. How had I just become a mother? I didn't even know what my baby looked like. I had had no contact with her. I had lost over a litre of blood and no-one was even with me. I felt overwhelmed and angry. How had I let this happen to me and my baby?

Later that day when the psychiatrist came to see me, I put on a brave face and smiled. I still hadn't held my baby yet. When asked how the birth went I said it was calm, it was okay. She already knew it hadn't been okay. I was having significant flashbacks of the vaginal exams, and I felt like I had been raped. I had been raped in my birth. It is the only way to describe it. I tried to block out these feelings and carry on as if nothing had happened.

A lot later that day I got to hold my baby, my miracle, my strong and brave amazing girl that had chosen me as her mother. I called her Mila Emerson. I didn't know how significantly her birth had impacted me until I embarked on doula training. I spend my time trying to make light of the bad things that have happened to me and have always had the attitude of

'I have to get on with it'. I always have to be strong. I try to make jokes and laugh at myself rather than ever fully embodying the traumatic experiences of my life and the lives that came before me.

The most significant thing was the disconnect I felt from my baby, my family and myself. I loved my daughter, that wasn't in question, but I felt so lost. Becoming a mum hadn't been all I had imagined it to be. I wasn't attending any mums' groups, I felt I had no close friends, my mum stayed for a couple of months but then returned to England. I was alone, again, in a toxic marriage, isolated, scared, depressed, anxious.

I left my husband when my daughter was just 7 months old. My mum flew back to Perth to help me and I tried to return to the old me – the one before having a baby, before being married. It was a difficult time in my life. I was so disconnected, my mum didn't even recognise the person I had become. My daughter was on the airport watchlist, and I felt trapped in Perth, I was suffocating.

You think I would have learnt my lesson after my husband, but I did not. I was desperate for connection but looking for it in all the wrong places, and a strip club probably wasn't the place to meet your next husband. After leaving my husband, I went back to working as a stripper (yep, in a past life I was stripper, that is a whole different story though), and met a man that I thought was my soulmate, only 4 months after leaving my husband.

We were on and off. He would be amazingly supportive and listen to me; I felt heard. He would show me kindness and love, and then he would lie and cheat. He would run away and could never fully commit. Yet I believed in the love we had for each other and the future we could have together. I allowed him to treat me this way because I needed the intensity of our relationship. When it was good, it was out of this world amazing and I would melt into his arms. Every time we were off, I found my power. It was a journey we both seemed to need, but could never walk away from each other completely.

About 18 months in, things were a little more serious and we were spending more nights together. I thought we had turned a corner; I think we both felt that. I embarked on doula training as I wanted to support women and advocate for them in a way that no-one had for me. For 2 weeks I was on a roller-coaster, one day wanting another baby and the next feeling like I still had so much more healing to do. On the second-to-last day of training, I decided I needed to have a baby. As I left training that day I said, "Bye everyone, I am going to make a baby," fist-punching the air as I walked out. And yet again, make a baby I did! The only thing was that the on and off again boyfriend broke up with me a week later.

When I told him I was pregnant, about 2 weeks later, his first response was, "I don't want a baby." I knew I was keeping the baby; that was never in question. This baby chose me as her mother. The next day he turned up and was all-in. We dived into looking for a rental together, and were very much back on. I booked an independent midwife and a birth photographer before I even reached 8 weeks. I didn't know that my partner not only had no money but that he had massive debt, and years of people-pleasing and addiction had led him down that path. If I had known, would I have done things differently? Most definitely, but I didn't know, and one of my biggest lessons in this lifetime has been 'you don't know what you don't know'.

You can do things differently when you do know. When you learn. Our baby chose us because we both had lessons to learn. The same way Mila chose me and her dad. We all have a path to follow in this lifetime and things to heal and learn.

We ended up homeless when I was around 15 weeks pregnant, which was when I found out about the money situation. I found myself longing for my mum; no doubt we would have argued if I'd had to stay with her for too long. Life just felt fucking hard. Mila would not sleep, she would scream and cry every night and I would end up driving around the block to get her to sleep at 11pm every night. We went into another lockdown, and every house we looked at I hated. I know you can't be picky when you are homeless but I wanted somewhere to settle and be a family. To help my partner pay off his debts and get ahead so we could build our dream home and life in the country.

My confidence and insecurities were on a roller-coaster throughout my pregnancy. I couldn't sleep at night and I would find myself looking for things my partner had done wrong, waiting for him to slip up again so I could tell him that I was right. Trauma is a crazy thing; you feel it in your body and it takes over. You can't breathe. Every time I would go through his social media or sneak into his phone, my heart would race and I would physically ache in my chest. I knew it wasn't right but I couldn't stop torturing myself. I was torturing myself. Tyson was trying to move away from his addictions and be there for Mila, the new baby and me.

At 26 weeks I started to get flank pain, exactly the same as I'd had with Mila. Instead of taking pain relief, I changed my lifestyle. I stopped driving any further than 10 minutes from home and started attending the chiropractor and acupuncturist weekly, both of which helped me. I couldn't sit down for long periods of time. I would get tired and I felt I had to move a lot.

Because Mila had been born at 36 weeks (even though I had been induced), everyone seemed to think this baby would come early and that I knew what the hell would happen to me at the end of my pregnancy. It is safe to say I was just like a first-time mum; I had no idea what was happening to my body. I thought I was educated from my doula training and hypnobirthing. But nothing prepares you for the physical and mental changes that come at the end of pregnancy. I kept asking my mum, "How do you know?" Her response was always the same, "When you know, you know ..." *"But how?"* I would cry.

I did not know, not at all. From 37 weeks, I thought it was the day, every day. My hips started loosening, they felt like jelly. I kept getting super excited and my heart would race. I felt like I was so close to the end of my pregnancy. I had the 27th of August in my head. I was sure the baby would arrive early. I told my doula friends that they could all be there, and I had the photographer booked, a private midwife and a student midwife. I wanted Mila there as well as Tyson. I was sure I would be comfortable birthing in front of an audience.

As each day passed, I grew more and more confused and more and more questions surged through me. I lost trust in myself. I wanted pregnancy to be over. I wanted to meet my baby. I grew impatient. I felt fearful. There were all these emotions coming to the surface. I had hit a wall. I tried to enjoy every day that I had with Mila. I tried to stay connected with my partner. I considered induction. I considered changing my birth plan and going into the hospital. Deep down I knew that I couldn't give my birth to the hospital, but the thought crossed my mind daily.

One Saturday night at 40+6 weeks, I thought it really was the day. I had started to lose my mucus plug and was having contractions. I was having hormone rushes through my body. We sent messages to everyone letting them know we thought it was the day. We had the birth pool set up. My partner and I prepared the birth space. We started timing the contractions. I spoke with my midwife and knew it would take her about an hour to get to our house. I told my partner I wanted to shower and then we could invite everyone over. He jumped the gun a little and let everyone know it was time to come while I was showering. It felt like everyone turned up at once, my 3 doula friends, private midwife, student midwife and photographer. The energy in my house suddenly changed or I had changed; I didn't want anyone there. I wanted to be alone. I couldn't switch off the uncomfortable feeling that I had. For a few hours I tried to shut everyone else out and just focus on my partner. I couldn't fully tune everyone out and my midwife thought it was early labour rather than active labour. I kept saying that the baby wasn't moving down.

I wanted to get in the pool but didn't want to take my clothes off – a far cry from the exhibitionist and stripper I had always been. I was self-conscious and wanted to be hidden from the world. As soon as I hit the water I wanted to sleep. Everything stopped. The contractions stopped. Anna, my doula friend and one of my closest friends, tried to bring my contractions back with acupressure points but nothing worked. I was starting to feel frustrated with myself, wanting it all to be over.

I went out for a walk with my partner to try and encourage the contractions. When we returned, my midwife said she had asked my doula friends to leave and sent my photographer and student midwife to have a lay down in the other rooms. I went to lay down in bed for a bit too. In the end, everyone left. Nothing was happening. I felt so disheartened, and again, the trust in my body was starting to vanish. I didn't trust myself.

In the morning, I asked Mila's dad to come and collect her, as I needed to be alone to feel into my body. I also had a lot of emotions that needed to come up but all the while Mila was at home with me, I had to be her mum and I had to be strong. After Mila left, Anna returned to help me try and get my contractions to come back. We walked, we danced, we talked. We did a guided meditation to see what came up for me. I cried and Anna held me and cuddled me while I slept.

It felt so good to be held by a girlfriend, something I felt had been missing in my life for so long. Our friendship and connection grew even stronger. I miss my girlfriends from home every day. I have been in Perth 7 years and am only now feeling like I have real friends in my life.

Nothing brought the contractions on though. My partner agreed to not return to work and stay at home with me until the baby came. I needed time alone but didn't want to be fully alone and needed to know someone was close if I needed them.

On the Tuesday, I felt called to find someone to massage my feet, something I have never sought out before. I knew deep inside that I needed it though. I sent messages to anyone I could to ask if they would rub my feet for me. Somewhere deep inside I knew labour was about to start. I eventually found someone local that would massage my feet at 5pm. I wanted to go out for dinner too as I knew it would probably be the last time it was just the 2 of us for a while.

Whilst at dinner I could feel the contractions starting and I felt alive again – something I hadn't felt for a few weeks. I felt as if I was human and not just this pregnant blob which I had seen myself as for the weeks before that. The dinner was rubbish and I was totally disappointed but was happy to just be out of the house. We didn't hang around and went home to try and get some sleep.

At about 10pm I suddenly woke up knowing that my waters had broken. It was the strangest feeling as I had been in a deep sleep but I knew that my waters had broken and that baby was coming. It hadn't been a gush of water either, just a small trickle. I woke my partner up and got him to set up the birth pool while I texted the team to let them know that things were moving (a slightly smaller team than a few days before, I might add). While my partner was setting up the pool, I finally started listening to the breastfeeding resources that my midwife had sent me. I was determined to breastfeed this time as I hadn't been able to with Mila.

At midnight, I climbed into the pool. I wanted to be sure the contractions didn't stop before we let everyone know it was time to come. They didn't, so I told my partner it was time.

By the time everyone started to arrive, I was in a trance. Feeling every contraction that was happening but I wasn't present in the room with everyone, I was deep inside myself. I struggled to get into the position I felt I needed to be in. The bottom of the pool was soft and I couldn't ground myself. I wanted to be in a deep lunge which just wasn't possible in the birth pool.

Around 4 or 5am I started to tell everyone that I couldn't do it anymore. I couldn't take it. It was too much. My midwife looked me in the face and said, "You can do this because you are doing this." I looked at my partner and said, "You have to believe me, I can't do this anymore."

It felt like no-one was listening to me but my midwife said that I could get out of the pool, have a vaginal exam and go to hospital if that was what I wanted. I remember just staring at her not saying anything. I wanted to tell her to fuck off but kept my mouth shut. I also knew somewhere in my body that I was fully dilated and I wouldn't manage the 40-minute drive to the hospital. My midwife suggested I move to the shower as the pool didn't seem to be working for me.

I remember being on the floor of the shower, wanting to go home, and by home, I meant back to my mum. My partner was in the shower with me and my midwife was outside of the shower talking to me through the glass door. Just looking at each other through the glass, I felt like I was being held.

I moved into my bedroom and declared that no-one but my partner and midwife were allowed to come in. I didn't want anyone to see me. I needed to be alone again. There was a feeling inside my body that still to this day I can't describe. I felt my whole body tense up. It went against everything I had learnt. The baby was moving down but it felt like my body was trying to stop it. I had no power over my body anymore and I couldn't come back into it to calm myself down.

I decided that I needed to sleep; I wanted it to stop. I tried to lay on my bed but as soon as I laid down I knew that that was a big mistake. I jumped off the bed and ran faster than I have ever run in my life (or so it felt) into the bathroom. As I sat on the toilet, it was like an explosion coming from inside me with a massive gush and the baby's head dropped down into the birth canal. I wanted to squat lower than the ground and no matter how hard I tried I couldn't seem to find the power that I felt I needed to push.

I started to push and felt my baby's head start to crown. My midwife told me to put my hand down and feel. I felt my baby's head. I wasn't feeling the euphoric feeling I had hoped to feel but instead I was trying to escape. I felt as though my body was trying to run away but in fact it was only my mind. After a few minutes of pushing, my midwife directed me to get down onto all fours. She then put her hand inside me and helped the baby turn as the shoulder had become stuck.

As the baby came flying out of me and was soon passed through my legs to me, I had become completely dissociated and was no longer present in the room. Something happened in the birth that I can't quite explain, but my body didn't feel like my own and the feelings I was feeling, even though I couldn't remember in my memory but my body seemed to recognise, were that I felt violated.

Each birth teaches us a new lesson and brings to the surface the next lessons we have to learn. There is lots of talk about your second birth being healing, and that it heals you from your first birth, but mine didn't. Instead, it brought up everything I needed to feel and face and heal myself. Which I am now on a journey to do. I am not telling you to scare you about birth or put you off, but to try and encourage you to face as much as you can and heal as much as you can before you get there. I still want to have another baby, I still want to birth again. But I know that my next experience will show me a new side of myself.

Lots of women do hypnobirthing and believe that their birth will be this peaceful and magical experience, and for you, it might be. But our births can also have us grovelling on the ground to God, for them to only reveal to us that we are God. That we are mighty and powerful and no matter how difficult the journey is today, we always have tomorrow to birth ourselves again.

Rachelli Yaafe

Hi, I am Rachelli Yaafe, a melting pot of different cultures, careers and life experiences. Born in England to an English mother and Israeli father, I lived in England until I was 18, when I started my nomadic life, with my first overseas living experience being 6 months on a kibbutz (commune) in Israel. After that I spent years bouncing between Europe and the UK.

In 2014 at the ripe old age of 27, I landed in Perth, bright-eyed and bushy-tailed. I had been working as a stripper for a number of years and the prospect of money had led me to Perth.

Since 2014, I have eloped to Las Vegas and been divorced. Given birth in a hospital and given birth on my bathroom floor. Started a handful of businesses and found my calling in working with women and birthing people.

I have always been an entrepreneur and creator. I started my first business at just 5 years old when I turned my bedroom into a beauty salon. When my mum started paying me for massages, I knew I was on to a good thing and had to expand. My mum caught me putting flyers in the neighbours' letterboxes at 5am one morning. Sadly, that business didn't really take off. I struggled to find anyone to take me seriously.

In 2016, I was struggling hard with making friends in Perth and didn't know where to look. I needed Tinder for friends. I am not tech savvy at all but I started a Facebook group called 'Be. Her. Friend WA' and started running events for women to meet and form friendships. This has since led me to contribute on the app *Miit*, which is a friending app that helps to connect you with people in your area at the same stage of life as you, e.g. married without children.

After I moved to Perth I started working as my then-husband's PA but he then ceremoniously fired me and gave me instructions to find employment, but NOT stripping. I had to think fast and quickly created Pixie Loves School of Sass. A dance class with a twist, I saw the importance of women connecting with their feminine and not just learning to be sensual and sexy for someone else but to do it for themselves.

When the whole world went into lockdown, I had no choice but to look deep inside at what I really wanted to do with my life. I am that metaphorical horse, the universe had led me to water many times before but now it was time to drink! I finally hung up my dancing shoes and started to look at what I really wanted to do.

I circled around the same things: healing, counselling, doula work, birth work, energy work, rituals, women and birthing people. In December 2020, I created a new baby and a new path for myself. I became Rachelli – The Naked Doula.

www.thenakeddoula.com.au
www.facebook.com/rachelli.thenakeddoula
www.instagram.com/thenakeddoulaperth

Emma Snelgar
STORIES FROM THE SYSTEM

Women are the creators of life. I don't care what any book says, it is women who have the power to bring new life into the world. We should be treating pregnant and birthing women with reverence and awe. We should be respecting women as the autonomous, powerful beings that they are. We should all be treating birth with reverence, deeply supporting our mothers through those early years of parenting and respecting our children in their own innate knowing.

How and where did it all go wrong? Overcrowded antenatal waiting rooms where women can wait up to 3 hours for a 10-minute appointment in our public system, feeling much like cattle lining up for market. Concerns and questions being glossed over, birth plans being dismissed and women being 'allowed' very little choice in the way in which they birth their babies. When I dreamed of becoming a midwife, this was not what I was anticipating.

I have always felt drawn to birth and babies from a young age. When I was 17 and was entering my preferences for university, I chose nursing, knowing that midwifery would be my ultimate goal. And that first week in university felt so right. Being immersed in all things birth felt aligned and familiar – I now know that I have been doing this for many lifetimes.

Those first few weeks and months working in the hospital were exciting, but it also started to feel frustrating. Why were so many women having multiple interventions and going for non-elective caesarean sections? Why did so many women blindly trust the obstetricians in charge, and end up with traumatic births? Why did birth not feel sacred in this environment?

As it turned out, midwifery was not going to be my final destination. I left not long after finishing my graduate year, burnt-out and disillusioned by the system that seemed to be setting up so many women to feel like they were failures. Inductions, interventions and caesarean sections were normal, and you were considered lucky if you had a woman experiencing natural, physiological labour and birth to care for. These women were protected, and the medical staff were kept out of the room as much as possible.

Why though – why was birth like this? Why weren't women respected as being the experts in their own body and birth? Whilst in that environment, too often I saw women actively handing over their power to the obstetricians or midwives. I asked women if they had a birth plan or birth preferences. Quite often their response was, "Oh no, I'll just trust what the doctor or midwife tells me to do." Over and over I heard this, and I began to realise – these women didn't KNOW. They didn't understand the physiological process of birth. The power that they have the ability to harness. They had never seen it, had never been shown it and were never taught it at school. Our deep conditioning to fear the pain of birth was almost always prominent. Birth has always been portrayed in the media as a sweating, screaming woman on her back in a brightly lit room on a hospital bed with 10 people looking up her vagina. No wonder so many women come into the birth space in fear!

Fear also actively works against the birth process. Our bodies so perfectly release hormones that work together to lead our bodies to birth. Oxytocin is the predominant hormone during childbirth, known as the love hormone. It plays a role in arousal and orgasm, as well as stimulates uterine contractions, or surges. It also plays an important role in facilitating bonding – when we experience that rush of love, that is oxytocin. For oxytocin to be released in both intimacy and childbirth we need to feel safe, private, supported and respected. It is not often that we feel this way whilst on a hospital bed with drips and monitors strapped to us, with bright lights and loud noises and people coming and going constantly. These scenarios are counterintuitive to the birthing process, and if the woman (or birthing person) starts to feel unsafe, her body can release adrenaline and go into fight, flight, freeze or fawn mode, which can slow or even stop labour altogether. Biologically, this is so that if we are attacked by a sabre-tooth tiger we can get ourselves to safety, and labour restarts when in a safer place. If this happens whilst in the hospital system, this is when the cascade of interventions can begin.

The cascade of interventions is something I saw almost daily whilst working as a midwife in the birth suite. This one intervention leads to another, which leads to another, and so on. An example of this is when a woman starts to feel unsafe at any point during labour, which can happen for a multitude of reasons, for example, if she has a painful vaginal examination, is spoken to or treated with disrespect or has been put onto a time frame – she goes into fear and adrenaline is released. Her labour slows, she gets put on a Syntocinon IV infusion to speed it up, her pain level dramatically increases, an epidural is inserted, a CTG monitor is put on, she's stuck on the bed, baby gets into a funky position or she can't push effectively on her back, and she needs an episiotomy and instrumental delivery. Or the epidural comes first, the CTG monitor gets strapped on, she's stuck on the bed, many hours later she's still only 6cm dilated, baby appears to be going into distress and mum ends up going for a non-elective caesarean section.

Most midwives would find these situations all too familiar; most are aware that there is so much more that they could be doing to support these women, but get disheartened when it happens time and time again.

Women have not been properly educated (the antenatal education programs that most public hospitals provide is sorely lacking) and aren't aware of quite how hard they might have to fight to protect their birthing experience. From the midwives' perspective, it can be really hard to advocate for the woman if she herself isn't aware that her birthing experience could be so much better.

We have been culturally conditioned to look outside of ourselves and to accept experts telling us that they know our bodies better since we were little girls. As kids, we are told to finish our plates regardless of whether we are full, teaching us to ignore our own cues that our bodies send us. We are taught to be quiet, only speak when spoken to, to dress demurely and to cross our legs. In school, we are taught to listen to the teacher, raise our hand and wait if we have something to say, to eat at set times, to wait if we need to go to the toilet. We have been taught not only to distrust, but to actively ignore our own innate knowing. Not only for what is right for our own bodies, but what feels right in making choices when it comes to our own lives. This cultural conditioning makes it seem normal to allow another individual to decide what is best for us, our body and our baby.

The sad reality is that the experts that are placed in this position of trust do not always deserve it. The support that should be directed 100% towards the women, is often instead directed across to other medical staff. Although more and more women are entering the field of obstetrics, it still seems to have a 'boys' club' mentality. One senior consultant obstetrician I worked with that was based in a private hospital and spent a day or two a fortnight at the public hospital that I worked at was heard to announce to the private hospital staff, "I'm off to see the poor people now," when leaving to come do his public shift. The patriarchal culture of men deciding what should happen to women's bodies is deeply entrenched in obstetric practice. This is not to say that they are not needed – they often do save lives. And some of them are genuinely lovely, but their involvement should be the exception, not the norm. And logically, whilst obstetric and midwifery staff know this, it is not often practiced in reality.

Obstetricians are experts in surgical births – caesarean sections and instrumental deliveries. In my practice as a midwife, however, their presence was constant as we were in a teaching hospital. This meant that births seemed to be medicalised more and more – that they were overseeing the midwives instead of working with them, and constantly feeling like they were looking for an opportunity to jump in and interfere.

Too often I saw seeds of doubt planted by the medical staff – fears of having a 'big baby', pelvic outlets 'too small', mum or baby 'getting tired', leading to interventions where more often than not, a completely healthy, normal-size baby has been born. Even the most seemingly supportive obstetrician has been known to cast little nuggets of fear and doubt, most likely not even intentionally, but out of their own fear of something going wrong and the consequences falling back onto them. And if a woman pushes back, some have even been known to pull the 'but your baby might die' card. Shocking, but sadly, true. Fear of litigation perpetuates a fear-based practice in a lot of obstetric services.

This has shown up in our most recent statistics here in Australia from the most recent (2021) Mothers and Babies Report which has analysed the 2019 birthing statistics:

- *1 in 3 women (36%) are giving birth via caesarean section.*
- *1 in 4 women are having an episiotomy (24%).*
- *The rate of spontaneous labour has dropped in ten years – from 56% in 2009 to 42.5% in 2019.*
- *The rate of labour induction has increased from 25% in 2009 to 35% in 2019.*
- *The rate of no labour has gone up from 18% in 2009 to 23% in 2019.*

- *The only thing that hasn't changed since the year 2000, is the rate of perinatal mortality.*

Let that sink in. Despite the rate of intervention significantly increasing, the rate of babies dying has not changed. So why intervene? Why hold the threat of babies dying over mums, trying to pressure them into interventions that they don't want or need? Really, it's no wonder that currently in Australia 1 in 3 women experience birth trauma (and that is only what is reported). And for any woman who is feeling traumatised, there is little in the way of support, and generally staff do not have the time to spend doing an adequate debrief. Staffing is always an ongoing issue in all hospitals. Babies are not counted in patient allocations – meaning that if you have 4 women in your care that shift you also have 4 babies to look after as well. And if just one woman needs extra breastfeeding support or one baby is under phototherapy, and you have one discharge to manage as well as an admission simultaneously, then the time available to spend with the women is extremely limited.

Deciding to leave midwifery was one of the hardest and yet easiest decisions that I have ever made. I no longer wanted to be a part of a system that was disempowering and traumatising women. I had a birth not long before where I knew I let that woman down – I had built a good rapport with her, then when it came to the critical moment, I did not feel like I could stand up for her against senior staff. As I was repeating what I had been told, I saw her losing her trust in me – she didn't feel like she was being heard, and I saw her shut down right in front of my eyes. I knew that I had let her down.

As a graduate midwife I found it so hard to stand up to senior midwives and the obstetricians who were much more confident and experienced. But really, I should not have had to stand up against anyone, in whatever situation. I should have been supported and we should have all worked together to support the woman. Time and time again I was left feeling lost and sometimes even scared, and one night I came home and cried to my husband after another hard shift, and I am not a big crier. I did not want to be in that environment anymore and I handed in my notice the next week.

I do not regret my experience as a midwife, although I am saddened that it was not the beautiful, wonderful environment that it should have been. My experience, however, helped me greatly when it came to birthing my own children. In my first pregnancy I did a hypnobirthing class, which was brilliant and really set me up to have the waterbirth of my dreams. My waters broke spontaneously and I went into labour a few hours later, and that night he was born in the water at a birthing centre. In the water I felt safe, supported and private. I was able to go completely inward and felt so in control of his birth. The midwives I had were so incredibly respectful of my body's ability to birth my baby and my own innate knowing in pushing him out instinctively. The rush of oxytocin that followed was like nothing I have ever felt before.

My second birth, however, had other plans for me (much like my second child's personality!) and I really got a taste of what it was like to be on the other side of the hospital system. My waters broke in the evening, and thinking the same thing would happen as last time, I quietly waited. The next morning, nothing much was happening so I called the birth centre and went in, having told them that my waters only just broke (giving myself an extra 12 hours on top of the time line I knew I'd be given). I was examined and went home to await events, time frame in place. I wasn't worried as I believed that my body would go into labour quickly, like last time. By that afternoon I was having erratic contractions but they were not establishing. I had to go back into the birth centre that evening, where I was told that my midwife had reached her maximum hours for that week and was not allowed to care for me. There were no other midwives available and I had to transfer to the main hospital.

I was still only contracting irregularly, and was taken to the assessment unit where we had to wait for hours to be seen. I was then told that I was to be induced early the next morning and I was going to be admitted to a 4-bed room on the ward. At this point I had had enough of everyone and asked the midwife looking after me if I could just go home instead and come back early the next morning. I did not want to stay overnight and I did not want to leave my husband in case anything happened. I was told very bluntly no, that that was not something I could do. I knew she simply couldn't be bothered with the paperwork, and so I argued (advocated) that I was going to have a baby the next day, that my whole life was changing and I needed a good sleep, and that I would not sleep well in a shared room in a noisy hospital. Again, I was told no, I couldn't do that because I had an IV cannula in my arm (for the 18-hour 'policy' for antibiotics that I really didn't want) and I would need to have it removed and reinserted the next day. I shoved my arm in her face and told her to take it out. Not very impressed with me, she went and spoke to the doctor. The doctor was lovely, wrapped it up for me instead, and I went home.

The next morning I was still only irregularly contracting. We were back at the hospital early and were given a room on the birthing suite, and it was at this point that I was really wishing I'd opted for a homebirth! After 3 hours waiting (it became apparent that although I was on a time frame, they were not) we had a midwife assigned to us. Prior to setting up the Syntocinon infusion to induce/augment my labour, she had to perform a vaginal examination. This was my first one this whole time (they are limited in the case of PROM to minimise risk of infection). She discovered that my membranes were still intact and my waters had broken up higher (called a hindwater leak, and had been continuously leaking this whole time) and this is why I had not established into labour myself. Of course, I was annoyed at the whole situation as, although I knew VEs were to be limited, if I had had my midwife, I feel like this would have been picked up much earlier. I really didn't want to have to be induced and I would have preferred the chance to establish labour myself after the ARM (artificial rupture of membranes), but because we had to wait so long, I was 'out of time'. I knew that these times were arbitrary, having done extensive research on this exact topic for my final assignment at university (my previous assignment being on waterbirth – ironic, no?) but by this point I knew that I was subject to their timeline and staffing constraints.

Once the Syntocinon infusion was running, I requested the wireless CTG monitor so I had freedom of movement. I then had the anaesthetist, the obstetrician and the paediatrician one by one pop their heads in, uninvited, into my room to introduce themselves 'so that they were a familiar face should I have need of them'. I told them all that I won't be needing them and that if I did, I wouldn't care who they were and to please leave my room. The fact alone that they feel like they should/can just enter a woman's private birthing space, interrupt whatever might be going on and announce themselves as the potential hero of a non-existent situation, speaks volumes about their belief in and respect for women.

Once I started feeling the heat of the Syntocinon infusion, I got in the shower. The beauty of being in the water whilst in labour means that no-one else really wants to get wet so they tend to leave you alone more. I was able to get deep into my zone, and focus inwards. I was vocalising so much more than I did with my first, and the other great thing about being in the shower is that those primal, animalistic noises really echoed. I was told that everyone in the birthing suite was blessed to join in on that experience with me. Another really great thing about being in the shower in a hospital is that the hot water doesn't run out!

The intensity of the Syntocinon-led contractions vs. physiological, oxytocin-led contractions, was so much greater, as my body was not able to produce those beta-endorphins which help the body transcend the pain. I knew I was transitioning when I felt like I couldn't do it anymore, and it was at that point where I heard my vocalising change from being very much in my throat, to dropping down a few levels in pitch and coming from my gut. I knew my baby was coming and knelt on the bed to push.

At this point I had 3 midwives in the room with me as my regular midwife had come to be with me anyway, although she had to be there in a non-working capacity, plus I had my assigned midwife and her second midwife. For 3 contractions in a row, I had all 3, one after the other, come up to me, rub my back and tell me how well I was doing. Each and every time, they pulled me out of my zone, and I had to ask them to stop touching me. The 3rd time repeating it I was not polite – "Will everyone stop fucking touching me," I believe is how it was expressed.

The fact that I had to say it 3 times, that they couldn't figure out from the previous time (and they also hadn't figured out that I was labouring in the shower to get away from them) even now baffles me. Midwives aren't taught in university how to hold space for women and they either pick it up along the way, or they don't.

When he entered the world and was passed through my legs, I didn't instantly feel that rush of oxytocin that creates that immediate surge of deep love, bonding and attachment. This was because the artificial Syntocinon was blocking the oxytocin receptors in my brain – something that most people aren't made aware of when being informed on the induction process. It literally took me aback on how it didn't happen, and I really noticed the lack compared to my first birth. When I scooped my first boy up out of the water, I felt so expansive and powerful that I literally felt like I wielded the power of the universe. When I looked down on this wriggling pink baby on the bed, I had to take a moment to process that he was here, that he was a boy, and that I didn't feel like the universe. But in that quiet moment, the world felt like it stopped and I looked at him and thought, *Oh, it's you. Of course it's you.* Bonding with him was more of a slow-burn process that took a few days, rather than the immediate intense fire that was with my first boy.

His birth was very enlightening on what it's like to be in 'the system'. Without my experience in midwifery and from my first birth, it could have been very different, even a traumatic birth. If it was my first birth,

I honestly do not know if I would have handled it as well as I did. But I knew that I was strong and capable, had a deep trust in my body and an innate knowing and trust of the birthing process. Because of this, I was able to clearly advocate for myself with confidence. I know that a lot of other women in my situation wouldn't have been able to do so, or wouldn't have even known that they could do so, as I had seen time and again. Too many times I have seen or heard of midwives and doctors rolling their eyes at women, especially now that I have started working as a birth trauma support practitioner. Of them ignoring their requests. Of them touching women without consent, not giving them informed choices and instead telling them what they are 'allowed' to do. This has to stop. Current research is clearly showing that the system of maternity care, both private and public, is not working. So much research all suggesting a better way that is being ignored. One must ask, why is that and in whose interest is the hospital system serving?

The system is broken. Women need to be taught about the physiological and hormonal aspects of birth. That they need to protect their oxytocin and be selective on who to invite into their birthing space. That they are strong and capable, and that birth can be so deeply empowering and transformative. Once women are equipped to be the lead decision-makers in their own maternity care and birth experience, the whole system will change.

Emma Snelgar

It's been a long journey to working towards my soul purpose. I have always felt that tug towards working with mothers and their babies, and I became a nurse after high school always with the intention to be a midwife. After working in midwifery for a couple of years I started working in maternal and infant research, where I stayed for 9 years. These years of experience have been invaluable in setting up the building blocks to scaffold me to where I had always intended to go, without even knowing it at the time.

After I had my own babies, I started to realise how much more support new mothers needed in the postpartum period and beyond. My own transition to motherhood was not a smooth journey. My first baby needed me so intensely, and my expectations and my reality waged a huge internal war and I felt like I was failing. I was seeking answers outside of myself to try and make sense of what I was going through, when what I really needed was a deeper level of support – physically, mentally, emotionally and spiritually.

After coming out of the fog of my second baby, I started to want more for myself, and I was feeling the call to step into a different kind of service. I started learning about matrescence, which describes the transition we go through from maiden to mother, and all the changes we go through. I have since completed various courses and training programs, and have created from them my own one-on-one program to guide new mothers through their own matrescence. My intention is for all mothers to work through their own layers of conditioning and limiting beliefs and to help them rewrite their story of what motherhood means to them and reclaim their identity, allowing more freedom in their motherhood experience and a deep sense of self-love.

I have also completed a healing birth practitioner course and work with mothers and birthing people who have experienced birth trauma to support them through their own healing, which is a service that I feel is so deeply needed. I help women and birthing people to unpack and rewrite their birth story and set them on the path to healing.

I have 2 very funny, happy boys, who now both sleep all night, and a wonderfully supportive husband. I am a voracious reader of mostly fantasy and fluff – I'd much rather be reading than doing most things, and I am continuing my learning journey to include more energy work and healing into my services and offerings.

www.empowermatrescence.com
emma@empowermatrescence.com
Instagram : @empowermatrescence

Bonnie Collins
CONNECTION

When I look back on my own birth and witness the stories of birth around me, I believe one of the most crucial elements is connection. I also believe this is the very beginning of where things go wrong. People in general are so disconnected from one another, and most importantly, from themselves. I know some might challenge that statement with the fact that we have more means and devices than ever before to help us remain connected, but I would urge you to consider that those devices have the exact opposite effect, and in fact, are a tool of escapism and numbing out, rather than facing the true connections and potentials for connection in and around us.

I believe this disconnect takes on extra layers, in particular, with women. We are so disconnected from our true nature simply because it isn't widely catered for in our society.

To be a woman and to be feminine is a constant battle as so much of what is asked of women requires them to step into their masculine energy. I'm sure you've heard the saying but I feel nothing is truer than women being expected to parent like we don't have to work and work like we don't have to parent – that in itself is a huge burden to carry and brings with it a mess of guilt, comparison and judgment to name a few things.

Sadly, it's been so normalised that women can/should and need to have and do it all, that now we only tend to celebrate when we are living in that space, and that space I believe, is the precursor to burnout, because the road to that life is generally one of being hyper masculine and because we were never meant to do it all and certainly not alone.

If we take it back even further, women supporting women was once far more than a catchy tagline or a trending hashtag – it was a way of life – and a way that worked. When women supported women, we could also better support our children and men which allowed them in turn to better support us. This is a beautiful cyclic gift I believe we are so missing in our current lives.

When it comes to birth specifically, connection to yourself, connection to the person you made a life with, connection to the people that hold space for you and journey with you, connection to the life you have growing inside of you; those connections, they are everything.

A woman that is disconnected from herself spiritually is disconnected from her truth and power and a woman disconnected from those is not embodied and confident or able to fully trust in herself.

A woman disconnected from her body is like a passenger trapped in a moving vehicle with no way of controlling or stopping it.

A woman disconnected from her partner is like a wave with no rock or shore to crash upon and is disconnected from the knowing that she is held or that she is safe.

A woman disconnected from her tribe is a woman disconnected from the innate wisdom and guidance of those that have gone before her, and the stories and knowledge that weave a knowing and a clarity that would act to help guide her journey.

Even just one of these areas lacking a solid foundation will impact your birth story immensely. When the foundation or the pillars are lacking, the disconnect and the crumble is imminent.

In my own experience (somewhat unbeknownst to me at the time), I had a level of disconnect across all of these areas. When I look back at my pregnancy and birth, which has taken me a very long time to do, I am heartbroken for the young woman that travelled that path, largely alone.

From the very beginning of my pregnancy I wasn't supported in the ways necessary. From having to visit the doctor multiple times before I was taken seriously and had the pregnancy confirmed, to having my plans to birth naturally scoffed at and dismissed. Belittling comments made by the very health professionals that should be supporting you can and did very easily chip away at my confidence. I began to doubt that I was able to handle having this baby or that I knew enough about my body to make the right decisions for my own health and my babies.

I was crippled by severe morning sickness from the very beginning and it lasted the entirety of my pregnancy, with the only day I didn't vomit being the day I gave birth. I was losing weight when I should have been gaining weight and was so exhausted it was dangerous at times. I was working an hour commute from home at that time and on multiple occasions had to turn back because the sickness would come on so suddenly that I would vomit on myself. I worked for a construction and engineering firm and found myself feeling the need to constantly defend myself and convince people that I was genuinely unwell. It was a predominantly male workplace, and even though a large number of the men that worked there were parents, I was constantly compared to other women who 'handled pregnancy better than me'.

After a car accident close to the 7-month mark, I decided to finish working and again felt that even though I was sure it was the right decision for myself and my baby, I was still trying to explain and defend my actions to those around me and felt so judged for being lazy.

My then-partner was working in a fly-in fly-out role, so I was often home alone and would for nights at a time sleep on the ensuite floor simply because it was easier to be closer to the toilet.

Birth New

I felt like I was doing something wrong, like my body was failing. I waited for the pregnancy glow I'd heard of but it never came. People would often make comments like, "It can't be that bad," and, "Surely it's not every day," and it was at this stage, when I needed a village more than ever before, that I found myself more isolated and more alone. I was at this time estranged from my own mother, and on very rocky ground with my soon-to-be mother-in-law. Even the connection and intimacy with my partner changed as my body changed. I had lost myself and my life as I knew it was slipping away.

It was around this time that I found that I was able to lean into the energy of my sister (in-law). She had had 2 babies and through this we had become closer. She was the only person around me that made sense, that understood and that could make me feel less of a failed mess for 'only being able to focus on growing a human'. I asked her to be my support person at the birth and I will be forever grateful that this beautiful soul was there. Not only because of the love and support that she was able to offer me, the insight and guidance she provided having birthed before, but also for the clarity that I would need to seek out later as I tried to piece together what transpired whilst giving birth. And of course, for the special bond she shares with my daughter. I know with confidence that my daughter will always be more supported than I was simply because of the women already placed in her life, and for that, I am eternally grateful. I remember going into labour on the Monday afternoon and being so excited to finally meet our little girl. The contractions played away for hours and then suddenly stopped, and I couldn't believe it – was this false labour? You've got to be kidding, I was already 4 days past my due date and I'd had enough. But what had me concerned was that all movements had also stopped. Given how extremely active our little girl usually was, this meant a late-night trip to the hospital for a check-up where we were relieved to find that everything was okay. Turns out, that was all that was necessary to kick things right back into gear and by the time we arrived home I was in active labour again.

I called my sister, who came to our house and by 1am was telling me we should probably head to the birth centre. But I didn't want to get it wrong again so we waited while I laboured at home in-between what are still some of the funniest inside jokes we have between us. Once I finally decided to go to the birth centre, it was clear to me from the back seat where I found it impossible to sit or lay or do anything because of the pain I was in, that I should probably have listened to my sister and gone sooner. So much of the birth is still a blur to me; I know by Tuesday afternoon I wanted to leave and pretend it wasn't happening. I'd had that many shift changes of staff by Wednesday that I wasn't even sure who my midwife was, and I was so angry and disappointed in myself and in my body for not 'just having the baby already' that I could barely speak and with every check they would do that told me again I wasn't dilated enough, I simply cried. I had gone more than 24 hours with no drugs, the birth pool and shower were the only things to give me any relief but I got to the stage where I was losing myself between contractions and collapsing with what I assume was pure exhaustion and defeat.

Eventually I had my waters broken and I recall everything speeding up, except the part where I actually delivered a baby. The next low then followed – "You'll need to be transferred to King Edward Memorial Hospital." The team at the birth centre were wonderfully reassuring that I had done the absolute best I could, but in my mind, I had failed at something I was born to do and the judgement I layered on myself was thick.

The minute I left the birth centre, I felt what little grasp of control I had slip away. I was exposed in a passageway having contractions while waiting for a bed whilst the nurses stood by, and I felt completely unsafe and uncared for. When we were put into a room I was hooked up to so many contraptions, I had no idea what was happening and my body was moved and placed where it suited the doctors and nurses without communication or consent – I felt *in the way* at my own child's birth. By the time it was decided that I would need to have an epidural, I was handed a bunch of paperwork to sign. I struggled to read them and concentrate, and when I asked for help I was met with fear of the gravity of signing off on the potential 'worst-case scenario' so it became another thing I just had to handle.

The epidural gave my brain a chance to reset, I was able to breath and be without pain, to speak to people in the room and feel actually present, to acknowledge that one of my beautiful midwives had stayed with me and come across to the main hospital. I don't know how long that moment of ease lasted, but I soon found more intervention being thrust upon me; doctors and nurses speaking about my baby being in distress where I could clearly hear them but wasn't acknowledged, the obvious disagreement of my midwife, and the multiple student doctors and nurses coming in and out that I don't recall ever being asked about or agreeing to.

Suddenly I was being told it was time to push; I had waited days to hear that sentence, and now that it was here, I was powerless. Literally, I couldn't feel anything, the disconnect from my body was no longer just a mental game but it had been medically enforced; how was I supposed to push when I couldn't feel half of my body? I was offered a mirror to try to visually connect with the sensation of pushing, which to my surprise did help a bit (our bodies are truly amazing) but when things started to escalate and monitors chimed, bells rang and all the people started to gather, I really wish someone had thought to remove that mirror. Looking away from the scene a moment too late I caught the gaze of my sister; she was crying, she looked to my midwife and there was something in their exchange that told me I wasn't crazy, something about this wasn't right, but I was pulled out of that moment by the feeling of someone handing me my beautiful baby girl. I remember thinking that none of it mattered now because she was here and she was okay. But even as I thought the words, I felt a part inside of me feel the crushing weight of affirmation that you don't matter, that what you've just gone through didn't matter and I knew I would have to revisit these moments. My baby was here, she was okay – but I wasn't.

I was again pulled from one moment into another as I heard the words, "What happened here? It looks like a massacre." I looked away from my baby to see blood everywhere, all over me, the bed, the floor, up the side of my midwife's face and I didn't know whose it was – I panicked, thinking it was my baby's and for a split second I thought I'd dropped her or something but then I heard a laugh and, "Oh no it's nothing, we just dropped the placenta."

The amount of feelings and emotions our body can encompass in any one moment is still something that to this day blows my mind.

When it came to the afterbirth, I had asked to do skin to skin, to have delayed cord clamping and it felt like a fight at every corner to get these things. Eyerolls, snarky comments, being ignored and dismissed to the point where my midwife physically stepped in to support my requests being heard and adhered to. A bed was brought in for my partner so he could rest while those things were done and I was having the procedures I required. I was then alone in this room with my baby in my arms, elated, devastated, overwhelmed, and then I felt the room closing in on me – I buzzed repeatedly, desperate for a nurse, as I knew I was going to pass out and there was no-one to take my baby. I sobbed until a nurse arrived and took her, she did ask what was wrong and I said I felt I was going to faint so she took the baby but no-one came back to check on me.

A little while later a lady with a food trolley came past, and she recognised me from the day before and asked if I'd had any food. Not since Monday, was my response. It was after 11pm Wednesday by this point, and this woman, whose name I don't think I ever got, gave me a sandwich and sat with me holding my hand while I ate and cried in silence – she was an absolute angel. After she had left, a nurse came in and told me that I'd need to get up and shower before going back to the birth centre. I told her that I still couldn't feel my legs so she went and got another nurse to help me up. With a simple, "See, there you go, you're on your feet," she stepped away from me and I hit the floor because you know what – I couldn't feel my legs! I was given a chair and left in the shower.

We eventually made our way back to the birthing centre where the 3 of us could stay for the remaining few hours of the night together. I don't know if I slept, I know I spent a lot of time staring at my new baby wondering how I could possibly be what she needed, and praying that I could be stronger for her than I'd ever been for myself.

There is a photo of me taken the morning after she was born; it's one that's been joked about a number of times as I have a look on my face like 'what the hell have I done' – but in truth, that look and that sentiment were no joke. I was so deeply internalising everything that had just transpired, the obvious ways I was unseen, unheard and unsupported and the not-so-obvious ways that highlighted to me that, no matter how unwilling I was to receive the message at the time, I was alone in this, that no-one was going to help me and if I couldn't take care of me, how would I take care of her?

It was a silent process of putting on my armour and bracing for the outside world. I didn't have time to feel hurt, sad or let down, I had to be her mother. It didn't take long before that armour was needed; pushing back at who I was comfortable having visit whilst still in the birth centre, pushing back at the home visits where my baby was passed around and argued over until I locked us in a room and refused to come out until everyone had left. I'd finished birthing but the art of pushing had remained and I'm so glad it did.

We spend so much time preparing for motherhood by looking into the practical needs – prams, cots, car seats, monitors, etc. when really the better place to invest our efforts would be into planning how to support the people going through this transition. Who will be your people, your tribe, when things get tough? What will you do to monitor your mental health? How will you stay connected to yourself, your partner and your own identity? I've heard it said that we spend nine months preparing to meet this new human being, but that no-one tells you that new being is you – the mother – and very few words in my life have ever hit like those did.

It has been a long road to learn how to be in my power and how to push back, how to be connected, how to fully embody and embrace all the parts of the woman that I am and the mother that I am. I mentioned earlier how many emotions the body can hold at one time and I am so grateful for this. I'm equally, if not more, grateful that the body has the ability to hold onto them for me until when I am ready to process them, as this has been a very long and slow process for me. Even the process of writing what you read now stirs up new layers to work through.

Women are intrinsically amazing creatures.

Connected women are a power and a force that the world so very much needs.

As a woman connected to your spirituality, truth and power you hold the key to balance the disconnect within and around you, calling people home to themselves and birthing new and better ways of being.

As a woman connected to your body, you know the strength and softness you possess to create, birth and to nurture life, and this breeds a connection to your voice – which should always be heard.

As a woman connected to your partner, you have the ability to celebrate, nourish and value them in such a way, that they reflect back to you, a safe haven to be exactly what you need to be, to step out of the masculine energy so often asked of you by this world, and to be held in all the waves of what you feel without feeling its chaos.

And as a woman connected to her tribe, you walk forever forward with your sisters around you, guiding, teaching and growing one another; carving out new paths for the next generation so we can heal the division from ourselves, each other and everything beyond that.

Birth New

If you are a woman seeking connection, I would invite you to first connect with yourself. Start by acknowledging your wholeness and worthiness just as you are, regardless of what you have been through, what you have achieved, what roles in life you play, just YOU. Connect with that beautiful woman within and watch the connection spread and grow from there, knowing that the external doesn't matter because you can always return home to yourself.

Please. Connect.

Bonnie Collins

Hi, I am Bonnie Collins. I am an advocate for positive body image, self-love, positive thinking, doing the hard work and taking ownership of your own journey.

I am a Pilates instructor, barre instructor, author in *Rising Matriarch* and *Heartcentred Leadership*, coach and the owner and operator of SWAI, a place for movement, health and happiness. Offering a space where you are invited to be seen, to be heard and to discover YOU – that is, after all, always enough. It's never about finding ways to change who you are but embracing all the different parts of you and building a relationship with each aspect so you can discover what sets your soul on fire and share that light with those around you also.

Born and raised in Perth, WA, I grew up as one of 8 children, so caring and nurturing others has always had a place in my world, even more so now being a mother to one incredible daughter.

Having worked for years on myself and with others, repairing the disconnect, I wholeheartedly believe that the most important relationship you will ever have is the one you have with yourself. The unison between the mind and body is designed to be a beautiful thing, and something I want everyone to experience. I also know that this is not an easy journey and not one we are meant to do alone, so no matter where along the path you are, I am happy to meet you there and help coach you back into your body and to stir up some energy and to get you feeling more connected to yourself, your power and your potential.

I am passionate about empowering women to be connected with themselves as I believe that there is great healing to be gained in that space, not just for individuals but for the greater collective. I hope to inspire and encourage more of that, not only for the sake of the individuals I work with but to show our children that there is always more and to inspire them to aim higher.

www.swai.com.au

bonnie@swai.com.au

Facebook: bonnie.collins.9216 & movement.health.happiness

Instagram: @swai_movement.health.happiness & @bon_collins

Sarah Elise
TRUST IN YOUR POWER, REMEMBER YOU'RE MAGIC

Our birth culture and maternity system in Australia, and in many other countries around the world, is facing huge challenges right now. Interventions in birth have become so routine and accepted as a normal part of the process, our innate birthing wisdom is being lost. Before the 20th century, women birthed in their family home, surrounded by their loved ones or midwives. Infant and maternal deaths at this time were largely due to poor health and hygiene, but most labours progressed beautifully. Birth was sacred and celebrated, not typically feared like it is today. Any fear, whether real or imagined, can cause our labour to slow down or stop completely. This is such a common situation when birthing in cold, clinical settings, surrounded by strangers and machines. Home is generally where we feel unhindered and unobserved, so it is here that we can fully surrender and allow our birthing hormones to take over. For this reason, we are told to stay home for as long as possible in early labour. The beautiful interplay of birthing hormones is at its most potent when labour begins spontaneously, and I am so grateful to have experienced this for 2 out of my 3 births. Mother and baby triggering the onset of labour in a way we are only just beginning to understand, and then working together at every stage of labour, birth and postpartum. In the absence of a true medical need, why would we not support birth in this way? We truly have the best of both worlds right now. We understand the risks of infection, the importance of good hygiene and we have access to the best emergency medical care within minutes, should we need it. So, it's never been 'safer' to give birth. Yet too many women are entering motherhood feeling traumatised by their birth experience or feeling like their bodies have failed them, which just isn't true.

The question we need to be asking is, not just how are we feeling physically after birth, but how are we doing mentally or emotionally? It doesn't take many conversations with friends or family to see big issues here. Sometimes silence follows, but often there is a dramatic story that cannot wait to be shared with the closing line, 'as long as baby is healthy, that's all that matters'. My heart breaks every time I hear this. This is not okay. Mothers, fathers, you matter too! Even with its intensity, we can still enjoy labour and birth and want to do it again and again. Also, how many times have you seen someone announce their baby has arrived, to read the words 'mum and baby are doing well'? This sounds like the minimum standard to me and always makes me wonder how the mother is really feeling. Our maternity system needs to be aiming so much higher than this, and as consumers, we must demand better care! Just because something has been done a certain way for many decades, does not mean this is the best way or the only way. Our current interventions in birth have been continuing to rise in recent years, however for 20 years our perinatal mortality rate has remained basically unchanged. So, despite an increasing percentage of inductions, augmentations ('speeding up' labour that has already begun), episiotomies and caesareans, we are not saving the lives of any more babies. Are we not all starting to wonder what the point is at all? There would have been different reasons given to these women, but I'm sure many would have been told it was the safest choice to ensure their baby didn't die. Sadly, the statistics in our Australian government Mothers and Babies Report (2019) simply do not support this. The problem with our maternity system is that it does not trust or respect the physiology of birth, and birth NEEDS to be trusted. There is often so much rushing of the process, watching the clock rather than the woman, and too many coercive conversations and fear-based decisions made by care providers or the birthing parents themselves when feeling so unsupported. None of this helps us emerge from our births feeling like the powerful, capable and intuitive mothers that we all deserve to be, and that our babies need us to be!

Luckily, we do still have choices here in Australia, and the most important one is not always where we are giving birth but who is on our birth team. I've known many women to have incredible births in public and private hospitals when they have chosen a midwife or obstetrician who is aligned with their values, and so is the best support person for them. Likewise, many who were birthing in hospital or birth centres, but couldn't be sure who their midwife or obstetrician would be on the day, had hired a doula as their continuity of care. And all my friends and colleagues who have chosen to birth at home say that they would never birth anywhere but there again! What ties all these amazing births together is that the birthing people were always treated with respect by their care providers and they were always the centre of their birthing experience. Just knowing that no-one can force you to do anything you don't feel comfortable doing is key too. It is not fair that so many birthing people with negative stories felt coerced into decisions or mistreated in the birth space or didn't even know they had choices. Never forget that you have power over your body and baby. And your intuition is heightened at this time so always remember to tune in and listen if faced with difficult decisions. It won't lead you astray. It is true that only you can make these decisions, just as only you can birth your baby. It may be confronting to feel this weight on your shoulders, yet this is often what it takes to truly step into your power, and it is so worth it.

Birth New

This takes me to my first birth experience, where my whole journey to becoming a mother and doula began. My labour began at 2am one balmy night in the middle of summer, just as a thunderstorm and the first rain in 60 days was upon us. I woke to feel a 'pop' and had wet the bed like you see in the movies. I was excited and nervous with anticipation for what lay ahead, so I couldn't get back to sleep. Thirty-six hours later, my surges had still not begun, and after enormous pressure from the hospital, I reluctantly 'agreed' to be induced with Syntocinon. The drip started at 11am and right away, all I could feel was a constant lower back ache. Not getting any breaks from this pain was tough but with the support of my incredible birth team, I kept going, focusing on my breathing and hypnobirthing music. At some point I asked for gas and air which really helped me breathe slower and deeper. Then an obstetrician came in, demanding to know how I was 'progressing' as I had been at it for 'too long' (it was also 6pm on a Friday – home time for some!). At this moment I remember thinking, *This is too much, the induction hasn't worked and I am done.* In my mind I was preparing for surgery but instead I heard the 4 words I never thought would come, "You are fully dilated." A surge of adrenalin hit me and I was up on my feet once again. It is incredible how one minute you can be lying on the floor, muscles fatigued, excruciating back pain, and no fight left, then next minute you are roaring your baby down inch by inch. I actually loved this bit, it felt so much better to be physically 'doing' something after the complete surrender that was needed before. Around 2 hours later, I finally pushed my baby out into this world, into my husband and midwife's welcoming hands, and then was holding my firstborn in complete disbelief.

I can safely say I had no idea what I was capable of before that day. It was the beginning of a massive transformation, much more than just maiden to mother. It was an initiation and a remembering of who I truly am; what my unique gifts are and how I can best help others. I will always be grateful for the challenges this birth sent me. It helped me to fully understand the depths some of my clients must go to, to birth their babies, and led my work down many new and exciting roads. Yet, I do have regrets. I can't help but wonder whether my surges would have naturally started the night I ended up birthing my baby with the induction. My intuition says yes. I do believe that if I had given my body even just one extra night, and if my poor brain hadn't been bombarded with pressure and tough decisions in the days leading up to this point, that labour would have begun that evening anyway and my baby probably would have been born only hours after he was birthed with the induction. Was it really all necessary? I felt overwhelmed with all of the hospital's talk of 'risks' and started to doubt that my body would go into labour on its own. I really felt let down by the maternity system. We need to start presenting information to birthing people with no bias and give them options about their care. If I hadn't felt the pressure to be a 'good girl' and do the 'right thing' that day, I could have given myself the space to listen to where my intuition was guiding me. I did go on to have completely different and magical birth experiences with my next 2 babies, hiring independent midwives and birthing at home. My second birth felt so much easier than the induction, I laboured on my own and called my midwife so late that she only made it 15 minutes before my baby was born! My midwives got to know me on such a deep level in pregnancy that they could almost read my mind in labour. It was such a relief not having to worry about when to leave for the hospital, and once baby was in my arms, I just needed to take two steps and I was tucked up in my own bed. Having the same midwife visit every day for a week, then once per week for 6 weeks is the gold standard in postpartum care. Independent midwives are truly woman-centred and don't make decisions about your care for you. There was zero pressure leading up to birth which meant I could completely surrender and trust the process. This is what every birthing person deserves, no matter where they choose to birth.

***

Taking back our power and authority over our bodies begins way before conception. For decades, women have felt shame about their body, right from the beginning as innocent young girls. I have memories of playing at home with my sister, maybe 5 or 6 years old, sitting on the floor comfortably with my legs apart and wearing a skirt, and my dad quickly demanding that I close my legs as people will see my undies! Caring what my father said, although not fully understanding why, I did as I was told and there began a disconnection from my true self with thoughts of being ashamed or needing to hide parts of myself. Then, at around 8 or 9 years old, my mum handed me a book titled something like 'what is happening to me' and that was it. I have no memory of any open discussions about puberty, sex or birth. In fact, even growing up in a house with predominantly women, I still felt embarrassed every time I had to ask mum to buy me more pads or tampons. Then in high school it didn't get any better. I went to an all-girls school, yet every time I had to change a pad or tampon in the toilets, I would be mortified every time a wrapper would make a rustling sound as this meant someone would know that I had my period. Basically, anything to do with menstruation, sex/self-pleasure and giving birth were taboo. I am not blaming my parents. Both have always done their best with the knowledge they had at the time, just as we do now. This is generational. Humans are constantly evolving and learning, and now more than ever I feel times are changing. Although, there are still many cultures around the world where women are oppressed and not as privileged as women in western countries. As someone who has access to all this incredible knowledge and wisdom and is free to live my life now without this shame, I feel in my bones that I have a responsibility to share this far and wide.

It has been a gradual remembering for me. It began while studying my Chinese medicine and human biology degree in Melbourne. I met some incredible, strong women in that course that were so open about their periods and sexuality. As I began to practice Chinese medicine, I was soon drawn to working almost exclusively in the areas of women's health, fertility and pregnancy. But even then, it probably wasn't until my own journey to conceive that my mind and heart were truly opened to women's mysteries and all the possibilities. Embracing every aspect of our amazing menstrual cycles, understanding how to optimise periods to be healthy and pain free, learning how to check my cervix and discharge throughout my cycle for ovulation signs to either assist with creating new life or avoiding pregnancy, and tracking my cycle, noticing when I had the most energy or when I needed to rest – all became effortless and my new normal. What a gift! After birthing and raising my beautiful boys, I moved through years of feeling grief and disappointment that I would never be able to share all this female body wisdom with the daughter that I so longed for. It seemed like such a waste. I was never taught this as a young girl and knew this would help my daughter grow up with acceptance, love and admiration for her incredible body rather than shame. But always one to look deeply for lessons in tough times, I realised that the universe must have bigger plans for me, and it was no wonder that, after having my two boys, I was feeling such a strong pull to work more intimately with pregnant and birthing women. So, I started my training to be a doula. I decided to channel my longing to share all this wisdom with a daughter, into sharing this wisdom with every woman that crossed my path. One by one, any woman that stepped into my Chinese medicine clinic was taken on this journey to relearn and deepen their relationship with their bodies. So not 'getting what I wanted' initially, opened up many more doors in my life and brought my career to a place where I have never felt so much love. So much so, that my work no longer feels like work, which is the greatest blessing.

As I felt so content in my business, I started to attract the most beautiful clients. I was definitely in my flow here, but at home it was another story completely. I could not shake this feeling and longing for another baby. I now realised that I could not control the sex of my baby (I had tried so many things to conceive a girl the second time … timing of sex, no orgasm, diet changes, supplements, moon phases, you name it!), and in fact, the tighter I clung to this dream and tried to force it, the further away the dream became. My husband felt so done with 2 children and we had so many arguments about this. For him, it was mostly a fear that he couldn't financially provide for another child, but also that we were just so busy already. Yet my heart would not be quiet and the longing to add one more child to our world would not leave. By June 2019, I was utterly exhausted with the constant disagreements and feeling in limbo with my life. I remember one day vividly, after a massive argument and another 'no' from my husband, I took off in the car to do the weekly food shop with tears streaming down my face. I was broken and defeated, feeling like I had no choice but to let this dream go for good. Then a crow (my spirit animal since I was a child and I didn't even know what a spirit animal was) flew right in front of my car, nearly hitting me! I then parked the car to find another crow perched above me on the parking sign basically staring down at me, cawing away. I took a couple of slow, deep breaths. When crows fly into my life, I have learnt to pay attention. If you Google 'crow symbolism' you'll read that they can support us to develop the power of sight, transformation and connection with life's magic and the mystery of creation. I love this! Their presence reminded me that I wasn't as alone as I felt in that moment and there is always a way forward. As soon as I entered the supermarket, the song being played caught my attention –

"Well you couldn't be that man that I adored
You don't seem to know, or seem to care what your heart is for
I don't know him anymore
There's nothin' where he used to lie
Our conversation has run dry
That's what's goin' on
Nothing's fine, I'm torn
I'm all out of faith, this is how I feel

I'm cold and I am shamed
Lying naked on the floor
Illusion never changed
Into something real
I'm wide awake and I can see the perfect sky is torn
You're a little late
I'm already torn"
(Song: 'Torn' – Natalie Imbruglia)

The tears started again! Then, I am not kidding, the next song to come on was –

"All that she wants is another baby
She's gone tomorrow, boy
All that she wants is another baby, yeah
All that she wants is another baby"
(Song: 'All That She Wants' – Ace of Base)

I couldn't help but smile now. What are the chances! I could feel the universe telling me my intentions had been heard and I was being supported. Driving home, feeling more at peace although still terribly sad. I heard this –

"I've got time, I've got love
Got confidence you'll rise above
Give me a minute to hold my girl
Give me a minute to hold my girl
My girl, my girl
It takes one hard second to turn it around
It takes one hard second to turn it around"
(Song: 'Hold My Girl' – George Erza)

And just like that, I had hope again. That feeling that I couldn't shake was back. It was as if this beautiful daughter of mine was right there guiding me to not give up. Yet I knew I couldn't keep pushing for it to happen like this. It was creating so many issues in my relationship and heartache for me. So, I shifted focus completely. I was so grateful for my gorgeous boys and the life we had together. I began to surrender to the fact I may never have a daughter and felt at peace with this. Perhaps her spirit would always be there guiding me, yet she would never be here with me on earth. But deep down I think I knew I would have another baby; I just didn't know when.

Then, in October 2019, my husband's beautiful mum passed away after a long illness. Everything changed for him, and he suddenly felt this strong desire for another baby too. And just like that, our 3rd baby was conceived. As with all our children, we waited until birth to find out the baby's sex and it was an absolute joy and surprise to discover she was, in fact, a SHE! I had been calling in this soul ever since our second son was born, almost 3 years earlier. We possibly even had 2 chemical pregnancies over that time, where a home pregnancy test showed a faint positive but then my period would arrive just a couple of days late. Those years were such an emotional roller-coaster. I now believe that it wasn't until my husband was 100% onboard too that this soul would choose to join us. When we conceived our first 2 children, it was something that we both wanted and consciously chose to do. Which is something that I see regularly in the clinic too. When there is no medical reason found for someone's fertility struggles, it can help to look outside the box at something like this. Conception, pregnancy and birth are hardly ever black and white. They are sacred and magical, and it is such an honour to live and work in this space.

Sarah Elise

Hi there, I'm Sarah Elise, Doctor of Chinese Medicine, menstrual health coach, fertility, pregnancy and birth doula and mother of 3. I truly believe that both the natural world and our body is always communicating with us if we can just remember to tune in and listen. My life's work is to reconnect women with their incredible body, restoring trust in their power and wisdom to conceive, grow and birth their babies.

Aquarius sun, Cancer moon and Cancer rising, a free spirit and an empath, I have always felt deeply connected to the moon, the universe and to nature. Nature is where I go to feel grounded and recharge, so you'll regularly find me walking along the beach, diving into the ocean, exploring bush trails nearby or spending time with my kids at one of the many local parks.

I was born and raised in Perth, Western Australia, but moved to Melbourne in my 20s to further my studies in herbal medicine and acupuncture. I graduated from RMIT University in 2009, achieving a Bachelor of Applied Science with Distinction, majoring in both Chinese Medicine and Human Biology. This degree also took me to Nanjing,

Birth New

China, for 5 months, where I had the life-changing opportunity to be immersed in traditional Chinese culture and experience life as an expat. I now have my roots firmly planted in Perth once again, where I live on the west coast with my husband, my two sons and my daughter.

Since growing and birthing my own babies, my desire to learn more about birth has been never ending. Over these years, I have completed training as a doula and reiki practitioner, as well as studied hypnobirthing, optimal maternal positioning and birth mapping. Pregnancy, birth and motherhood have cracked me wide open and given me the opportunity to find my voice, be reminded of my power and to step into my calling as a healer and birth keeper.

www.doulaperth.com.au
Instagram: @the_sarah_elise/
Facebook: sarahelisedoulaperth

Cat Fancote
BIRTH HAS CHANGED ME

"Still two lines," I said unenthusiastically as I climbed back into bed after peeing on another (positive) pregnancy test.

Leigh and I had been together for 4 years and were somewhat reckless with contraception. I assumed that if I hadn't already fallen pregnant like the rest of my super fertile family, then it likely wasn't going to happen. Ever.

"Well, I'm a bit excited," said Leigh, snuggling in for a spoon.

sigh "Well, someone has to be!" I replied sarcastically.

I was not excited. I was overwhelmed.

I booked an appointment with our family doctor. I recall feeling like this whole experience was very surreal. The idea that my body was growing a tiny human was very slowly beginning to feel exciting, and despite being ever so tired, there were no other physical signs of pregnancy. *Is this even real?* I thought to myself as I waited to be called into the doctor's office.

The doctor confirmed my pregnancy with a urine test, and then nonchalantly announced that she did not specialise in maternity care and that I should find a doctor that does. *Huh?! Where do I find that type of doctor?* ... I didn't say that aloud but maybe I should have. I felt so silly, as if I should have known what to do next. But this people-pleasing 'good girl' didn't know; so

I just nodded my head, thanked her for her time, and left the appointment. I think back and wonder how I didn't know what the process was?! I was 24 years old, I was an aunty 10 times over, my sisters had been through this multiple times already, and I … I was just a deer in the headlights. It was blindingly apparent that I knew nothing about being pregnant, nothing about my options, and absolutely nothing about giving birth!

And so that is where it all started: my path to becoming informed.

I won't lie, the path looked really fucking scary at first. My social circle at the time was essentially a bunch of social drinkers – and whilst they were happy for Leigh and me, they couldn't relate to this stage of our life. My beautiful best friend Ash was excited for me, but having not been through pregnancy herself yet, she was just as naive as I was.

Mother universe sent me an earth angel by the name of Ebony – my older sister's lifelong friend. Ebony was inspiringly still breastfeeding her second baby, now a toddler, whom she had birthed at home, and was more than happy to answer any birth-related questions I had. I didn't know anyone else who had birthed at home besides this gorgeous woman. Ebony took me under her wing and provided me with resources and support, and welcomed me into a community of women who were making conscious parenting choices.

The next few months were a ride! I threw myself into learning about what happens to the human body during pregnancy and childbirth. I immersed myself in birth videos and slideshows, and I scoured the web for birth stories. I connected with family friends who had birthed in hospitals, in birth centres and at home. I went to prenatal yoga classes and Australian Breastfeeding Association meet-ups, I learned about the cascade of intervention and all the wildly inappropriate things that were done to birthing women throughout history, and then I did my best at relaying information and knowledge to Leigh.

I felt a fire in me grow. I was not going to be a sheep and just 'let' the system narrate my birth story. I was freshly empowered and I wanted as little intervention as possible. I wanted to birth my baby in water. And I was going to plan a homebirth!

Leigh was not onboard with this idea at first; "Can't we just go to the hospital like normal people?" he said with a confused look on his face. I could feel his uncertainty, but I suspected that it was stemming from a lack of knowledge and overwhelm. A feeling that I knew all too well. I had been there just weeks beforehand when that unhelpful doctor shrugged me off. But I knew differently now. I knew that birth was a normal physiological function of the human body and that how we approached it would have an impact on our baby's wellbeing.

I applied for our local community midwifery program and soon after met with my assigned midwife; a welcoming middle-aged woman with a British accent. Instantly I felt safe. Her energy was kind, nurturing and bubbly – with a little bit of that 'no-nonsense' charm. When I questioned the necessity of standardised testing and procedures, Linda (my midwife) had this wonderful way of explaining what she was required to say, but also letting me know that I could review the evidence of such practices and decline them if I felt called to.

My estimated due date came and went without a hint of labour. I don't recall even experiencing any Braxton Hicks. I was quite happy being pregnant and I trusted that baby would come when baby was ready.

It was 8 days past my due date when I found myself unable to sleep due to uncomfortable pain in my lower back. By the morning I presumed it was early labour and the excitement of what was to come began to build. The next 2.5 days were a blur; with a posterior positioned baby, radiating back pain, consistent surges that did not seem to progress (but still required me to brace myself or position myself on hands and knees) and a birth team of beautiful people waiting on me hand and foot.

I had no choice but to surrender to the process. The only way out was through; and 'through' pushed me beyond every physical, mental and emotional limit that I thought I had.

Birth New

At 41 weeks and 4 days our baby boy, Henry Leigh, was welcomed earthside. Almost 3 full days since those first backaches kept me awake to when I was finally holding my squishy baby in my arms. I was both exhausted and exhilarated.

Our painstakingly long, yet incredible birth experience featured:

A tricky little posterior positioned baby that needed time to wriggle into my pelvis.

Seventy hours of combined pre-labour and labour, including 2+ hours of pushing.

Two full nights and days of regular, relentless surges. Surges that made me feel like I had no control over my body and forced me to let go.

One unpleasant hospital visit for monitoring, an ultrasound check up, and a shot of morphine.

An empowering opportunity to exercise my right to body autonomy and decline interventions from an unexpected bully obstetrician who used lines like, "I can't trust what your midwife has done," and, "Women in your position are at high risk of caesarean," in an attempt to coerce me.

One amazingly patient and trusting community midwife that supported us to make informed decisions every step of the way. This woman truly knows what it means to be a midwife, going above and beyond to ensure that I had the most positive birth experience.

A voluntary change of plans to birth at our backup hospital so that labour could be augmented by artificially rupturing my waters.

A delicious and healthy baby boy birthed with gentle vacuum assistance.

My beautiful best friend, Ash, by our sides for the whole time. Holding space. Supporting me. And also ensuring that Leigh was well cared for too.

A lovely birth photographer that spent so many hours with us, and then unfortunately wasn't present for the actual birth because I did not value her (more on this later).

And whilst dozing in and out of consciousness and feeling physically and emotionally depleted, I was embraced by something or someone that was not from this world. I felt my body being enveloped and held in the warmth and safety of angel wings. The most phenomenal hug I have ever received, and I will never forget.

Was it the birth experience I had envisaged? No. But did I feel empowered and supported? ABSOLUTELY.

I often wonder how my pregnancy and birth journey would have differed if the doctor that confirmed my pregnancy did offer maternity care. I suspect that I may not have had the opportunity to educate myself to the extent that I did, or to head down the path of planning a homebirth. And for this I am grateful.

The flow-on effect from having such an empowering birth experience was that I then felt confident to continue making informed choices for my family. Choices that included, but weren't limited to, bed sharing with my baby, extended breastfeeding, babywearing, and conscious, attachment-focused parenting. All of these things led me to connect with more like-minded women, and the friendships that were formed over those years have been deeply valuable to my experience as a woman and mother.

Henry was only 15 months old when I had an overwhelming urge to have another baby. I recall coming home from a toddler's birthday party and saying to Leigh, "Can we make a baby?" His response was, "Um. Now?" Laughter ensued, and by the following month we were expecting baby number 2.

Again we planned a homebirth with the community midwifery program. This time around the process of being assigned a midwife felt disorganised and messy, and it became apparent that we may not receive the same type of continuity of care with this pregnancy as we had with our first.

Despite the uncertainty of midwives, preparing for birth the second time around was easier. I had already learned so much with the first pregnancy and birth experience, and had continued to learn through listening to other women speak of their birth journeys. Actually, sharing of birth stories was a regular occurrence at our weekly attachment parenting playgroup.

One of the women I met through that playgroup became a dear friend. We both had similar labours for our first babies, and Amelia was now expecting her second baby too. Amelia gave me the most incredible gift by inviting me to attend her homebirth. I cannot explain how powerful it was to be present and witness this woman birth her baby on her own terms, whilst also being pregnant myself. It added to the fire in my belly and my obsession with the magic of childbirth.

I was over halfway in my pregnancy when I finally met my assigned midwife. She was lovely, but I had this feeling in my gut that she wasn't the midwife that would be present for my labour. I longed for that connection with a woman who 'understood' the magic of childbirth, and that would know how to support me regardless of how this birth would pan out. So I decided to hire a doula. Emma's energy was just perfect and we connected easily. During our prenatal visits we would spend hours drinking tea and chatting about all things birth. Leigh even remarked, "Are we paying her to have cups of tea with you?" Yes! Yes we were! We were paying Emma to be my birth friend and I was 100% okay with that.

At 6 days past our estimated due date I had lunch with Ebony and my sister. We joked about ways to get labour started, even though I was actually very content still being pregnant. Ebony suggested belly dancing … "To wha, music?" I laughed. "Shakira!" she replied sarcastically. That evening with toddler Henry in the bathtub, I decided that a good dance was in order, and found some Sharkira on YouTube as per Eb's suggestion. Henry thought my dancing in the bathroom was hilarious, and we continued to dance together in the loungeroom after his bath, revelling in the oxytocin.

As I breastfed Henry to sleep that night I noticed a familiar backache. I wondered if it was just a result of the dancing, or if it was an early sign that labour wouldn't be too far off. "Maybe labour will start tomorrow?!"

I said to Leigh before heading to bed ourselves.

I managed about 2 hours of sleep before Henry stirred, and whilst I breastfed him back to sleep I could feel the backache becoming much stronger. So strong that I could no longer lie down. I ninja'd my way out of bed so as not to disturb the sleeping toddler, and decided to call my doula. Emma told me to go have a shower and report back in an hour. One more surge after that phone call and I realised that I could not shower alone. I told Leigh to get up and fill the pool, and I called Ash to come over. Ash arrived in good time and instantly got to work rubbing my lower back and providing counterpressure. I needed to get in the water but I was scared to in case it was too soon, so I asked Ash to call my doula and the midwife – surely one of them could tell me if it was okay to get in the water.

Ash informed me that my midwife was at another birth, but they were sending a backup midwife. Then she helped me to the toilet so I could wee before getting in the water. I got stuck on the toilet. The surges came thick and fast. I wanted to move, but I couldn't. I looked up and saw Emma's familiar face. Ahhh she was here – thank goodness. The midwife arrived and I didn't recognise her – I didn't really care though, I just wanted to hop in that damned pool. At this point Henry woke up asking for me. He took one look at me on the toilet with all these people around and attempted to pull my pants up!

Leigh settled Henry in the toy room as I stepped into the blissfully warm birth pool. I recall Emma positioning herself near my head, whispering words of encouragement into my ears. She placed warm towels on my back and used essential oils to massage my sacrum. I recall the midwife checking baby's heart rate and then gently whispering, "Baby is happy. Baby is perfect." Ash and Leigh took turns playing trains with Henry and supporting me poolside. Earlier in my pregnancy I had read about 'horse lips' in a book by Ina May Gaskin. Horse lips = loose lips. I thought it to be an amusing technique and requested that Leigh remind me to practice my horse lips when in labour. So when Leigh did actually remind me of the horse lips, all I could do was laugh!

The midwife suggested that I use my fingers to see if I could feel baby's head. "What? Already?" I really thought it was way too soon for that, but I checked anyway, and sure enough, I could feel something firm just inside my vagina. What an amazing experience. I was doing this. I was birthing my baby at home, in water, just as we had planned. A few involuntary pushes later I was reaching down into the water to catch my baby. I paused momentarily before bringing her to the surface, allowing her to stretch out and begin her transition to this world.

She was here. Baby Hazel.

The oxytocin high lasted for days. I was on cloud nine and so incredibly proud of myself. Reflecting back on my first 3-day labour and comparing it to this labour, which was less than 12 hours from those initial signs – I couldn't believe the contrast. Despite how different my two births were, one thing remained the same … the feeling of being loved and supported.

From Mother, to Birth Photographer, to Doula

I developed a love of photography when Henry was a baby. Leigh gifted me a DSLR camera for my birthday and I took every opportunity to use it at playgroup, kids' birthdays and mother blessing circles. I even took it along with me to Amelia's homebirth – which was the experience that inspired me to learn how to use the camera properly rather than just on auto settings.

Two more of my beautiful mum friends invited me to attend their births and document their stories, and soon after that a woman I had just met asked to hire me. If I was going to be paid to do this amazing job, I needed contracts and insurance. And so my birth photography business was born.

On reflection of my own experience of having a birth photographer for Henry's birth, I came to the harsh realisation that I did not value the photographer enough. And the reason I did not value her was because I had not invested money into her services. It's like being gifted movie tickets for Christmas and never getting around to using them because their value to you was essentially $0. So when my labour was long, and I was disheartened by the change of plans, I said 'no' to having her in my birth space at the last minute. I can just about guarantee you that, had Leigh and I invested our money into her services, we would have wanted what we paid for. This lesson was hard to swallow, but it was an important lesson that set me on the path of valuing myself as a birth photographer and ensuring I charged appropriately.

I documented 4 births in my first year of business, 9 births the following year, and 16 births the year after that. It was safe to say that I was in my element and not turning back.

Birth photography is an interesting thing. For many it is a way of documenting their baby's birth story so that they can look back on that special day like you would with your wedding photos. It's a way for them to share the legacy with their children, and their children's children.

But there are even more benefits to having your birth photographed, including having the details captured that you probably wouldn't have noticed or remembered because the event was such a whirlwind.

Now what if your birth doesn't go to plan? What if your labour isn't anything like you expected and you ultimately experienced some sort of birth trauma? I want you to know that your birth experience is still completely valid, and special, and unique, and absolutely worthy of being documented. Having those photos to reflect back on can be extremely useful when processing and healing from any trauma. Helping you to understand why or how certain things happened, helping you to put together a time line of events, helping you to see that despite things not going to plan, there were still moments of strength and support and excitement and love.

There is one particular birth that I often reflect back on. This birth was a scheduled caesarean, carefully chosen by the mother due to her baby being in a breech position. I was in theatre with them that day and captured baby's first moments. During the surgery, baby swallowed fluid and as a result had 'wet lungs' and was struggling to breathe. They whisked baby off to special care whilst mum was still in theatre being stitched up. Several hours later, mum got to briefly meet her baby as it was being transferred to the children's hospital in an incubator crib. She didn't get to hold her baby, nor could she really see him with his oxygen mask on. Through her sobbing she announced, "I don't even know what his face looks like." My heart broke for her, and in that very moment I realised I could show her photos of her baby's face. This strong and vulnerable mother was able to connect with her baby via images that I had captured! They were reunited the following day.

Over the years I have attended births of all types. I have witnessed women in their absolute power, and I have witnessed women succumb to awful coercion and fearmongering from their so-called 'care providers'. I have witnessed care providers obtain true informed consent before performing vaginal exams, and I have witnessed them just say things like 'I need to check you now' without any attempt to ask for consent or even explain why they need to put their fingers inside her.

I wish this wasn't true, but sadly I have even heard obstetricians use language like: "This is either going to be an easy vaginal birth, or an easy cesarean birth," "You are not pushing effectively. You're too tired. Let's just go to theatre," and, "If this baby isn't out in 3 pushes, it's not coming out vaginally."

I have seen and heard women and their birth partners be dismissed when simply asking questions about their care, and it is truly heartbreaking and sickening, especially when I know how different it can be.

In contrast, I have witnessed many many women be supported by midwives who make it their business to be present, understanding and respectful of the mother's needs and preferences. Midwives who hold space. Midwives who hold hands. Midwives who hold showerheads! Midwives who rub backs and shoulders, and perform acupressure and rebozo techniques. Midwives who listen and offer their perspectives and knowledge without an ulterior motive. Midwives who will fight to be in theatre with their women so that they can be that familiar face, and ensure that baby and mum can have immediate skin to skin, and not be separated unnecessarily. Midwives who obtain INFORMED CONSENT.

Through these experiences I have learnt so much about how to support women, and their birth partners, to feel seen, heard, respected and loved. I have developed confidence in my understanding of birth and a deep knowing of what it means to truly hold space. It has become abundantly clear that what is required for parents to have positive birth experiences comes down to them being treated as the drivers of their own birth stories, and not just participants.

Becoming a doula was not something that I chose to do for my career, it is simply ingrained in me. It was the magic of birth and the magic of women that led me here. And I trust that this magic will continue to lead me to be the best version of myself in all aspects of my life.

Cat Fancote

Hello, I'm Cat Fancote, professional birth photographer and doula, and mother of 2 wonderfully unique homeschooled kids.

Born into a large extended family settled in Perth's southern hills, it was inevitable that I would become a 'people person'. Through my community-style upbringing I learned to embrace my empathetic side, my sense of humour and quick wit, and my ability to sense others' energies.

As a mother I feel that it is my role to guide my children to be the very best version of themselves, and not place unnecessary and harmful expectations on them to be anything other than authentic.

In addition to being a photographer, I am also a self-proclaimed birth nerd and passionate advocate for women's rights and body autonomy. My aim is to encourage and inspire women to seek knowledge and support so that they may make informed choices for their unique circumstances. I do this not only through my role as their birth photographer/doula, but also through my social media content, and by voluntarily facilitating a local in-person birth circle.

In recent years my photographic works have been awarded in birth photography competitions both nationally and internationally, as well as published in various print publications worldwide; including Germany's largest-selling Sunday newspaper *(BILD am SONTAAG)*, and a highly distributed Swiss magazine *(Schweizer Illustrierte)*. My photos have also been featured in many online publications such as *HuffPost*, *BuzzFeed* and *National Geographic*.

Photographing women in labour, giving birth and immediately post-partum lights my soul on fire. I want women to be able to reflect back on their birth experiences and see how beautiful, fierce and capable they are – even in their most vulnerable moments.

My innate ability to read the energy of a birth space allows me to capture the labouring woman's essence, the love and connection with her birth partner, and many additional details that will aid in retelling their birth story. Through this emotive visual imagery I provide a glimpse behind the veil of the birthing world, spanning a wide variety of birth stories. This offers everyone an opportunity to see not only what birth looks like, but what it FEELS like too.

Woman, mother, sister, daughter, lover, friend, photographer; I am all of these things and still so much more.

www.birthphotographyperth.com.au
Instagram: @catfancote.capturingbirth
Facebook: catfancote

Shani-Faye Chambers
BIRTHING ON MY TERMS

I had never really truly considered whether I would have children or not. At 35 I had been single for 10 years, so had never gotten to the point of thinking about or planning to have kids. I was a career woman. Sure, I wanted to fall in love, more than anything. But work was my priority and I had never felt safe enough with a man to go there. With time ticking away, in the back of my mind, I had come to the conclusion that it may never happen for me.

But on the morning of my 36th birthday, I woke up, sat up and just knew I was pregnant. To a man who I was casually seeing for about 2 weeks and had just ended things with because I could see we had no future.

A baby? Wait. What? Nope! I can't do this, I am not doing this! I do not want to be a single mother!

I had HUGE plans for 2020. I was meant to be flying to the USA and Amsterdam to present at international conferences, I was meant to be flying to Peru, I was meant to be travelling Australia and overseas teaching my beautiful work. There was no way I could do that pregnant!

"You'll move everything online," said Spirit. Very loud, very clear. Stronger than I have ever heard before. Wait, what? No, I am not having this baby! I couldn't, could I? "It's something you need to consider, speak to the father, if he wants the baby, you'll be having it."

Sure enough, the father was really happy! So we decided to go ahead, as two strangers, not in a relationship, having a baby together! (Crazy, right? But that's a whole different story!)

Every step of this journey, from pregnancy, to the birth, to raising and providing for my little girl has shown me a level of strength, a level of power that I never knew was possible. Bringing this baby into the world showed me that I have all the power and all the resources I need to create absolute magic in my life.

One of my biggest worries was that I was not financially secure. Spirit said I would make more money than ever before and I would be really good with it. Spirit was right. I moved everything online due to COVID-19 cancelling everything a week into this pregnancy, and I started making more money than ever before.

I instantly had great plans of how I wanted my birth to look. I was going to hire a doula, the most reputable one I could find, and I was going to have a homebirth in water, and it was going to be magical. I had no preconceived ideas about birth being traumatic or painful or hard. As a hypnotherapist and kinesiologist, I knew I had all the tools to make it easy and pain free. I was visualising the most beautiful moments at home, surrounded by the people who loved me and I felt safe with.

But that only lasted a few days. Maybe a week. I was suddenly unable to see or think about the birth. Weeks were ticking away. Friends and family were asking about my birth plan and if I had a doula or midwife yet, and that I'd better hurry up and book something.

Then I realised something was wrong. I was avoiding the birth plans at all costs. So I started to try to apply to birthing centres, midwifery programs and I even messaged the doula for a consultation. And I was a mess. Bawling my eyes out on the phone to the doula, I couldn't quite understand the reaction I was having to something I saw as so beautiful, exciting, magical and safe. I was having a huge reaction to the upcoming birth. I was 17 weeks along and nothing had been organised.

I had been seeing my kinesiologist to keep me balanced throughout the pregnancy, balancing the hormones, my hips and pelvis, my emotions, my energy – everything we could think of to make the ride smoother. I told her I had birth paralysis. I told her I couldn't book anything. That I was having a huge emotional reaction to it, despite mentally being in a great place about it. That's when I realised it wasn't my stuff.

It was my daughter who was scared. She was scared to be born. That's what I was feeling. That was my resistance. I went on a deep dive with her, to uncover what was going on for her. My daughter and I had been together in many lives, swapping roles of mother and daughter. And every single lifetime had ended tragically, it had ended short.

When a baby is in the womb, they are in an extremely aware and all-knowing space in the spirit world, yet they are starting to integrate into the earthly plane, with all their old stories, pains, traumas and memories.

Despite knowing exactly what she was coming into, having the full awareness of the life she had designed for herself, the one where everything gets to be perfect for us, the memories of the past were terrifying her. And she didn't want to come out. She was safe where she was, in my womb, where nothing could separate us.

So we had to do quite a bit of work on that for her, in fact, we did a lot of work with her all throughout the pregnancy. She was quite telepathic and was able to tell me and my team of epic healers exactly what she needed to clear, needed to heal, and the contracts she needed to change.

So with a couple of sessions, I was back on my way, excited for the birth. I had left it too late for the Community Midwifery Program, so my second choice was King Edward's birthing centre. It was attached to the hospital, but not a hospital. So there was no medical intervention unless absolutely necessary.

I booked in with my doula for the gold package, all the trimmings. We had sessions leading up to the birth, which were so helpful. I read the HypnoBirthing book and I discovered all the ways that the medical system actually makes birth harder. Even the things you see in the movies, you know, where the woman in labour is squeezing someone's hands super tight? It was all wrong. All of it. A tightly squeezed hand will tense the whole body, and a tense body does not make for an easy labour.

I was so excited, in such joy and trust about the labour. I had known for the first half of the pregnancy that I would go over 40 weeks, that she would come late … But something had changed, I was suddenly feeling like she would come early. Maybe it was all the work we did? We had changed and healed so much for her and she was coming in differently, maybe that meant a different date too? I asked my kinesiologist to check in and see what was going on. Yes, the birthdate had changed. She was now coming early, 2 weeks early, on the 6th of November.

I was pretty happy with that. It was the best date for numerology, it was the day after I finished work, it meant I didn't have to get super uncomfortable, and it felt good. I was excited!

A week later I was diagnosed with gestational diabetes. My midwife informed me that if I couldn't keep my levels down, I would have to take insulin and it would change my birth plan completely. I would be moved to the hospital, and quite likely be induced at 38 weeks.

I was devastated. Beyond devastated. I wanted my natural birth. I wanted the waterbirth. I didn't want to be induced on the day they decided! I wanted to have my baby when she decided she was ready. Which was the 6th of November …

Then I realised that the 6th of November was the 38-week mark. That's when they wanted to induce me.

I spent the day in tears, and I allowed myself the space to grieve. But I also knew I had to trust the process. They wanted to induce me for the day we had already been told she was coming, which was a huge sign for me. So I decided to do everything I could to control my sugars and avoid the insulin which would change my birth route.

Unfortunately I couldn't manage my sugars. They were the tiniest fraction over the borderline each morning before eating which meant I needed nightly insulin. They started monitoring me, monitoring baby's heartbeat and movement and ordering extra scans to measure her. I was up at the hospital 3 times a week for those last few weeks. It was really not what I needed, it was a lot of extra stress, worry and concern. But deep down I knew she was fine.

She was measuring quite small, and GD babies are usually quite big, so sure enough, the doctors wanted to induce at or before 38 weeks.

With this knowledge my kinesiologist started balancing me for labour. We wanted her to come naturally, we wanted to avoid the induction. I also started seeing an acupuncturist to help induce me. I would see her 2 or 3 times a week for the last few weeks.

Each time I went in for monitoring I could see my own contractions, my own Braxton Hicks, getting stronger. My body was showing all the signs of getting ready. Finally the doctor came to see me and I was booked in for the induction on the 5th.

It all felt good. As much as I did not want to be induced, I had chosen to surrender to the process completely. I am all about mindset, and I know everything is purely a perception. I chose to listen to empowering and positive induction stories, I got excited, I kept up with the kinesiology and acupuncture as well as talking to my baby, and talking to my body. My doula really helped me feel safe, and knowing I had her in my corner was really valuable.

On the morning of the 5th I called the hospital at 7am as instructed to see when I should come in.

"Someone will call you back, dear." By 11:30am, still hearing nothing, I called again. "Oh yes, sorry, quite busy, someone will call you back." By 5pm and sitting around all day ready to go, I called again. "Ahhh, yes, sorry about that, it's been a crazy day. We have just had a shift change, I'll see where we are at and call you back." At 6pm they called to say it's looking like it will be tomorrow now. There is a chance a bed may become available tonight and if there is they will call me, but just rest as it's looking at being tomorrow now.

I was so upset, my mum and I had been waiting around all day for nothing. We could have been out shopping or seeing a movie. I was really upset about it. Then 30 minutes later they called again. "Can you come in at 9:30pm?" I was so excited! Yay! We are doing this! I let my doula know and we were headed in for 9:30pm.

I really wanted a big room, one that could fit my doula's birthing pool – I was adamant that I was having a waterbirth even though they said I couldn't. Apparently the monitoring equipment used for inductions can't get wet, but my doula assured me that they had waterproof ones there. She was really great at helping me navigate the change to the hospital birth. She assured me it would still be magical and she would help advocate for my choices.

I took a big box of chocolates for the midwives on duty to butter them up. They were ecstatic about the chocolates and immediately gave me the biggest room. I stupidly packed for a week, so I unpacked all of the things, set the room up with crystals and knick-knacks and waited for the midwife to come for the initial internal exam.

We had a chat about my options, the balloon or the tape to open the cervix, and decided on the balloon. I got up onto the table and prepared myself for the internal examination. I requested an exam a couple of days prior to see how ready I was for the induction. Along with the discomfort, my body was showing very little signs of readiness, and I left feeling really upset. So I really wasn't looking forward to this exam.

"Oh!" said the midwife. "Umm, you are quite far along, your cervix is already open? Can you feel that?"

"Feel what? Your hand? Yeah, a bit?"

"No, you're having a contraction!"

"Oh really? No, I can't feel that."

The midwife explained that my cervix was too open to need the balloon induction, and we decided to do a stretch and sweep to see if that could move things along, as well as the tape. After the stretch and sweep, the nurse went to go get the tape, and when she returned and got everything ready to go, she put her fingers in and WOOSH my waters broke all over her! Then bang! First big contraction started at 11:11pm.

I was in labour; no induction necessary. I was over the moon, my body knew exactly what it needed to do. The contractions were coming hard and fast, and I was straight into active labour.

I was loving it, I felt so in my power, so in control, so proud of what my body was doing. But the contractions were getting stronger and I needed my doula.

About 1am in-between contractions I called her to come in. She didn't believe me. "If you were in labour you wouldn't be able to call me." She was really upset with me. I was in active labour, my app said that I was and so did the midwife. I had paid $3,000 for her to be there and she was arguing with me saying that she didn't need to be. I wanted the birthing pool. I wanted what I paid for.

The midwife eventually convinced her to come in. She half set up the pool, put the TENS machine on me, told me to lie down and get some rest and then she left the room.

So I laid down, and found myself painfully stuck in that position during my next contraction. Worst advice ever. How am I meant to rest when I am having strong contractions every 2 minutes? I was so upset by her lack of care.

Luckily my mum was with me, giving me all of the love and support I needed. My mum was amazing, she never left my side. She knew exactly what I needed and when. I couldn't have asked for a better birthing partner.

At about 5am my personal midwife's shift started and I was so relieved to see her familiar face as my doula was nowhere to be seen. "When am I allowed to get in the pool? That's all I want."

"Anytime you like! Why is it only half set up?" she asked. I didn't know. I had no idea where my doula was or why she had only half set it up. My midwife finished setting it up for me, and I hopped in.

OMG it was like heaven; the warm water, it made me feel so supported. The contractions were so much easier in the pool. I didn't want to get out. But eventually I had to, as I started violently throwing up and shitting myself at the same time (glamorous, right?) so I went into the shower, letting it all go whilst having such strong contractions. I started to get heartburn as well. The heartburn was worse than the labour. I had reached that stage in the middle, that part where you want to give up. My doula had warned me about this. And here I was. I didn't want to do this anymore.

At 9am the doctors came in to see how I was doing, and at this stage, I was really struggling, the lack of sleep, the heartburn, the vomiting etc., had really worn me out. I wasn't getting the support that I needed from my doula either. The doctors wanted to induce me. They explained that as both my baby and I got more tired I would find it harder, and if baby got stressed, I may need an emergency C-section.

Honestly? I just wanted the C-section at that stage, or maybe some drugs. My doula who was meant to be advocating for me was silent. My mum piped up and asked the midwife, "Louisa, what would you recommend?" My midwife was amazing, she said, "Let's just wait a couple of hours, and see where you are at." By this stage I was only 4cm dilated and so ready to give up. The gas bottle couldn't reach the birthing pool so I hadn't even had any gas.

Then BAM! Along came the vomiting and diarrhoea again and back in the shower I went.

This was my turning point. I knew I had to give this my everything, fully surrender to and lean into the contractions, or give up and go down the medical route. Then Louisa came in with a portable gas bottle like some kind of knight in shining armour! And all was well again!

Sucking deeply on the gas, I managed to regulate myself, I was able to lean into each contraction, and I was able to get out of my mind and out of my body. With each contraction I repeated the mantra, "Your body and your baby know what to do, your mind doesn't need to be here, get out of the way." And I managed to remove myself, completely surrendering to the process.

It all became so magical again; I was *loving* my labour, I was stretching and squatting and leaning into each contraction to work with my body. And I was sucking back that gas like there was no tomorrow. And by the 2-hour mark, I was 9cm dilated. Baby was on her way, I could feel her. With some of my contractions I could feel the *ring of fire* starting … and it felt so magical, so exciting, I was in-between worlds, I was so elated. I knew that if I pushed she'd be here, but I was waiting for her. I was savouring and enjoying each moment.

"She's going to be here soon, I can feel her," I said to my doula. She explained that it would still be a few more hours, and that she was going to go and move her car so that she didn't get a parking ticket. At that moment I knew she was going to miss the birth. But I didn't care. She wasn't helping at all and it was so empowering for me to know I didn't need her. So I let her go.

"I can feel her crowning with the contractions," I told my midwife. "I can't see any crowning?" she said. I rolled over with my back against the pool for the next contraction … "OMG she IS crowning!" my midwife exclaimed, so I pushed for the first time. "And I can see her head and her shoulders, OMG your baby is here!"

Apparently they don't usually come out that quick.

It was 12:17pm, 13 hours after my first contraction, and she shot out so fast her cord snapped! There was blood everywhere and doctors and nurses were all rushing in. It was chaos. I had to get straight out of the pool and onto the bed seconds after giving birth as we were both losing a lot of blood.

But I had this beautiful little baby girl in my arms, crying and needing comfort. I was so calm, despite the crazy around me, I knew all I had to do was to assure my baby that everything was fine. Because it was, everything was perfect. She was here, she was amazing. We had done it.

The doctors managed to clamp the end of the cord and get my placenta out safely. My babe was so sticky and covered in vernix I had no idea what to do with her. I hadn't even been around babies much, like how do I even hold her? But I was gushing with oxytocin, adrenaline, love, pride, I was so ecstatic. I had managed to do it all on my own.

Now, 13 months later, as a single mother, I have just bought my first home. Becoming a mother has taught me so much, it's given me so much and it's allowed me to step up so profoundly. I see so much disempowerment going along with motherhood, especially single motherhood. But it's all bullshit. Life is yours to create the way you want it. And with the right tools and mindset, you really can.

Shani-Faye Chambers

Hi, I'm Shani-Faye Chambers. I'm a kinesiologist, master hypnotherapist, pranic hypnotherapist, multidimensional energy healer, international spiritual teacher and trainer, founder of Sacred Ancestral Clearing and DNA Healing, co-founder of The Temple of Divine Intelligence and founder of the Wellness Chambers.

My journey into the world of healing started at a young age; being introduced to reiki and completing my reiki 1 training when I was 10 years old set me up for a life of understanding and working with energy. A gifted child, I struggled a lot emotionally, mentally and spiritually. Spending most of my childhood quite suicidal, I was introduced to kinesiology when I was 14. After 2 sessions, my entire life changed. No longer struggling, no longer suicidal, I realised just how easy healing was when you have the right tools.

A very intuitive soul, I always knew my life path, and that I was here for big things. I have been heavily immersed in spiritual training and healing since my late teens. After over a decade of training and overcoming many personal issues, addictions, traumas, sexual abuse, toxic relationships and body dysmorphia among other things, I finally opened my doors to see clients professionally in January 2014. Word spread quickly on the effectiveness and wisdom of my sessions.

As a highly sought after and booked-out therapist, I rapidly realised that I had to level up again and reach more people. I embarked along the path of overcoming my fear of public speaking so that my gifts, talents and healing could be spread further.

In 2018, after much healing and preparation to be able to take the stage and share my story, I channelled through the Sacred Ancestral Clearing and DNA Healing that put me on the map as an international spiritual teacher. Since then I have channelled through and birthed many New Earth and ancient healing processes and trained over 200 practitioners worldwide both on my own and in my joint venture, The Temple of Divine Intelligence, which I founded with Emma Romano in 2019.

I am available for private consultations in person and online, as well as short and long workshops, online programs, retreats, practitioner training and mentoring. I currently live in Port Kennedy, Western Australia, with my beautiful baby girl.

www.thewellnesschambers.org

Sarah Howard
BIRTH BROUGHT ME HOME TO ME

There has been a burning in my soul from a young age about birth. I have childhood memories of telling my mother that I wanted to deliver babies when I grew up and also feeling embarrassed and ashamed. I wanted to see vaginas for a living? It felt really weird and odd yet I still dabbled with the idea of wanting to know more. I brought home a book about the human body and how babies were made because I was so curious and needed to know details of how it all worked. This desire was eventually silenced by social norms and my shame. I always had an affinity for babies and children and pursued a profession of being with them in child care settings. My husband and I were married for seven years before we chose to start our family. In those seven years the people around us having children were doing it differently than what I desired, they seemed disconnected from their bodies, and I knew I wanted something different. It was as if this yearning inside of me as a child that was curious about birth was being awakened.

After a few months of trying we saw two faint pink lines at the beach we camped at every Thanksgiving in California. The line was so light we weren't sure this was real. A week later at home I took another test and it was undoubtedly positive. The planning began: the two things I knew about how I wanted to birth were that I only wanted my husband to be with me and knew that I wanted a birth that was minimally altered and as much of a natural progression of the process as possible. I knew I wanted a midwife as my provider and found one through the group at the hospital that took my insurance; after reading all the bios from the list I found a good fit. I thought about homebirth for a moment but I had no examples of people birthing at home so that seemed too scary and a bit radical. I would have a hospital birth with my midwife. I built a relationship with her and I saw her at every appointment; she knew what I wanted, seemed to listen to me, and I had connected with her nurse. Preparing for birth, I read books and I found a childbirth preparation course that went beyond positions and explaining the process of birth. It was a 3-day workshop encouraging me to dive deep into my relationship with my body and my baby and my partner and exploring the changes we could experience through this process. This class was my introduction to a different way of being that my soul was searching for and I didn't even know it.

I needed to have a hard conversation and share with my mom that I did not want her in the room while I brought this baby earthside. I had always been the good girl, I didn't ruffle feathers and I did things to please other people despite how it made me feel because my discomfort and disappointment was more comfortable than that of other people and the confrontation of it all. I mustered up the courage to talk to my mom; it was so hard to tell her this, I knew it would hurt her feelings and that is the last thing I wanted. I also knew that it would hurt me more if I didn't speak up. I love my mom and I am grateful for her. The energy she carries does not radiate calm and in stressful situations her energy rises, it does not fall. I needed to create the vibe I wanted in my birthing space. During my pregnancy she shared with me that she was worried I would not have the experience I desired because of her experiences. My mom was induced during my birth and she did not go into active labour; I was born via caesarean section and weighed 10.5lbs. Her experiences and concerns were valid, of course, but I felt added stress and anxiety hearing them while I was already worried about that in the back of my mind. I invited her to come to my home during early labour and asked that when we left for the hospital that she would not come. I thought she heard me and understood. She was disappointed. Despite feeling that I caused her pain at the time, I am so proud of myself for saying what I needed out loud; I chose me and I am so proud of that version of me.

My due date came and went and the battle against the machine of the hospital system began, including talks of induction and fearmongering conversations about my baby possibly dying if I did not comply. I did not want to be induced, I knew that my baby wasn't ready and that they were safe. The rules I needed to follow in order to continue were to have another ultrasound and extra appointments to listen to baby. I acquiesced to having a membrane sweep after 41 weeks and the ultrasound showed a healthy large baby. I was approaching 42 weeks and my midwife told me I would not be able to go past that (and I believed her) so we needed to schedule an induction for that day. She shared that she would not be on call that day so she would not be attending my labour. *Wait, what?* I was thinking. *I trust you and have a relationship with you but you aren't going to be there?* This was so much to digest. The night before my induction I took some castor oil and panicked and called around to hire a doula at the last minute. I did not think I wanted a doula present if things had progressed on their own but with navigating an induction, I wanted someone to advocate for me. I hired someone and went to sleep. I woke in the wee hours of the morning and thought I had diarrhoea pain. I stumbled to the toilet and did not need to poop after all so I laid back down. It wasn't until I did this a few more times that I realised that this was not upset stomach pain but actually contractions.

We went to the hospital later in the morning where the moment I stepped in I felt all my desires were resisted. I stated that I wanted to stand or sit on the birthing ball while they listened to baby and the nurse tried

Sarah Howard

but was unable to and told me I had to lay on the bed to do this. I already felt worn down by my first small request being denied. While I laid there feeling defeated and not managing my pain well, my mom, stepdad and sister walked into the room. I was utterly shocked, like jaw-droppingly shocked. They soon left as I think my reaction let them know it was not okay for them to be there. Things continued to be challenging; I did not want my water to be broken, I had it written in my birth plan and I had planned this with my midwife. The midwife on call checked me and as her hand was inside of me she asked me if I wanted my water to be broken as she could feel the bag. I was stunned like a deer in headlights. Why was she asking me this? I did not want this. I have never felt more vulnerable, her hand was inside of my body and I could sense her annoyance when I did not answer quickly, so I said yes. Something happened to me after that; I feel like I left my body, I was not there, I was somewhere else coming back into my body for moments, but I completely dissociated. After my boundaries and desires were denied over and over again, I felt like I had thrown in the towel, as there was only so much I could withstand and I had hit my limit. I progressed to almost complete at 9.5cm, then my cervix was swelling. I was exhausted and done, so I asked for an epidural to get some rest as my last effort to have the experience I wanted: to be able to push my baby out of my vagina. Spoiler alert: it didn't work. I wasn't progressing, they shared we could wait a little longer, that it could possibly still happen but that it wasn't looking good. I decided to go ahead with preparing for a caesarean as it wasn't an emergency at this time and I wanted some sense of control. I started to advocate for my doula to come into the operating room with my partner but was met with the news that no-one would be coming with me, the epidural wasn't working and I needed to be put under general anaesthesia. I could hear my mom crying outside of my hospital room, she had not left. Hearing her stung, I was angry; I asked her not to be there and she didn't listen. I asked for things in labour and I wasn't heard. My desires and needs were not met. I birthed via caesarean a beautiful 10lb 6oz baby girl while asleep. When I woke up my husband and I found out that she was a girl and it was a sweet surprise.

The birth of my first baby was the impetus of my awakening, my rebellion. When I reflect on my life before birth I feel like I was on a conveyor belt, going through the motions of what I thought I was supposed to do: go to college, get married, get a job and start a family. I wasn't looking beyond me to expand my ideas and mind. I was forced to face a truth: that my good-girl ways were no longer going to serve me, they had kept me safe up until now. I caught a glimpse that I was not here to make other people happy and that playing life on safe street needed to end. I got a taste of it, licked the surface, but it would take longer for me to take more actions that would change how I was living. I went back to work at 8 weeks postpartum and resumed the life I had before, just with a baby, but it didn't feel good. I muddled through, feeling so different and frustrated but I continued wading through for the next 2 years.

We decided to have another baby and I became pregnant with a baby that was due to arrive in July. I had a miscarriage at 8 weeks while camping at the same beach we discovered we were pregnant with our first baby. No-one knew that we were expecting again and I did not want to share my grief at the time. I quietly digested the reality of what was happening with my toes in the sand and the wind in my hair. I used to think how horrible it was that it happened there and now I reflect on how special it was that I was there at a beautiful beach with my partner and little girl. We tried again and became pregnant quickly.

This pregnancy, I felt an urge to leave my job and to stay home but the thought of being a stay-at-home mom had a lot of negative ideas for me. Remember, I did the things I was supposed to do, I went to college, I got the degree and now I had a career that I was supposed to follow through with. I was thinking of all the things I should do while my heart was telling me to stop. I had a lot of bad feelings about being a stay-at-home mom, I think from how they were depicted in the media and television and movies. They were frumpy sad people that did nothing but rot away watching television and eating bonbons all day. If I dig deep, this is the disturbing image of them that I saw; that they had lost themselves to being a mother and that they did not enjoy their lives. I saw that everything I worked so hard for would be over, that I would no longer be relevant in my career field and that I would succumb to this sick idea of what a stay-at-home mom's life is. I battled this idea day in and day out, yet something whispered to me that I would be okay. I was so scared that I had fought to be taken seriously, to be a professional, to be seen as the smart woman that I was; how could I walk away?

My pregnancy was going well and I deeply desired a VBAC. I searched for a provider that would be with me through the entire process and I found her. She was kind, wise and calm, her vibe was exactly what I was looking for. She was a private midwife that I would be able to build a relationship with and she would be at the hospital when it was time for me to birth. My partner was with me and we did not hire a doula this time as I felt prepared with my midwife to be supported. Achieving a VBAC was one of the hardest and most beautiful events of my life and when I pushed my baby girl out of my body I was in complete shock. I looked at my husband and said, "I did it." I birthed my gorgeous 10lb 9oz human how I wanted to. I felt a sense of redemption and I took back my power. I felt supported, safe and heard which I had not felt after my first birth.

I didn't go back to work. I stayed home, and you know that part about me fearing losing myself? The exact opposite happened. I started to unfold and bloom and discover parts of me that had been hidden, the parts that the good girl was hiding to keep safe. The previous version of me had been burned to the ground. It was hard and ugly at times but I was growing and changing. Growth hurts, and I hurt a lot in those early months. Postpartum and a grey Pacific Northwest winter added to the challenge. I was able to move through it and little by little I dove deeper into my mind and worked to rewire the parts that no longer served this version of me. I started connecting to my mind, body and soul like I never had and it was so juicy and delicious.

In the time between having my second baby girl and becoming pregnant for the 4th time, I learned so much about myself. I don't know that I would have been that version of myself without becoming a mother. Each rebirth of Sarah allowed space for so much new to grow and flourish. I listened to my body and soul and followed them no matter how scary it felt and I truly trusted myself. I learned that I was a bad bitch, that my desires and me being fully expressed and happy were the most important thing. That my boundaries deserve to be honoured and respected. I found magic in connecting to my bleed and the moon. I started a job as a lactation specialist in the hospital bringing my inner child closer to helping birthing people.

When I found out I was expecting for the 4th time I knew this one was going to rock me, although I wasn't sure exactly how. The global pandemic was happening and I decided I was going for it. I wanted to welcome this baby at home, and I wanted my girls to be able to witness birth and be there with me. Remember the version of me that was afraid of homebirth? She was gone and I felt comfortable and confident in this decision. The stars felt like they were aligning as the midwife that I fell in love with during my last two pregnancies had started to attend homebirths. I couldn't believe this, it was kismet. I would be able to have my cake and eat it too; to have my baby at home with my midwife.

I had a deep desire to take radical care of myself during this pregnancy. I understand that this comes from a place of extreme privilege to be able to afford (in time and money) the things I was able to do for myself. I started assembling my care team: a pelvic floor therapist, a massage therapist, an esthetician, an embodiment coach, acupuncturist and a therapist. Caring for myself became a full-time job and I do not regret one bit of it. I started therapy mid-pregnancy; I still had trauma I was carrying from my first birth and wanted peace. Through talking, processing and EMDR I went

Sarah Howard

from feeling anxiety and pain when thinking about it and a 9 on a scale of 1-10, down to a 2. I wanted to heal and be in the best place possible before this next birth, and I had no idea just how important this would turn out to be. I needed to protect my energy and boundaries and I made the difficult decision to not share with anyone, including my mom, when I was in labour. I deeply feared hurting people's feelings but knew that I had to choose me if I was going to have the best experience for me.

I expected this baby would come early, at least closer to 40 weeks, but they had other ideas. I was approaching 42 weeks and my midwife would no longer be able to attend at home if we got past that date. I was feeling anxious and sore and tired, the birthing tub set up in the dining room felt like it was mocking me. On the eve of 42 weeks my baby decided it was time and labour began. The next morning my partner started to fill the tub and I called my midwife. I absolutely loved being home and having my children there with me. It was the most calm and beautiful thing to have them pottering around, playing and checking in with me, pouring water on my back and gently stroking my belly with a paint brush. I reached completely dilated and my waters broke and I was feeling the urge to bear down and push but things were not progressing. I got out of the tub and up to my bed and my cervix was swelling. The fear and worry from my first birth came rushing in but with my husband and midwife I was able to hush the fears and keep working; changing position and resting and waiting. Night fell, I went to the bathroom and checked myself and I could feel my soft cervix, puffy and swollen. I went back to my bed and told my midwife I didn't think this was going to work as I could still feel my cervix swollen. She confirmed, and we decided that we needed to go to the hospital. My partner called his brother and he arrived shortly after. I was sad that we needed to leave the girls; with current protocols at the hospital, I knew I would not be able to see them again until we got home. When I made the slow walk down the stairs in pain and feeling sadness, I saw them cuddled up with their uncle. They were calm and relaxed;

it was the most amazing feeling. I felt so much peace as we pulled out of the driveway. All the work I had done to protect me and make this a calm, supportive experience had rippled on to them. At the hospital my midwife was in the operating room assisting and again the peace I felt despite being back on that table was remarkable. Our baby boy was born via caesarean section at a whopping 12 lbs 7oz with both of his parents in the room. My midwife calmly carried him to the isolet as he needed help and spent time being worked on while I looked on. It felt like 100 years but he was stable and he was laid onto my chest and he instantly stopped crying and calmed.

Surrounding myself with a team of women that I completely trusted and adored was pivotal in my experience. Caring for myself with such reverence during this most recent pregnancy supported me and healed me in so many ways.

I want you to know:

The way you feel while pregnant and birthing your baby matters.

Birth will change you, it's supposed to. Welcome it.

Your boundaries and desires are important; they must be shared.

You are a bad bitch, don't ever forget it.

Sarah Howard

Hi there, I am Sarah Elizabeth Howard. I am an American mostly stay-at-home mom learning to break all the rules I learned growing up. I am unravelling from the good girl to the wild woman that listens to her intuition and does what feels good. I am committed to connecting to my mind, body and soul for the rest of my days; to learning more about me and how I flourish so that I can be the best version of me. I am doing the extremely challenging work of healing generational curses. I have a deep calling in my soul to connect and gather with other women.

Learning about human design and astrology lights me up and I have found so much clarity and support from what I have learned so far. Connecting to my cycle and bleed has also changed my life and I love talking about it. The moon is magic.

I grew up a military child living in different parts of the world and then married a man that was in the military. I always had a way of connecting to babies and children and worked with them and their families for over 10 years in various settings, including on a college campus, a military base and inside of a women's correctional facility.

Birth New

I have been pregnant 4 times and am a mother to 3 young humans. I believe that parenting is a practice, it is not something you master. Parenting is the most humbling experience. Our children are our mirrors and will reflect our best and worst selves back to us so we can review, grow and keep practicing.

Nature, dancing and long hot baths are my current most effective medicines.

I work as a lactation specialist in a hospital per diem and am lit up by connecting with and supporting people that have had babies.

I want to cultivate relationships with other mothers and encourage them to chase their happiness and joy, to find what lights them up and cheer them on while they follow it. I believe that happy and thriving mothers will change the world.

Instagram: @thesaraheliza

Sara Evans
UNRAVELLING THE MYSTERY

We are all born. But there is something incredibly taboo in that we don't share our births with one another. For many of us, giving birth remains a mystery – whether it's the intimate details of how birth unfolds entirely on its own, or we don't know the details of our own births, or perhaps we may have birthed a baby but still have no knowledge or understanding of what need not be a mystery. The silence surrounding birth – what it is and what it can be – is a kind of censorship of our souls. Not just for the women who have given birth, but to the women that are yet to give birth and their families too. What we see and hear about birth is usually clouded in fear, rather than honouring and acknowledging the momentous transition that it actually is.

I spent most of my own life not actually realising or understanding how incredibly normal and simple birth is. No-one ever talked about it except to scare us from sexual exploits! My arrival into this world was not a smooth one, it was only because I was cut from my mother's belly that I survived my birth at all. And that's all I know – that was the discussion. My mother always seemed proud of the vertical scar that ran from her navel to pubic bone – a visible symbol of an enduring labour and birth. I myself wouldn't even realise the significance of this scar she wore so well

Birth New

or giving birth until it happened to me. And even as I write this there's a sly smile across my face as becoming a mother was never really on my radar. Like, at all. The transformation that takes place when we become mothers is completely incomprehensible until we come out the other side, and even then, it can take a while to fully comprehend. For me, there's a sweet irony in that becoming a mother quite literally opened me up to a whole new world. I found within me 2 great passions: birth and yoga, and somehow these 2 have combined to become my profession. A labour of love all on its own.

I have been in relationship with yoga since the age of 6 years old. I remember making butterflies with my body, expressing shapes and stories through movement. And as is the story for many who come to yoga, yoga and I were in a non-committed relationship. We were off and on for many, many years. But every single time I found yoga again it felt like I was coming home to myself. While I've made many shapes with my body over the years thanks to yoga, one memory stands out that didn't happen on a yoga mat or even in a class. I was sitting on a train that was travelling from Subiaco to Fremantle, enjoying that childhood notion of gazing out and watching the world pass me by. When we passed Mosman Park station along the Stirling Highway, I looked up and locked eyes with a bright pink sign which said 'The Home of Yoga'. And for me, at that moment in my life, I had such a strange thought cross my mind. I remember thinking so clearly to myself that when the time came for me to carry a child, I would immerse myself fully in a practice of yoga – that that would be the time when I would fully commit. I shook my head and laughed it off, as I still thought I didn't want or even need children in my life.

I was 23 years old and even if I did want kids, it definitely wouldn't be for some time. I didn't know it then but that sign sparked something within me that day. There are so many passing moments in life, but this one in particular stands out so vividly. I could never have dreamed just how significant that one moment, a single thought – from an actual, physical, bright pink sign – would go on to be a pivotal moment that perhaps planted the seed of an intention. Sometimes it's in those fleeting moments that we take for granted that we conceive our connection with our deepest darkest desires.

I was rudely awoken by the news that I was pregnant. It didn't happen in a way I would have hoped or planned, of course these things rarely do. The two lines on the stick were a confirmation of why I had felt so shit the weeks prior and confirmed that I was carrying a baby. The shock of that news was accompanied by guilt. Obviously, my body was ready to receive, but I, in my heart and soul, was sure as hell not! And then like some kind of cruel joke, when I was finally coming to terms with the pregnancy a few weeks later, I lost the baby. Whether it was the wisdom of my body or the knowing of this little soul, their barely formed body fell from me.

I've always believed that in losing something, we're often given a great gift in return. In losing this baby, I was given a period of grace and gratitude to do the work needed to shift my mindset towards becoming a mother. I was being called to ready my emotional and spiritual self for this next phase of my life. A reminder to come home. Yoga. The practice has a universal knowing; it weaves its way back into your life exactly when it's needed most. Either you find it or it finds you! The Home of Yoga – that meaningful moment on the train years before – was not about a yoga studio or a place (although it actually existed as both of those), it was a reminder to come home. There was a lesson for me in finding yoga so that I could come home to myself, and in doing so, nurture another. Once again, I fell pregnant. This time I was ready, excited even. After the delicacy of the first trimester, the second trimester was like a burst of fresh air. Everything felt like I was doing it for the first time and I relished getting to know myself and my baby in this way. The world around me seemed to shrink and start to go slow as my body became my whole world. Together we were in our own little cocoon. My body was nurtured more than it had ever been before, I had made it a ritual and my yoga played a huge part in how I cared for myself. Yoga is more than movement and making shapes, it's really a practice of being fully present in each moment. I was completely immersed in every little thing. Yoga was in everything I was doing and being. As my belly and my baby grew, I felt a deep sense of trust, an appreciation of my whole being – the expansion and conscious growth was beyond the physical. I loved every moment of it.

There are so many unknowns in the lead up to birth and I felt a nudge to learn from other women but I knew only one person who had given birth. She thought I was crazy for wanting to hear about her birth! She would only share with me anecdotal snippets of how her birth surprised her in more ways than one, that for her it was an unexpectedly wonderful experience. She provided no specific details except to say that I would probably shit myself … as if to scare me off from wanting to know more! While she held her birth story close to her heart, I do recall the shift I saw in her as she moved into motherhood. Since giving birth, she was different. There was a self-assurance and a vibrancy that seemed to light her up. When I remarked this shift to her husband he simply grew a big smile, nodded in agreement and gazed lovingly in her direction. And so the mystery of birth continued to be elusive.

Like most women, I made the incorrect assumption that all birth was done in the hospital. It had never been presented to me any other way, and so in planning my birth alongside my husband, it seemed that the best option was to 'go with the flow'. Together we attended antenatal classes at the hospital which were informative, light-hearted and fun … except when they showed us the epidural needle. No thank you. In my mind, 'going with the flow' would give me my best chance at a natural birth and help me avoid an epidural. What I know now and wish I knew then was that by choosing a 'going with the flow' mentality, we as the birth giver relinquish our power and by doing so, we lose the ability to influence our own experience of our birth. Surrender carries with it notions of waving the white flag, of giving in, but this is a fallacy. There's a sense of allowing and acceptance in surrender; leaning in to the experience and allowing it to unravel itself in the way it is intended. These two things are not the same. Knowing these subtle differences on an experiential level can be hard to comprehend; it's not a matter of intellect but one of faith.

Whether you want to call it contemplation, planning or preparing for birth – it's an absolute necessity to consider how you want that experience to be. And while I was happy to go with the flow, I also wanted to express my fears about how the birth might go, my biggest fear being giving birth via caesarean. During my pregnancy, I had gained a clearer understanding of what that scar on my mother's belly meant and I did not want my baby to be pulled from me. I didn't want my experience of childbirth to be a visibly painful memory, of that I was certain. Whether we care to acknowledge it, anxiety, fear and uncertainty are an ever-present reality of everyday life, and in the lead up to birth, the waves of our emotions rise even higher, creating a conflict of wanting to do what we 'think' is right while at the same time honouring our intuition.

So all in all, I had 3 wishes for my birth: labour or birth in water, try for drug free and avoid a caesarean. Knowing that labour would be a challenge and potentially painful, I had no desire to be numbed from the experience of birth. Ned and I had discussed these 3 desires together. Fortunately for me and many women who have come before, there was a blissful kind of ignorance in not knowing or having any context of what labour might look or feel like, but regardless, I wanted to do my best to be a part of it: mind, body and soul. Waterbirths at that time were reserved for hippies at home, apparently (and not at all common in the hospital at that time in 2008 – but thankfully times have changed since then), but even so I did not want to be drugged during my labour. There was an unspoken understanding between my husband and I that by making that acknowledgement to one another that I did not want drugs, and that the task of upholding our choice would ultimately fall on him on the day our baby would be born. I really don't think either of us truly understood the depth of what that responsibility would entail, nor did we realise just how deep our unspoken understanding of one another was at that point in time. I had chosen him to be by my side in life and there was no other person I wanted to share this birth with other than him.

The people we choose to invite into our birth space ultimately have an intricate role to play as the process of labour unfolds. While so much of what we experience throughout our pregnancy in the medical system is about control – doing the right thing, checking off boxes and so many instances where we hand over our own power or get told what to do – when it comes to giving birth, the only thing we can ever truly control is the energy in the room. And it's often the birth partner who is unknowingly given this monumental task of holding space so that the process can unfold in the way it's intended to.

As I was reaching the pinnacle of my pregnancy and preparing to meet my baby, it was Christmas and stinking bloody hot at 44°c on my supposed 'due date'. Although I felt heavy and slow, I still felt incredible. When I was still pregnant a week later, an induction was scheduled in the interest of the staff roster at the hospital over Christmas, not in my interest or my baby's.

On the eve of my induction, I got very little sleep. My mind played out so many scenarios contemplating the unknown of what might happen in the next day or so. Here I was, literally on the cusp of becoming a mother. The blissful innocence of not knowing and having no context about what to expect certainly worked in my favour for this first birth. There was excitement, anticipation and sheer terror!

I had no way of comprehending then that the woman who woke up on the morning of my induction was going to be an entirely different woman going to bed that night after giving birth.

It took less than 30 minutes for the Syntocinon to kick in. The resistance that played out in my mind was met with the wisdom of my body, and thankfully that force was greater, as she knew what needed to be done.

Sara Evans

The instinct to move was unstoppable, each wave of the contractions was pulling me deeper into some kind of other world. Ina May Gaskin, in her book *Spiritual Midwifery*, talks about labour as though it's some kind of trip – and I was certainly experiencing something reminiscent of trips I had taken in my life – so there was a welcome familiarity, and as much as I was fighting it, it did manage to carry me inward to a whole other dimension. I didn't know it at the time, but I understand fully now that in those moments I was letting myself be carried off. Labour can go one of two ways; either you fight and resist yourself and the process, or you trust and let go. I am indebted to many years of yoga for the subtle teachings of learning how to hover in that space between our physical and spiritual realms. Letting go in labour ultimately becomes a kind of out-of-body experience. Even as I write this, I can picture myself in that room laying sideways on the hospital bed, rocking myself into oblivion, transcending time and space in such a way that I could lean into the experience, even though at the time I was actually laying down!

Time stood still. It was just the 2 of us in the room. The communication between us on that afternoon was largely unspoken; there were very few words, except when I would yell 'do it harder', wanting the firmness of his hands to find the sweet spots on the back of my body that would intercept the intensity of each contraction. Although there was touch, the connection between us was beyond a physical one. While the physicality and firmness of his touch provided a kind of psychological reassurance, his presence and energy extended beyond that in such a way that I felt safe to let my guard down, to reveal my inner self and to be vulnerable. He was holding the space on the outside so that I could go within. Just as I was peaking towards the transition phase of labour, I was at a point where I doubted my ability to continue – the intensity required every ounce of my strength. This was the only time I consciously opened my eyes. I pulled him close to me, pressed my nose to his and locked eyes, "This fucking hurts!" I pushed him away, secretly hoping he would offer me the sweet relief of some drugs. I am too proud a person to ask for them outright, and he knew me well enough to know that was my intent. But rather than offer the drugs I so desperately wanted at that moment, he offered me reassurance. Reminding me of my strength and admiring me for the work I was doing. Having gotten that out of my system, I could return to my labour.

Labour lasted for just 6 hours. Although a relatively short amount of time, those hours felt like an eternity, every moment of labour was visceral, it was other-worldly. Completely unlike anything I had ever experienced.

The dream for my child that came through me came true; he moved from my womb and slid ever so slowly out into the world. As he emerged, the fear of my own birth which I'd held for so long seemed to fade. Here I was, staring into the eyes of my own child, a boy. I would like to say the love was instant, but it wasn't. I felt many things in that moment, a mixture of overwhelm, awe and pride. The lessons learned in labour are incomparable to anything else; those inward moments that were deep and dark is where the seeds of my own awakening were planted. And in giving birth to my son, those seeds cracked open and slowly began to spring to life. Like all good things, they took time to nurture and mature. What was immediate though, was the ecstasy. I was riding high on the rush that birth revealed to me. Post-birth I felt like a goddess – absolute in my power, every feeling and emotion in the days afterwards was electric. Giving birth had taken my relationship to another level – the love, appreciation and understanding we had for one another was next level, a powerful catalyst from which to begin our journey into parenthood. The regard and reverence with which I was held in those hours became an unspoken oath in the direction this birth has taken me in the 14 years since my son was born. As the wisdom of his birth began to settle into my being, it became apparent that my story of birth was not universally shared, and to my disbelief, it was more often unique!

The insight that we gain from carrying and bringing life forth is limitless. Not only does birth provide the insight and intuition needed to bring forth our children, but together with the subtle more spiritual aspects of yoga, it ignited within me a desire to want this experience for other women. And in becoming a mother, I discovered my dharma – my life's purpose. The receptivity of a woman with child knows no bounds; by allowing our wisdom to shine, we find our own inner light. We cannot tell it to one another, for our stories are our own. We come to know it as a mystery that unravels itself from within.

Sara Evans

As a student of yoga for more than 25 years, I praise my practice of yoga and the unwavering support of my beloved Ned in helping me emerge from each of my births feeling strong, supported and empowered. I moved through both my births and the transition into motherhood from a place of love and self-assurance. As a young mother, yoga was like an anchor in a storm and so it was the catalyst to my 18-month study of yoga, so that I could offer this insight and experience to other women and mothers through yoga. My 3rd 'baby', Bloom Yoga, was born in 2010. What began as a desire to share my passion for yoga and birth organically grew to become established as a small, boutique, commercial yoga studio serving Perth's northern suburbs; the first and only one of its kind at that time.

For me, yoga is the ultimate expression of our cyclical rhythm. Much like motherhood, it's a constant evolution that requires us to truly examine ourselves from the inside out; the good, the bad and the fugly. My yoga and the classes I share are a creative expression of feminine fluidity, infused with my light-hearted humour while revealing the depth of my skill as

Sara Evans

a long-time student of yoga. My nature is warm, inviting and down-to-earth, and I have an innate ability to see each student for the individual that they are.

In addition to wearing many hats as Bloom's boss lady, I am a senior yoga teacher, highly respected as a prenatal and postnatal specialist, qualified yoga therapist, birth educator and yoga teacher trainer. My most treasured passion is mothering my 2 children, George and Morgan, who collectively revealed this path of my dharma. They continue to be my greatest teachers in love and life.

www.bloomyoga.com.au
Instagram: @bloomyogaroom
Facebook: bloomyogakingsley

Kirsten Lyle

A SACRED RITE OF PASSAGE

A sacred rite of passage.

A truly transformative time.

A rebirth like no other.

These are all things that I have come to know, and that we are all told, about birth. But recently as I have been diving deeper into my own womb space clearing, connecting and remembering, I've been having inklings and stirrings of an even greater truth and magic that is unfolding in the unravelling of a woman as she creates and brings through new life and spirit to this earth. The missing key or puzzle piece that has been staring me right in the face for so long. A secret knowing that priestesses of times gone by have held onto and finally gifted to me as I have claimed my role as a birth keeper.

The moment of birth is not the *pinnacle* of the experience.

Right now, you're thinking – *What? How can that be?* Of course, the moment you get to meet your child is the climax of pregnancy, labour and birth. The moment that you have been waiting so long for surely cannot be anything but the highest point in the experience … How would you feel if I challenged that? If I told you it was the exact opposite. The nadir, the depth, the rock bottom? I want to share with you why it is so and why that moment is instrumental in the birthing process.

The womb is a place we are all familiar with. A place we are all connected to at the being of our physical journey on earth. This beautiful cave-like home is also the source of our creation energy, whether that be a child, a business, a painting or a relationship. Every time you create you tap into the energy of the womb. Journeying or meditating into the womb space is not like meditating from the mind or heart space. I describe it as a cave because I feel its beautiful earthly, underground, dark essence. Not in a way that is unilluminated but in a way that is a void. A deep crevasse of nothingness and oneness held in our body. A creation point, a portal to pull your creation into your body to manifest into the physical.

As humans we are cyclical beings. We see those cycles within ourselves as bleeding women and reflected around us in the oceanic tides, the moon's phases, the flowers blooming in spring and the leaves falling in autumn. We spiral in and out, constantly in motion. Constantly in flow. Creating a beautiful web of energy that holds the archetypical energy of all phases of life. We break down the seasons of the year into 4 quadrants … The phases of the moon into 4, the weeks of our inner cycle into 4, the phases of life into 4 and the trimesters of pregnancy into 4. Each holding a beautiful reflection for each other and mirroring our inner and outer energy. Knowing that each of these cycles have different time frames for the length and duration again mirrors our own experiences, growth and change. Being in the maiden stage of our life does not mean we hold only the energy of the maiden. It means just as the year always holds all 4 seasons, one is just at the forefront at that present moment in time. When we get to know our inner cycle, we can see the patterns and energy that are being reflected to us. For example, the autumn, luteal or premenstrual phase of our cycle is a time for spiralling inwards before our bleed. Preparing for the letting go. It's often when we notice the things that are no longer serving us the most. Some people call these realisations symptoms or PMS but when we let our cycle illuminate what is feeling good within our body, we can work *with* what's coming up instead of against it and let it go.

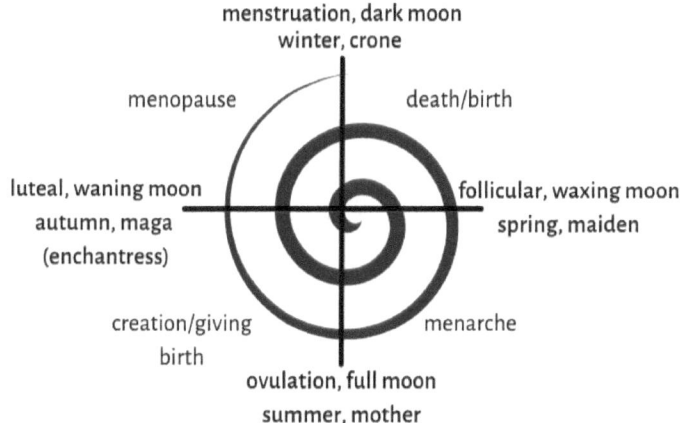

'Birth as a sacred rite of passage', 'positive birth', 'birth without fear' – these are all buzz terms you will hear in birthing communities. My issue with these phrases is that they have expectations attached to them. They make birthing people feel as if they are expected to do birth in a certain way, to experience birth in one 'right' way and we all know that doesn't happen all the time. When there is expectation on a journey that does not unfold, we are often left with feelings of inadequacy. Unworthiness, like we did something wrong, and we feel shame in our story. These terms to me are like spiritual bypassing for birth. They are practices that sideswipe or avoid facing unresolved emotional issues, psychological wounds and unfinished developmental tasks. It is basically saying let's all just throw some love and light and manifestation at the birth I want and forget about the birth that will help me move through social conditioning, limited beliefs and help me truly reach my potential as a spiritual being having a human experience. All that without even taking into account the birth the baby needs.

When I, as a birth keeper, think of *Birth New*, I think of all the birth education courses and classes that are on offer to help birthing women and families reach this beautiful, empowered, positive birth but they all make me feel like they are missing the point. To empower someone, you must first take their power away. These courses offer an outside view on what is happening and will happen within your body. They ask you to focus on an outside view. They suggest you move in specific ways, sound a specific way and release fear in a certain way. All ways that they feel is best for your 'positive' birth, these aren't necessarily the ways your body needs to move or sound or hold or release fear and this is what I feel women stepping outside of the hospital system to birth really understand. They hold all the power in their birthing experience. Instead of looking for a new way to birth, perhaps what we are really looking for is the old way to birth. In community, surrounded by love, surrounded by trust with the ability to let go of what is no longer serving us.

A sacred rite of passage does not need to be 'positive' to be transformative. A rite of passage is an experience or event in a person's life that alters and changes them in a way that cannot be undone. It is marked by a separation or a leaving of the familiar. A transition, a time of testing learning or growth and a return, a period of incorporation and integration of the new. Do you think the cicada nymph's journey out of the ground feels familiar to her after living there for 13 years? Do you think she is comfortable in the hard rigid shell before she molts to reveal her wings? Do you think she can fly effortlessly on the first try? Does she question if she is doing it right, does she look for someone to show her the way? Or does she simply allow her inner wisdom, instinct and her ancestral remembering that is ingrained in her DNA to guide her? If we lose the terms 'positive' and 'negative' and focus on our experience as just that – our human experience – I wonder how that changes your story? It's like that saying, does a tree falling in the forest make a noise if there is nobody to hear it? Do we still hold the same perception of events if there is no expectation on the journey? Two people can have the same birth experience and outcome and one could describe it as a traumatic event while the other recounts a positive story; the only difference being the perception of events, our expectations of the journey and being able to accept the experience.

Just because it's sacred does not mean it's going to be easy.

When combining the magic of our cycles, our innate wisdom and ancestral remembering of the womb space with the knowing of a rite of passage, we come to the juicy stuff.

Separation – The start of the spiral inward

For some, this separation from the familiar starts even before conception when the babe, still in the astral plane, starts to share their desires to join us on earth. For other people, the descent starts after conception as your body starts to transform from a familiar place of home to one that is shared by a tiny growing being. There are so many shifts within our body at this time. Physical changes, chemical changes and spiritual changes. Leaving the maiden phase and stepping into the mother energy is often marked with fatigue, sickness, heightened moods and intuition. We are drawn to other people; we want to share these changes and ask what is normal. We crave having a form of validation in what we are experiencing and something as simple as hearing someone say, "That happened to me as well," can bring so much comfort but it's here right at the very start of the journey that I feel is like a sliding-doors moment. Who you choose to seek that validation from is going to have an effect on your ability to spiral inwards.

For me, the first time I fell pregnant was the first time I truly learnt about pregnancy. Even what to do after you have taken a pregnancy test and it comes up positive was so foreign to me. The first thing I did was see a doctor; it was pointless. He literally told me if a home pregnancy test says I'm pregnant, well then, I'm pregnant and to come back in a few weeks and we could do a scan so he could tell me my due date. And just like that I had someone telling me what was happening within my body instead of giving me the knowledge or tools to find that out myself. Appointments were made for me; I was told when to show up and what test to do without even getting a proper explanation of what the tests were or how they could affect my pregnancy or my care. At first, I was under the care of a midwifery group practice so sometimes at my appointments I at least saw a familiar face, but I was soon kicked off the program and referred to a private obstetrician where, without me even realising it, this outsourcing of information became worse. As my due date became closer, more and more ultrasounds were given to 'make sure baby was okay' and to see how big she was. Internal exams were performed to see if I was dilated well before my due date. All this poking and prodding and external information did was create fear and distrust in my body and its ability. I was never once asked how I was feeling or what my internal dialogue was telling me. My inward journey was limited by the need of my caregivers to know what my journey looked like in statistical terms and on paper. My separation from what felt familiar was scary.

Falling pregnant with my youngest was a different experience altogether. I knew I was pregnant before taking the test. I could feel the familiar signs within my body. I knew my bleed was late and just like in that first experience I was not surprised when two lines appeared, but instead of heading straight to a doctor, I contacted a privately practicing midwife that would support my birth at home. I knew the date of conception so when contacting her I informed her of our estimated birthing month, not day. Now I must say from the experiences I have had attending free or unassisted births as a birth keeper, that is what I will choose for myself if I birth again. It is a next level unravelling and spiralling inwards and discovery of deep trust and intuition, but for this chapter, I am going to use two of my own experiences to help highlight the different paths our journeys can lead us on. Every appointment I had with my midwife I was asked if I could feel baby or what position I thought baby was in. I was asked what I was feeling, if I felt well within myself and if I had any concerns at the beginning of each appointment. All of these questions were opportunities to connect in with myself and baby. To listen to what my body was telling me and to my intuition. All 'routine' tests, ultrasounds and procedures were optional if I felt called to know that information. The reasons for the tests and what would happen with the results were all explained to me and then I was able to go home, do my own research and make a decision that felt best to me. By the end of my pregnancy, I knew what was 'normal' for my body and my baby. I had so much trust in my body that anytime someone questioned my ability to birth at home I could confidently state all the reasons I was better off there than in the hospital system. My separation from what felt familiar was liberating.

Transition – The descent into the darkness of transformation. The journey to the death of a piece of ourselves

Labour is one of the most testing experiences in life; you learn exactly what limitations you have allowed to be placed on yourself. My first limitation was time. My 'due day' came and went, and again, I became fearful that my body wouldn't work or do as it was supposed to do. Once I was in labour I didn't trust I was handling the pain as well as I should have so I allowed myself to be coerced into pain relief I didn't really want but thought I needed. I had the ability to listen to my body taken away from me and I wasn't able to move in the ways I wanted to because of the pain relief I didn't want. My trust was placed in the people around me to know what was best for me and my baby. There was no listening to what I needed; I could barely keep my eyes open, let alone think. I was instructed when to wee, when to drink and when to push. There was no 'journeying to the stars to bring my baby to earth'; I was out of it but not in the beautiful meditative state I had heard about. I was hyper focused on anything I could hear in the room as it was the one sense I felt was still working. I was all in my mind with no concept of what was happening in my body. There was no descent into the darkness of my womb. There was no meeting my limitations, there was no rebirth.

This labour was again past my 'due day' but there was no concern about time. There was no worry about my baby's position or size or when labour would happen. I was able to trust in the process, I was able to surrender into the process. I had no fear or expectations because I could trust that the journey that unfolded was what it needed to be. When labour started there was no questioning if this was it because I knew. Not because a monitor told me I was having regular contractions or because someone had checked my cervix but by what my body wanted, how my body wanted to move and by how it was showing me it was opening. I knew my baby was fine because I could feel him moving and when I sat and connected with him my intuition told me he was fine. I became unaware of the people in the room and was able to focus on the sensations in my body because I wasn't distracted by questions or monitors or time. I could feel my baby's soul drop into his body; I could feel his descent through my body. I had journeyed so deeply into the birth portal it was all I was aware of. In the final moments all I remember is the darkness. I had to smash through what felt like my physical limitations to birth my baby. I found pieces of myself, the strength, resilience, wisdom and power that the women of my ancestral line held and I left small pieces of me behind in the darkness like a snake shedding her skin. A true transformation.

The return – I was now a mother

Sure, I felt joy when I looked at my beautiful baby girl but for months after her birth I stood and cried in the shower. I couldn't quite put into words how I was feeling except for 'that's not how it was supposed to be'. I had felt educated, I had felt like I had done my research on how to have a 'positive' experience, but my experience felt far from that. I felt ripped off. I felt like I had been used, the trust I put outside of myself abused at the convenience of others. It absolutely affected my moods and therefore the way I parented. It took me years before I could confidently say I was okay with her birth. She was born in a time before social media took off so finding the people to speak to or even the language to explain how I felt was extremely hard. I stayed in the inner spiral for months, not feeling ready to journey back out. But the changes that unfolded within me after that integration period were immense. Without this birth I would have nothing to compare my own other experiences with.

The return to my new normal after my homebirth was a lot quicker. The 'high' of what I had achieved lasted a good few months, and I spiralled back outward into the community faster and with a lot more ease than previously. I can't ignore the ways in which I was changed forever though. I felt invincible, like I could now achieve anything I put my mind to. Comparing this experience to my first made me question everything that the Australian maternal health care system is and it is the reason I finally listened to the call and stepped into birth work. It was something I had felt called to for many many years before, but meeting that inner wisdom that I could only find in birth, made me realise what a big part of my soul's journey it would be. Without those pieces of myself dying I never would have been able to move forward on this path to the new me.

Witnessing women give birth in a hospital system, I rarely see them get to a point that is so within themselves they are able to meet their limitations and move through them while feeling safe and nurtured. They aren't given the space within the system to form a relationship with themselves that develops the trust they need to birth in a truly aligned way. To find the moment where all layers are stripped, all facades, all masks. The moment where she is raw and primal and pure. Where she is in her true essence and in that moment just after her babe is born, where she reconnects to and remembers all of the power within herself … All that she holds. She cannot reach the depths to allow the parts of herself to die and be reborn, ready to move into her parenting journey with deep trust and knowing in her own capabilities. She never reaches the foundation of her inner spiral and therefore the integration of the experience is harder.

As a birth worker I feel it is my responsibility to explore my own depths. Without seeing the darkness and the 'shadow' self of my own human experience, how could I relate to yours? If I didn't know the course of the journey into the underworld of my own self, how would it be possible to hold you in your space as you travel deep into the unknown? As you dance with the cosmos, with the energy of oneness, of death. A new cycle can only be started when we allow the old to end.

Are you ready to let a part of you die?

Kirtsen Lyle

Welcome, dear one, I am Kirsten Lyle. Birth keeper, energy weaver, best-selling author, ceremony holder, mother, lover. These are all some of the ways in which I could be described. My soul's work is nourishing people as they transition through pivotal times in their lives such as menarche, matrescence, birth, death and rebirth, while holding the sacred space for them to remember the innate wisdom and power they hold within. The unique light I shine on the world allows you to feel safe in trusting yourself.

My energy work includes reiki attunements and womb clearing massage that offer a loving embrace. I am dedicated to creating a safe intimate container where you are able to be open to receiving the messages brought through from the universe that remind your body and spirit that they are capable of releasing what no longer serves you and heal yourself on a soulful level.

As a birth keeper I am a heartfelt companion; my role is to journey beside you without bias or judgement. To hold you, as you hold the energetic portal and bring new life to this earthly plane. I feel the most in my element when I am intuitively supporting you while you birth yourself and your babe. My own experiences birthing 4 children and rebirthing myself multiple times has made me a wealth of wisdom and knowledge. I also have a unique perspective of birth from the physical and metaphysical experiences I have had in multiple birth spaces.

I grew up in the northwest of Western Australia, spending a lot of time snorkelling, boating, camping, reef walking while the tides were low and hanging out with my horse. There I completed my floristry apprenticeship before moving down south and embarking on the next chapter of life. This is where I met my now-husband and experienced becoming a mother myself. Each time I have birthed I have transformed myself. My children continually remind me that I have the power to create, the importance of coming together in circle and ceremony, and the ways in which we can combine parenting with sacred celebration.

I want you to feel safe, supported, seen and held while you transform and know that there is no part of you that is unlovable. I want to be the light that guides you while you travel into the deepest aspects of your being to reignite your own light.

www.kirstenlyle.com.au
Instagram: @the_kirsten_lyle
Facebook: kirstenlyledoula

Brigitte Benary
RED NECTAR

As I sit here in my large round peacock chair, I begin to explore how I feel when I think about my womanhood, my birthing journey, and what it means to me. I consider what has led me to this place – sitting in my big chair – a place that I am safe. My chair envelops me every time I sit in my studio. The funny thing is, this chair was purchased with my clients in mind, so that in their therapy sessions they might feel a sense of their own regality, like a queen on her throne. My vision in my work is for all women to experience their own sovereignty, embodying the full extent of their feminine power.

As circumstances would have it, it is me who is the recipient of this feeling as I sit in my glorious chair. As I look back on my own birthing journey, now a mature woman at 54, I see many subtle and not so subtle themes, stories, threads of my life tapestry.

I take a breath and try to formulate my thoughts and explore where it began …

What comes to mind is when I menstruated for the first time. I was extremely young; my physical body was mature for my age, however I was unaware of the process, and not prepared for what was happening emotionally or intellectually.

In my innocence, I remember the uncertainty, the mystery, so many questions about what was happening to my body. I now know and appreciate this beautiful red stain as a life force, giving me the power and potency to enter the wisdom of my womanhood and to one day create a new life. However, at the time, I had no concept of these possibilities. I was surprised and shocked at the sight of this unexplained blood. This was not uncommon in those days – a lot of girls, including myself, had no idea what was going on.

But I do remember the stain and the vivid red colour of my flow. How it represented the unknown. Now, for me, it's about the mysteries of the feminine. What happened at that moment was my feminine journey beginning to unfold. Curiosity began. "What is this? What is happening to my body?"

I didn't yet understand the meaning of this physical ritual, the emergence of this rich, abundant nectar and the threshold that my body had stepped over. This red nectar created and contained in my body – in all feminine bodies – is such a rich resource of creation and wisdom. Young women today may be fortunate enough to be educated and informed of its power; of the abundance, boldness, potency and the magic of the nectar released from us every month.

I could never have imagined how it would weave through my life.

Somehow I just accepted what was happening, and in my innocence, I don't remember asking too many questions. I vaguely recall my mum explaining to me that this was a natural progression in life. She was prepared with pads and spare underwear for me, for exactly when the unexpected happened. I remember her telling me that she had been waiting for the time my body would begin its flow. She honoured me in her own thoughtful and practical way, which allowed me to take the experience in my stride and with so much more ease.

I embraced this new responsibility of maiden within my life, but I guess at times, I felt my period to be an annoyance and inconvenience.

My cycle, unlike most of my girlfriends, was always a full 5-7 days. This meant my body was changing hormonally for a longer duration, so the down time, away from this shedding, felt very short from one cycle to the next. My bleeding was heavy and in some way I felt cautious and possibly on edge, nervous not to leak onto my clothing which would have been so embarrassing as a young girl, trying to stay unseen and unnoticed in this very early maturing.

From a young age I dreamed of having a lifelong partner, a husband and having children. Four children, to be exact, as the vision had always been so clear! When I met my future husband David at 16 years of age, it seemed like life was allowing this vision to come to fruition. But after some time the universe had other plans for us, and we parted ways for a number of years as we explored our own lives on different paths.

I believe in destiny and things happening for a reason, and a few years later David and I rekindled our relationship. It was impossible to ignore that we were to be life partners.

Our vision was always to have children, but as time passed I began to question my dream of a family. I hadn't realised that I was scared about the unknown and the new responsibilities, and I questioned my ability to mother.

In early 1994, I was invited to sit in a women's circle. This was the gift that began to open up a new understanding of feminine mysteries for me. It allowed me to connect with other women and share the fears and hesitations I had been feeling for some time. Perhaps, being able to speak with other women in this way, I felt acknowledged and no longer alone in my story, which led me to feeling more at ease stepping into motherhood.

Once able to fully embrace the idea of starting our family, we began earnestly to chart my cycle and time our unions in the hope of falling pregnant. I remember the excitement and the joy that my husband David and I had when, after 10 weeks, we announced to my parents over dinner that we were pregnant. Less than 2 hours later I saw the spots. I remember cramping. I recall pain I had never experienced before. I was lying in the fetal position in a state of utter confusion. Once again, I had no idea what was happening to my body.

But then, I felt the clots. I remember the blood, the heaviness of my red nectar flowing uncontrollably. Not knowing what was happening, I just had to allow my body to do what it naturally needed to. It was eliminating the life of a soul that wasn't meant to be. The flow of the red nectar served this. My body was letting go of something Mother Nature was not happy about. I didn't understand at that time in all the excruciating pain and suffering, releasing and tears, my body had its own natural way. My body knew. I stayed with the grieving, the pain and with whatever my body needed to do at that moment.

I remember my husband David watching me and trying to do everything he could to support me. My parents arrived at some point to see if they could help in any way and apparently one of my soul sisters was there too. I must have been so deep in my experience, I didn't recall her being there. The rest of that evening I was lost in a blur of severe pain and suffering.

I felt certain the child I was carrying was a girl, a young life with an old soul, complete with the wisdom that this time was not hers. What was held deep within me was the unexplainable loss. What lingered was the wisdom that was contained inside my belly.

The miscarriage was the clearing of my womb, nature's way of cleansing and shedding. It was preparing my body to renew my womb for a new soul. I felt so blessed to have an organ that was healthy and able to wash the dust away like a wet stormy day, albeit a day where it feels like the rain would just never stop.

We cried and mourned the loss of our little girl, but we were so certain we wanted to have a family we decided that this one terrible loss was not going to hold us back. We were willing to try again, as hopeful young people, longing to give life.

Birth New

It wasn't easy at first. Our friends were getting pregnant around us and we both danced the fine line of grief and joy for all of them, as they were also longing to grow their families. We hung on to hope and trust that it would happen as it was meant to be, and that timing was everything.

Even to this day when I think about the pregnancy, the little girl we lost, I feel a pang deep within my heart, my eyes well with tears and remember the grief and terrible loss I experienced physically and how we felt together emotionally. Now I am able to reflect and know that it may have happened for a reason. Possibly to test us, challenging how committed we were to each other and whether we were truly ready to begin our family.

I wish to honour my husband David for his ability to care for me during this time. I can only imagine what it must have been like for him to witness my pain and loss, and not be able to do anything at all to alleviate the suffering. This he did while experiencing a loss of his own. I am deeply grateful for his love, devotion and commitment to me and to us. His undeniable courage to bear witness to this death. All too often our partners go unnoticed and the silence of their own loss lays deep within, unexpressed and unacknowledged.

When the timing was meant to be, our trust and belief held us in good stead and I fell pregnant very quickly after my miscarriage, with our son Jessy. Pregnancy was easeful, I was healthy and loved every moment of nurturing this child within me. He was a gift and we were so grateful after the loss of our first pregnancy. Jessy's birth, however, was a difficult one, to say the least.

My baby was nearly a week overdue when my doctor examined me and found my blood pressure had risen to dangerous levels. He decided that it was time for me to give birth for the safety of us both, wanting to induce me. I refused for some time, reluctant to use any intervention. I fought against what I believed wasn't going to be good for me or my baby, and I held my ground and found my voice. As I reflect back, there are so many moments through his birth when I see that I didn't yet fully trust my instincts. I felt I had my voice at that time, however I was not yet feeling confident in actually being able to express my wishes and stand firm in what I needed.

Once admitted to hospital, my obstetrician did an internal examination and used prostaglandin gel to help stimulate contractions and begin labour. He told me to 'go and grab some dinner, it could be hours away before anything happens'. We didn't think too much of it at the time and trusted what he had said. There were no hours to wait. My contractions started before we could even get to the front door of the hospital. As a consequence of the intervention, Jessy's birth was very quick. It took only 3 hours.

I recall during his birthing, standing in the shower with the annoyance of the water dripping on my skin. I couldn't wait to get out, all I wanted to do was walk. So much about his birth was empowering, I experienced a strong motivation to feel the earth beneath my feet and keep my legs moving to keep my body in motion, feeling the sense my body knew what it needed to do.

Even though I had some medical intervention, I trusted my body could manage as I walked the path of birthing. My body was enacting my baby's travels down the birth canal as if I was being guided by something much greater than myself. I was prepared for this new birth, for my baby to come through and as I felt my womb labouring, I willed for my birth canal to open and expand. I had my husband by my side, letting me go through this process, witnessing me in this experience of trusting my body. He respected that I didn't want to be touched. I just wanted to be left alone and walk my journey home into motherhood.

As my baby left my womb and began to make his way down the birth canal, contraction after contraction, I embraced each of his movements by moving my own body and using the gas to alleviate the intensity in the moments in-between each contraction. At some stage his movements slowed right down and they had now hooked me up to a baby monitor to ensure his safety. I continued to immerse myself in the experience every step of the way. After a time, the contractions started again, and he was on the move. It was time to push. He was coming hard and fast. The birth was close but for some reason still unknown to me, he was stuck and couldn't make his way out.

I remember my doctor saying to me that my blood pressure was rising, the baby's blood pressure was unstable and the baby's life would be at risk. How does a young woman who is finding her voice choose, when she is caught between holding ground for herself, but also making sure her newborn will be safe? I was not educated enough to know about having a birth doula as an advocate solely for my needs during this journey. I hadn't yet solidified my inner strength nor was I fully aware of the power of my intuition at that stage. Despite having to go against my instincts of no intervention, I felt the surge of fierceness well up within me of a mother lion wanting to protect her cub and knew that its life was the only thing that mattered.

David reminded me of the scurrying and sudden busyness in the room to make sure that Jess arrived safely. I don't remember anyone discussing with me what was happening but it was all moving very quickly. My obstetrician needed to use a ventouse to draw Jess out as quickly as possible. I continued to push with all I had and very soon our new son was born. Not only did they use the ventouse to assist in his birth but I also required a small episiotomy because of it. Not quite the ending we had hoped for or envisaged. I did not have time to reflect nor think about anything that had just happened during the birth, as it wasn't over yet. When I was supposed to be in the bliss bubble of those first moments with my new baby, fate had decided otherwise.

I began to bleed; the red nectar began to flow – in fact, it began to gush from me. Once again, the theme of blood permeates. This nectar of creation shedding away from my body. During birth, a piece of placenta had torn away and I was bleeding uncontrollably. The doctor told me that he needed to stop the bleeding, and that I had to go into surgery.

It all happened so quickly with not a second to spare or think. And so I was wheeled away.

David was left standing there in the hospital room with our new baby in his arms. He looked at me with fear in his eyes, in shock and scared out of his wits, not knowing whether I'd live or he'd be parenting our son alone.

But we were truly blessed that day as the next thing I remembered was waking up in my room, having this beautiful baby by my side, and being a family for the first time. I think about that period of time I went through after birthing my son Jessy, and there are so many ways that I could look at that situation. I could focus on the negative things and blame the medical system for what went wrong. But I chose to go with my natural way of reflecting. I'm grateful that I was saved, to share wholeheartedly, and that I'm the mother of my son, Jessy. This incredible opportunity through giving birth to give life, to tap into the feminine wisdom and power that I receive from within my womb.

When I reflect on those first few months of motherhood, I remember the struggles that I had felt letting go of my old life, being a businessperson who was about to have a child and was in control of everything. Now I was in control of nothing. Coming home with our newborn heralded a flood of emotions. Hormones raging, physical needs of a baby ever-present, and my own physical healing after the trauma that was my birth experience. Not knowing when it really began, I felt the enormity of what lay ahead, the overwhelming pressure of my inner critic and the expectations of my perfectionism weighing on me. My emotional state was fragile and even though it was just under the surface at first, it began to slowly deteriorate. Three months had passed before I was even able to get out of my front door. My midwife and mothercraft nurse assisted in ways that they could, but it was never stated, never diagnosed, and my postnatal depression was never really addressed. It was however as clear as crystal for all those closest to me and they did the best they could to support me at the time.

David took on the role of father with pride and honour. He would encourage me to rest and take on the feeding duties wherever he could. He received great joy, forming a close bond and connection with our son which remains to this day. Once David returned to work, I struggled to manage, yet continued to put one foot in front of the other, being so grateful for Jessy's beautiful sweet easygoing nature and the joy he brought to us.

When I became a mother I had been given an opportunity in my womanhood to shed the innocence of the archetype 'maiden', the remnants of a stereotype of a young woman. As a maiden, I believed I was in control of everything and thought I could create anything. I thought I was infallible, and needed to do everything to transition into motherhood and the start of my new life. As a woman, I now know and understand that this process was far from a straightforward one, and that it would come with many challenges and trials along the way.

Beginning by taking small steps with my new baby son, and getting to know a new life, a new Brigitte; the mother, carer and nurturer.

At the time, I felt I was being guided by a feminine force of nature. It was a sign that it was time for change. Time for new questions in my life. Who was I? Was I that same businessperson I was before? Who was this woman who had now birthed a new child? Who could I turn to for help and how do I receive guidance to navigate this new path? These questions signalled the beginning of a quest for me, one which is still unfolding in my life today.

I know in my heart there are sacred messages in everything that I have experienced, and it was at that point, this wisdom started to slowly develop into this new archetype of mother.

Working my way through my PND, I found a new energy and sparkles of joy over time, embracing and loving motherhood. It certainly had its big challenges, ups and downs of no sleep and no or little personal space for me, just as all new parents experience. Our vision of expanding our little family crept in once again, as we wanted to have our kids close together in age. It felt like the timing was right and I had a good feeling that things would go smoothly.

Falling pregnant with our daughter Ella was easeful. I was fit and healthy, I had embraced exercise and had a positive mindset to bring another life into our family. The beautiful months of pregnancy flew by, busy with a toddler, our little Jess was a sweet blessing. Happy-go-lucky, full of joy and the easiest company any mama could have asked for. It was so divine to nurture a little male soul in the world as I came from a family of all girls, except for my dad.

I was now weaving art back into my life, creating mosaics in the times when I could have some space. My creativity was my soul food. It's what nourished my spirit and I drank it in as much as I could each day, until our little girl was due to arrive in June.

Our gorgeous pocket rocket arrived on time, short and sweet without any hiccups. I had replenished my inner world enough to hold my own ground throughout her birth, which was extremely quick. After only 2.5 hours she was in my arms. Her arrival was easy and natural. A true force of strength announcing, "I'm here!" which is so much a part of her character to this day.

There was, however, a concern because of my previous haemorrhaging. As a precaution I was given medication to stop further complications. Even though I wasn't sure that I needed the intervention, the choice seemed correct at that time. I still wonder about that.

What I do know is that Ella was perfect, sweet and beautiful. All I had learnt as a first-time parent, the strength and resilience I had gained by going through my journey of postnatal depression, was redefining and expanding me. Brigitte: woman, wife and mother of 2 children.

Having a daughter, I felt like I had been given a treasured gift, which also turned out to be a huge unexpected learning curve. Ella's strength of character and tenacity, even as a baby, was a reflection for me, a mirroring of what I had unconsciously longed for. Ella was able to decide and choose for herself, using her voice to achieve what she wanted, when she wanted it. When she showed her strength, I had to find mine. Strength that I had not yet developed and didn't know I had the capacity for. As a young mother, I did not expect to find my daughter as my teacher. For me, it was everything I wanted to be able to do – speak my mind, say what I wanted to say and have the conviction to say it with certainty. It was when Ella was around 8 months of age, and I was struggling through the challenges of the day to day with this strong and powerful baby, that the doubts and emotions started creeping back in again. At that point, when I felt all the signs, lashing out in my frustration for inner peace, I knew that I had to get help. I could not do it alone. With a support network around me that guided me, I found a psychotherapist who led me on a deep dive journey to bring me back to my creativity, back to self-acceptance and to my intuition. Most importantly, she brought me back to my feminine voice and to trusting myself once again.

As I continue on my never-abating journey of discovery, I reflect on the past few years. I've now come to learn that we hold emotions, stories, tales and beliefs in our bodies from within our family systems, which we inherit through our lineage. There comes a time in most of our lives when we realise that these stories need to change. Sometimes our body talks to us with regard to difficult aspects of our health such as anxiety, depression and other issues. In my case, my body speaks of bleeding, miscarriage and haemorrhage.

As a woman with a deep connection to my feminine spirit and soul, I carry those stories, beliefs of my family lineage within my womb, particularly being stored in the cervix. Through my work in birthing and womb space, I've come to understand that when a baby comes down the birth canal through the walls of the cervix, it gathers some of the mother's life patterns, beliefs and stories as it's born.

The healing of the womb is a beautiful way for us to reclaim and rewrite the themes of our stories, with the rich blood nectar. The feminine has a sacred opportunity each month, one which we have never been taught to understand, being the potency of this gift from Mother Nature. I now have a deeper understanding that the mysteries of the feminine have power and richness within them, and if we become present and attentive to the language of our body, it is constantly talking to us through our cyclical shedding.

My children had grown to young adults when, somehow in the crazy busy day to day of my life, I had missed the language of my own body. Once again, the heavy bleeding and irregularities of my cycles told me that something was not okay. My cycles felt long and constant, I was suffering mental stresses and failed to make decisions in my life that brought my soul joy. At that point, I had to seek medical attention, to discover through scans and ultrasounds that I had grown sizable fibroids and was advised that either I could wait to see what happened or have a hysterectomy. For me, having a hysterectomy was not an option at first. I tried to follow a few different healing pathways. One way was to seek Chinese medicine and to also look into MRI laser surgery.

I addressed my body with the utmost of care and diligence during this time, fighting so hard to avoid major surgery. I changed my diet, took herbs and juices and addressed my mental health. There was so much to deal with and I was scared, but I also felt empowered to give my healing a chance with all I had. I found out about the MRI laser treatment very late in my research and unfortunately it became obvious I was no longer a candidate.

I continued my struggle and fought to hold on to my womb. It was as if I was fighting to hang on to the old beliefs, the old patterns, the old stories that I had stored in my body in this womb space. And I fought to not let them go. The signs were impossible to ignore now, I was being told that enough was enough. It represented so much of who I was and how I identified myself as a woman. I hung on for dear life, continuing to take my remedies, eat organically, juice and receive therapy and reiki as my body was continually releasing and shedding as if my feminine essence was leaking.

I questioned myself most days. Why was this happening? What was the lesson here and what more could I do to heal myself? I was doubting and questioning all of my decisions.

My feminine flow continued relentlessly and the nectar that had once helped me create life wouldn't stop. Most days I would hardly make it through the morning when at 11am I would have to go to bed unable to move, resting for hours at a time. It was so hard to let go, I shed many tears as all I had known was to fight and my determination was fierce.

Each day that I did not surrender, my body would send its message even louder to stop. It wasn't until the day that I woke up at 3am with a fright, totally covered in blood, that I took a huge breath and my tears began to flow in fear, knowing that I had been defeated.

I said to myself, *Brigitte, if you don't do something about this now you are going to die.* I was allowing my own life force to possibly take my life away. *It is enough fighting, struggle and tears, this is a divine sign, it's your time now.* At that moment I decided to have the hysterectomy.

Herein, the story of surrendering began again. I took myself by the hand and ever so gently began to guide myself towards letting go of everything: my old stories of suffering, not trusting myself, not feeling good enough to speak up, taking care of everybody else before myself and that I wasn't good enough or worthy enough. It was time to reclaim the knowledge of what was good for me.

By letting go of total control, my surgery happened in a matter of weeks. Again, it was as if the universe was just waiting for me to find my way to the right time. With the support of my healing, reiki, therapy, family and beloved friends, I found my way through my decision with more ease.

I remember the day of my surgery clearly. My husband David was with me, so attentive even though I could feel his worry. It was palpable.

His life partner, the love of his life, was undergoing major surgery and his last experience had been holding our newborn after I had suffered a life-threatening haemorrhage. It was so hard to see his concern and worry but I could not hold this burden for him. It was my time to surrender to things I could not control and focus on me and this new journey I was about to embark on in my life.

I held onto gratitude and filled my heart with love and a white light for this shedding of the old me. It was my time to let go of this beautiful vessel, my womb that had served me so well. I imagined everything around me with ease. When I entered the room before the surgery, I felt anxious, however, I had an overwhelming sense of peace, that all was okay and that the trajectory of my life was going to change forever.

Once the ordeal was over, I began my healing journey of nearly 12 weeks with the sole focus on resting. Clear instructions were to stay off my feet, no lifting and complete bed rest. Suddenly I was thrown into not being responsible for anybody else in my world except for me. Being surrounded by loved ones and the precious women in my life, I gave myself permission to be cared for, at a time that was really hard for me to let go of control.

It was sometimes overwhelming but those close to me were so amazing, nurturing and caring as I healed. My own tribe gathered around me, similar to ancient times in tribal communities gone by in the 'red tents' where women took care of each other through their monthly cycle, births and deaths.

I had learned many different processes over the years that I could use to help me through the good and bad days. If I felt the darkness of depression or the sparkle of joy creeping in, I would use my art therapy, reiki, meditation, visualisation and frequency music in a way to surrender and honour the unknown steps of this healing journey.

I realised deep down in my belly that this type of shedding was probably the biggest letting go I would have to do in my life up until that point. I kept reminding myself of the incredible journey that my womb had taken me on. The miraculous gifts of having been pregnant 3 times and giving birth to 2 healthy beautiful children. The gift of being able to cycle for most of my life. I kept leaning into gratitude and forgiveness for myself and for the decisions that I had made that had led me to be here standing at this crossroad.

It was at this point I gained a deeper insight into the feminine experience, allowing me to open the conversation about losing my womb with women around me. Although it remains largely an unspoken topic, I soon found that many others had also experienced hysterectomies, have had medical conditions which cause an inability to cycle or give birth, as well as many other life-altering journeys. Knowing that I was not alone allowed me to have the strength to examine whether the loss of my womb would alter my perception of my womanhood. I have now come to appreciate that being a woman and identifying as one is not determined by our physical capacity or even physical attributes. Womanhood has numerous dimensions, tangible and intangible, and the real power lies in a woman's ability to draw on her inner knowledge, intuition and her strength and courage.

As I began to heal, some days I felt well in my body and on other days this seemed out of my reach. The days slowly passed and the lessons were revealing themselves as I had decided to surrender my womb. When things didn't feel good, I would turn and move in a slightly different direction. I began to understand my own feminine compass as my body was healing and I acknowledged just how lucky I was that I had been able to give birth to my beautiful children. How lucky I was that I had had a womb and had been able to cycle every month. I kept holding those thoughts in my mind and in my body, my soul and my meditations.

This is now the underlying theme of my work.

My journey has guided me into following the birth space, the womb, to study women's incredible resilience and capacity for releasing, renewal, birth and transformation. The journey of becoming a Womb Spiral practitioner, birth doula and death doula, has led me to know the dark spaces of life intimately, experiencing joy alongside grief and loss. When we examine and attend to our grief, it slowly begins to dissipate, and we are able to reflect and draw on the knowledge that comes from our experiences. We are also able to explore the polarity of feeling joy in celebrating the lightness and expansion in letting go.

My understanding and knowledge has led me here so that I am able to share my expertise, and support women through their trauma, grief and loss, assisting them to find their courage, inner strength and wisdom. I utilise a variety of modalities in which I have been trained, including transpersonal art and expressive therapy, sandplay and symbol work, emotional clearing and intuitive guided healing. This work encourages my clients to develop a relationship with themselves and their intuition. I guide them to discover and acknowledge that in the path of pain and suffering, they may have the opportunity to find a deep sense of trust in themselves and their own inner knowing. By uncovering and shining a guiding light on their trust, they are allowed to feel a deep sense of self-worth, inner peace and freedom to create the life of their choice.

It is unfortunately inevitable that there will be grief and loss, but underneath this layer there is always, with time, an opportunity for the celebration of life and an appreciation for our magnificent, miraculous bodies and our inner wisdom. Let us not ever take for granted an ability to cycle, having deep gratitude for the gift of being able to create life and also to let go of what is not meant to be. My womb has served me well, through my births, death and transformation. I have learned to trust her guidance and I'm so deeply grateful for every thread of knowledge that I've gathered from my stories, weaving them into my life's tapestry to share in this chapter of my red nectar.

I wish to express my heartfelt thanks and gratitude to my soul sisters, my family, and for the unwavering love and presence from my husband David.

Birth New

My sacred tribe have walked with me every step of the way, sharing their wisdom and reflections so I may birth this chapter and share with pride, love and honour.

Brigitte Benary

My name is Brigitte Benary and I practice as an artist, transpersonal art therapist, sandplay therapist, guide, birth and death doula, Womb Spiral practitioner, Spiral practitioner, ancestral midwife, and guardian of the sacred fires.

My journey into the mysteries of the feminine began over 25 years ago whilst sitting in my first women's circle in Byron Bay, NSW. I recall watching the women gather together, sitting 'in circle', and in those first moments I knew this gift was an opportunity for me to find my way home. I was safe to speak my truth without any judgement, simply being present as 'Brigitte'. This experience was the first stepping stone onto many pathways, weaving me towards a deep feminine connection shaping the trajectory of my life.

Women work with me, weaving their way into sacred motherhood, learning to trust themselves to birth as mothers and to birth their own inner child, finding a deep connection to their freedom. The wisdom of my magic allows me to guide and hold ground creating a safe feminine container for each woman's journey. Navigating their way through painful emotions towards inner peace, I assist clients to find clarity in their situation, develop boundaries and create a road map to living powerfully in their truth. I teach clients how to authentically connect with their higher self, so they are able to make conscious choices and trust in their own decisions.

I feel honoured to be a guide, adding a sprinkle of my magic as my clients reconnect with the threads of their own life's tapestry, and receive the hidden mysteries of their own potent wisdom.

www.brigittebenary.com
Instagram: @thewhytewitch
Facebook: brigittebenary

www.ingramcontent.com/pod-product-compliance
Lightning Source LLC
Chambersburg PA
CBHW020317010526
44107CB00054B/1874